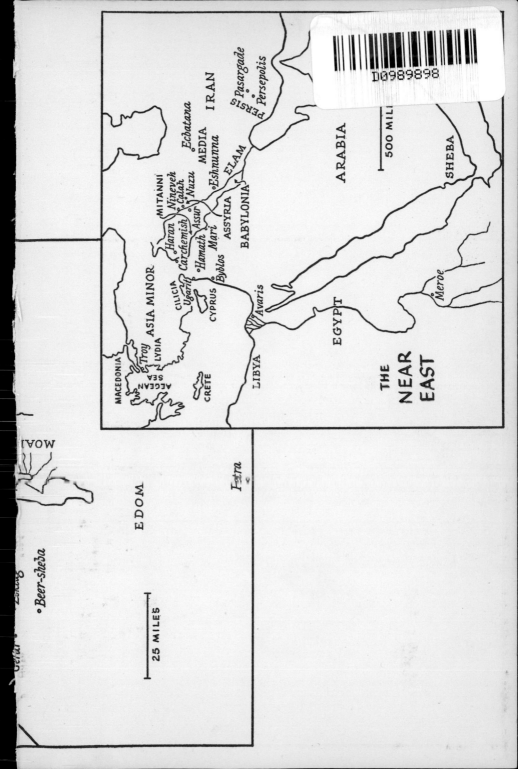

THE NEAR EAST

IRAN
MEDIA
Ecbatana
Pasargade
PERSIS
Persepolis
ELAM
Eshnunna
ARABIA
500 MILES
SHEBA
MITANNI
Nineveh
Calah
Nuzu
Assur
BABYLONIA
Haran
Carchemish
ASSYRIA
Mari
Hamath
ASIA MINOR
Byblos
ELAM
Troy
CILICIA
Ugarit
CYPRUS
LYDIA
Avaris
MACEDONIA
AEGEAN SEA
CRETE
LIBYA
EGYPT
Meroe

MOAB
EDOM
Petra
Beer-sheba
25 MILES

# INTRODUCTION
# TO
# OLD TESTAMENT TIMES

By
## CYRUS H. GORDON

VENTNOR PUBLISHERS, INC.
Ventnor, N. J.

# TABLE OF CONTENTS

Dedicated
to
my friend
Pater Professor Alfred Pohl, S.J.
who as editor of
*Orientalia*
and
*Analecta Orientalia*
is doing more than any other man
to further the scientific study of
The Ancient Near East

# FOREWORD

WHEN I began to teach Assyriology and Egyptology, it was evident to me that ancient Near Eastern studies must languish unless they are actively related to something vital in modern occidental culture. To be sure, an organic relationship exists at many levels, ranging from our exact sciences [1] to our most abysmal astrological superstitions; but nowhere is the relationship stronger or more challenging than in biblical studies. The Bible, a product of the ancient Near East, remains a living force in the modern West. Accordingly, I built my curriculum around the Bible, specializing in cuneiform and hieroglyphic texts bearing on the Old Testament. The results of this approach have been gratifying, qualitatively and quantitatively; because on the modern scene the only large reservoir of humanistic scholars with enough drive and stamina to master a whole complex of difficult sources, is the intellectual uppercrust of Bible students.

The modern study of the Old Testament resolves itself to an understanding of the Hebrew text against a background of discoveries in the Near East. Students working in this field have to grapple with the linguistic sources. However, all too often the student burning midnight oil over difficult languages, becomes so engrossed in linguistic minutiae that he fails to see the cultural and historic content of the texts he laboriously prepares for recitation. In general it is for such students that I have written these pages.

More specifically this book is a revision of my lectures on Old Testament Times and is designed as a textbook for my course on that subject. Since the course has to orient the new

[1] O. Neugebauer, *The Exact Sciences in Antiquity*, Princeton, 1952.

v

students, as well as help the more advanced ones correlate their knowledge, the following pages contain a comprehensive survey of the subject (to meet the needs of the beginner), into which are integrated new contributions (to lead the seasoned student into channels of productive research). To make the book as a whole intelligible to newcomers, I have tried to express myself as simply as possible and to reduce technicalities to a minimum. Mature scholars primarily interested in the new contributions, will at least have the advantage of finding those contributions in historic context.

I have endeavored to touch on a representative assortment of problems in the hope that every reader will find among them avenues of approach that will deepen his understanding and widen his horizons. There is no common mold into which all good students fit. The human equation with its infinite variety is ever with us. One student will have an interest in, and a capacity for, literature; another, social institutions; another, archeology; and so forth. It is hard to predict what a student will take to, and how far he will go with it. For this reason I have not hesitated to go into small details as well as broad considerations. What will appear trifling or banal to one, will lead another into rich pastures.

This book is meant to be used hand-in-hand with the Old Testament (preferably in Hebrew) to which reference is constantly made.

I owe thanks to the Social Science Research Council for a grant that helped defray the cost of preparing the manuscript. My deepest debt, however, is to a man whom I never had the privilege of meeting: the late Professor Eduard Meyer, whose *Geschichte des Altertums*[2] has made an indelible impression

[2] Second edition; I,1 (1907), I,2 (1909), II,1 (1928), II,2 (1931), III (1937), IV (1939); Stuttgart and Berlin. (The *Cambridge Ancient History* I-IV (1923-1926), which is the best work on the subject in English, is to appear in a revised edition.)

upon me. If I do not quote that still unrivaled history of the ancient Near East, it is only because it has become a part of me.

Unpredictable obstacles caused a delay of two years between the completion of the manuscript and its last revision before going to press. But the chagrin of delay has been compensated by the opportunity to eliminate some errors, to add some new evidence, and to amend certain statements where too much had been inferred from too little. On the important topic of the epic antecedents of history, my comprehension of the far-flung facts is still in the course of development, and may still be twenty years hence. Far from wishing to wait until I achieve perfection or finality, I prefer now to invite the reader to join the growing ranks of the scholars who are making such rich discoveries in this field. The present level of my grasp in this domain is sketched in the Appendix, which ought to be read before Chapters VI-VIII.

In dedicating this book to Father A. Pohl, S.J., I am paying tribute to an inspiring leader, who has selflessly sacrificed for oriental studies the most precious commodity a scholar has to give: his time. His vision and initiative—which know no national, linguistic or religious barrier—are producing the best in Near East scholarship today.

# Chapter I
# PROLEGOMENA

THE most important area for the study of human antiquity is the Near East, where we find a cluster of ancient civilizations which are not only the oldest and rank among the greatest, but are also well recorded. For no culture, however splendid, can be studied unless records concerning it are available.

The Near East included notably Mesopotamia, Egypt and Israel; but also Greece, as we shall see, was closely intertwined with them. The area is important not only for its own sake but also because it produced the origins of western culture.

Mesopotamia gave birth to Sumerian, Babylonian and Assyrian kingdoms whose art and literature are being unearthed in our own time. But even without archeological discovery, the Mesopotamian sexagesimal system of reckoning would live on in our sciences, ranging from the 360° circle (with degrees each of 60 minutes, and minutes each of 60 seconds) to our clocks on whose face the hour is divided into 60 minutes of 60 seconds each.

Egypt produced a civilization remarkable for its geniality and continuity no less than for the massiveness of its pyramids and temples. Yet even if all the monuments should perish, Egyptian influence would live on in us through our calendar of "solar" months independent of the phases of the moon. Ours is still the Egyptian calendar, albeit with Julian and Gregorian improvements.

Israel, unlike Mesopotamia and Egypt, was not among the

great forces of ancient power politics. Nor did Israel excel
in architecture, sculpture, painting and the minor arts. But
its genius in religion, ethics, literature and historiography
gave it an importance out of all proportion to its small population and land. Wherever Judaism and its daughters, Christianity and Islam, thrive, the influence of Israel lives on. Our
most familiar names like David or John, Mary or Susan are
Hebrew; our seven-day week stems from Genesis; our
modern literature and moving pictures often enough follow
biblical themes.

Since the study of the ancient Near East, or Bible World,
is the study of the roots of western civilization, it has a particular meaning for intellectuals in the West. For intellectuals
in the Near East, it has additional significance; for the antiquity of the Near East, as it is being discovered through
archeological excavations, has a growing effect on the new
nationalisms in the area today. The Egyptians associate their
claim to superiority with their descent from the ancient
Egyptians, whose magnificent civilization is being steadily
unfolded by archeologists and Egyptologists. Iraq is a country dedicating itself at high official levels to the rediscovery
of old cuneiform cultures that distinguish the land from other
Arab lands. Turkey associates itself with the Hittites about
whom it knew nothing a few decades ago; yet the spectacular
Hittite discoveries now in progress are a source of national
pride. Iran, which until the nineteenth century A.D. had lost
all memory of its greatest period of history, the Achaemenian
Age, is now turning back to that dynasty of Cyrus, Darius
and Xerxes for its inspiration in the challenging present.
Lebanon distinguishes itself from the surrounding countries
in accordance with an ideology whereby its people are the
descendants of the Phoenicians, and are accordingly different
from the other people around them. The newest nation at-
taching itself to a glorious past is that of Israel, and while

many factors go into the picture, it remains true that the momentum of Israel's long history, including notably the undying hope imparted by Old Testament prophecy, is an indispensable factor in the shaping of a new nation before our eyes. Israeli devotion to its archeological antiquities has been evident since the birth of the new state, even during the exigencies of its war for statehood.[1]

What sources have we wherewith to study the history of the ancient Near East? The most unequivocal sources are those in written form. The best known is the Hebrew Bible; next come numerous classic authors, first in Greek and then in Latin. Though even the Greeks came on the scene rather late in Near East history, they recorded many traditions which supplement more-recently-discovered native sources and so are of value not only for their own times but also for enabling us to work back into more remote antiquity.

In Asia, the first literature is the Sumerian, written in cuneiform in Mesopotamia since about 3000 B.C. Sumerian became the classical language of the entire cuneiform world, embracing Mesopotamia and the surrounding areas. It died out as a spoken tongue a little after 1800 B.C. but remained the classical language of western Asia for nearly 1900 years thereafter, until Accadian cuneiform disappeared in the first century A.D. Thus Sumerian has had a longer history as a classical language than either Greek or Latin.[2]

The main cuneiform literature of the Bible World is Accadian. Accadian, sometimes called Babylonian or Assyrian, is the standard Semitic language which gives us more written records of the ancient Near East, than any other source. The cuneiform offshoots of Accadian include Hittite, which in the second millennium B.C. was important in Asia Minor. A dif-

---

[1] For the pattern of revivals in the modern Near East, see my *Lands of the Cross and Crescent,* Ventnor Publishers, 1948.

[2] Sumerology has attained a new level with A. Falkenstein, *Grammatik der Sprache Gudeas,* Rome; I, 1949; II, 1950.

ferent kind of Hittite written pictographically and called Hieroglyphic Hittite, is now in the course of accelerated decipherment thanks to a newly found bilingual which we shall discuss in Chapter XIII.

Among the other cuneiform literatures is Hurrian which was used widely throughout the Near East in the second millennium B.C. This language is imperfectly known, though we have quite a number of texts written in it from Babylonia, Assyria, Asia Minor and Syria.

The most recent of the great literatures to be deciphered is the Ugaritic, from the city of Ugarit on the north coast of Syria in the early fourteenth century B.C., written in a cuneiform alphabet on clay. Ugaritic stands closer to biblical Hebrew literature than any of the other known literatures.[3]

The Achaemenian kings of Iran starting with the sixth century B.C. developed a cuneiform syllabary in which they carved their royal inscriptions on living rock or inscribed them on tablets of precious metal. The native language written in this script is called Old Persian.[4] Often the texts are trilingual, being written in Elamite and Babylonian as well as Old Persian. The most important of the Achaemenian texts is the long trilingual of Darius I, from around 520 B.C., at Behistun. The decipherment of the Old Persian provided the key to the Babylonian version, which opened up the vast treasures of Accadian, and ultimately of Sumerian, literature. The decipherment of Elamite has been slower because that language is not related to any well-known family.

Our sketchy survey of the cuneiform sources should at least show that there is no dearth of material, but rather so great

[3] For the grammar, texts and lexicon, see my *Ugaritic Handbook,* Rome, 1947. For a complete translation, see my *Ugaritic Literature,* Rome, 1949.
[4] See R. G. Kent, *Old Persian: Grammar, Texts, Lexicon,* New Haven, 1950.

a wealth of it that the historian is embarrassed and taxed because he has only one lifetime to devote to it.

Coming into Canaan (which means Syria plus Palestine),[5] we find another series of native inscriptions written in an alphabet. The Phoenicians have left us a number of texts, often of a funerary or commemorative character. The basic vocabulary and grammar are intelligible to everyone interested in the subject, provided he has a command of Hebrew. Other close neighbors of the Hebrews, the Moabites east of the Dead Sea, have left one moderately long historic inscription of King Mesha, who is mentioned in the Hebrew Bible. Moabite is even more closely related to Hebrew than is Phoenician. The Hebrews themselves, in addition to bequeathing to the world the Old Testament, have also left some inscriptions that have been discovered in modern times. In the northern capital of Samaria were found ostraca or inscriptions written in ink on pieces of pottery. The Samaria ostraca are wine and oil receipts. Though they are short and give us very little detail, they are rather interesting for ninth-eighth century Israelite administration and also for telling us something about the northern Israelite dialect of Hebrew as distinct from the Judean dialect that predominates in the Bible. From Judah in the south, we have other texts such as the Siloam inscription commemorating the completion of the tunnel that Hezekiah built (perhaps in anticipation, or as a result, of the war with Assyria in 701 B.C.) for augmenting Jerusalem's supply of water within the city wall. Also from Judah are the Lachish ostraca, which are the most important historic inscriptions left by the Hebrews. These date from the early sixth century B.C. and tell of military operations and signals around the southern cities of Lachish and Azekah during Nebuchadnezzar's invasion.

[5] For a comprehensive work on the area, see A. T. Olmstead, *History of Palestine and Syria*, New York, 1931.

The language with the widest distribution in our study is Aramaic.[6] Although there is evidence of the Aramaic language in records of the second millennium B.C., the historic texts begin in the eighth century in the city-states of Aram (or inland Syria), when it displaced Phoenician as the *lingua franca* in Syria and nearby coastal Asia Minor. By the end of the century, Aramaic had already won for itself the role of international language in official circles from at least Assyria to Judah (2 Kings 18:26; the date is 701 B.C.). The achievement is the more remarkable since the Arameans never forged a great empire but spread the language through relatively peaceful means, notably tribal migrations and trade. The Achaemenians used Aramaic as their interprovincial tongue, at least for the areas west of Iran. Parts of the Bible are written in Aramaic, notably large sections of Daniel and Ezra. A military colony of Jews in the service of the Achaemenian kings at Elephantine in Upper Egypt, have left a corpus of Aramaic papyri of prime importance. So great was Aramaic that it was destined to replace the native languages of all Semitic Asia outside of Arabia, and it remained unchallenged until the Islamic Conquest in the seventh century A.D.[7]

From Egypt we have a host of inscriptions on stone, papyrus, leather and other materials; in hieroglyphs, in a cursive simplification of hieroglyphs called Hieratic, and ultimately in a further cursive simplification known as Demotic. While Egyptology is full of difficulties, it is nonetheless simpler than cuneiform studies because it deals with only one language and

---

[6] A. Dupont-Sommer, *Les Araméens,* Paris, 1949.

[7] The language of the Syro-Arabian Desert tribes was predominantly Aramaic until about 700 B.C. The Amorite invaders of Mesopotamia in the third and second millennia B.C. had Aramaic affinities. It was in the first millennium B.C. that Arabic tribes began to displace the Aramaic tribes in the northern part of the Syro-Arabian Desert. The desert invaders of the sown have thus twice imposed their language on the Fertile Crescent; first, Aramaic, and now Arabic.

one script, even though the language, and especially the script, underwent considerable evolution.

The eastern Mediterranean produced texts in Minoan, Cypriote and Mycenean characters. Most, if not all, of those texts are Indo-European; some are definitely Greek. The decipherment is far from complete but it is safe to predict that the texts, when sufficiently deciphered, will prove to be of value for the history of the Asiatic and African, as well as Greek, mainland.

It is impractical to try to exhaust the list of written sources from the ancient Near East. To enumerate the most important ones, as we have done, and to convey an idea of the richness and variety of the written sources, are all that need be done here.

The written sources are supplemented by numerous material remains.[8] Of the latter, the most basic is architecture including cities with huge walls, streets, and buildings that range from palaces to hovels. Connected with the buildings are installations of permanent and portable types. Permanent installations include ovens for baking bread or bricks, baths with drainage systems and bitumen waterproofing, cisterns for storing the seasonal rainfall, pits for the storage of food, and so forth. Then there are many movable objects, of which the most common is pottery. Pottery is often the most valuable archeological criterion because while it is easily broken, it is not readily destroyed. The abundance of ceramic remains thus provides a clue for establishing a relative chronology (and for indicating trade relations, if some of the pottery is imported) when epigraphical evidence is lacking.

The excavator also finds tools of more substantial materials, for the erection of cities and monuments required instruments of stone, copper and eventually iron. After buildings

[8] For the material remains, see especially G. Contenau, *Manuel d'Archéologie Orientale* I-IV, Paris, 1927-1947.

were completed, they were supplied with furnishings, which under favorable conditions may be discovered. In dry areas like Upper Egypt, where organic matter is durable, we find wood and other perishable materials preserved. The same substances disintegrate in Asia where there is a seasonal rainfall that plays havoc with organic matter, so that all the excavator finds is a discoloration (often brown) in the soil.

Archeological finds also include the whole field of fine arts. There are reliefs and sculpture in the round, ranging from colossi to statuettes. Painting, unlike sculpture, is as a rule well preserved only in Egypt because of the accident of climate; though a few dry spots in western Asia have yielded painted frescoes. Then there is the work of the metalsmith and jeweler, constituting an attractive repertoire of minor arts.

Sometimes, when the original objects have partially or entirely disintegrated, their representations in art enable us to reconstruct them. For instance, in Ur, crushed harps were found with all the wooden structure eaten away and only the metal, stone and shell parts surviving. Yet, because of durable stone and mother-of-pearl representations of scenes showing such harps being played, Sir C. Leonard Woolley who discovered the harps, could restore the wooden and other organic materials, beat the crushed metal remnants back into shape and reconstruct the instruments as they appeared in antiquity.

The Egyptians frequently made models of servants at work on the whole gamut of arts and crafts and economic activity.[9] Thus the excavator often discovers a model brewery or bakery, with men and women at work; or a model ship complete with busy crew, so that even where full-size originals are lacking, these models plus other representations provide a vivid impression of modes of life, arts and crafts,

[9] J. H. Breasted, Jr., *Egyptian Servant Statues,* New York, 1948.

professions, trades, household activity, and entertainment in those times.

Coins appear on the scene rather late in history, in the seventh century B.C., and did not become common until some time after that. Coins occupy an intermediate or conglomerate category. They are a form of art, but not quite fine art; the work of the metalsmith, but lacking the individuality of his special creations. Though coins are a useful source of general history, they play no role in the scope of this book, until the last period of our investigation: the Achaemenian Age.

Now that we have considered the sources, we turn to the question of how to use them in order to derive a knowledge of history. Languages have a certain historic value in themselves. Thus the relation of Egyptian to the Semitic languages implies a degree of cultural history shared by the two groups of people. When we delve more deeply into the very remote past, we find that there are ultimate connections even between the Indo-European and Egypto-Semitic families of languages. This is a rich field but has not as yet lent itself to exact analysis in detail, though such limitations in no way detract from the potential historic importance of the problem. When languages share common features, either they have inherited them from a common origin, or acquired them through borrowing. English "father" and German "Vater" come from a common Indo-European origin which both languages have inherited without borrowing. Apparent phonetic discrepancies are normal in such cases and usually follow correspondences that have been (or can be) formulated precisely, under the name of "phonetic law." However, English "kindergarten" is borrowed from German, while German "Sport" is borrowed from English; for words tend to be borrowed along with the cultural contributions they designate. When a community is mixed linguistically, it tends to produce a resultant speech which may bear the stamp of especially one of the component languages, though the other component languages will leave some impression. The resultant speech will thus have features of its different component languages (and the latter may be of totally unrelated stocks). This type of fusion is known as linguistic alliance—a phenomenon that the historian must bear in mind alongside the more generally known phenomenon of related languages evolving from a common stock. Attempts to reconstruct prehistory from linguistic interrelations are as a rule less reliable than history based directly on written sources. Linguistic arguments become far more cogent when they are used in addition to (not instead of!) available written documents.

Though we are on firmer ground with texts, they have to be evaluated before they can be used for reconstructing history. Obviously the date and origin of a text have to be established before it can be applied to a historic context. Then it may be desirable to establish some facts about the author. If his name cannot be determined, it is often essential to find out at least his viewpoint, his purpose, what other compositions he may have written, or to what group of people he may have belonged. Important, too, is the evaluation of the text from the standpoint of reliability. Is it completely reliable? Is it completely unreliable? Or, as is usually the case, is it somewhere in between? If so, what elements are reliable and what elements not? The discipline of evaluating documents is known as philology and constitutes a basic aid to history. In fact the two overlap and it is often hard to tell where philology ends and history begins.

Texts can be used to build up historic pictures of different types and magnitudes. For instance, the tablets from Nuzu (a town in Assyria during the fifteenth and fourteenth centuries B.C.) constitute the private archives of leading citizens during four or five generations and the study of the texts enables us to show the social and economic development of the town during those generations with a degree of detail and intimacy that is rarely to be matched in the familiar cities of Europe or America of premodern times. Thus a homogeneous group of texts coming from the same time and place may provide a detailed record of society in that community at that time. But it is possible to go farther than that and here is where the subject becomes more intricate:

We can deal with interrelations. To take a simple example, we can study the thirteenth century treaties made between the Hittites and Egyptians, comparing the Hittite version with the Egyptian version. Each will contain different elements depending on the respective viewpoints; and by correlating the two sets of treaties, we get a more exact historic picture than could be obtained from handling only the one or the other. Or, we know that in the ninth century Israel had dealings with Moab that at times involved invasion and war. The biblical account is one of our sources. On the other hand, the Moabite inscription of King Mesha is another independent source. By using the documents of both the Hebrews and Moabites, we arrive at a controlled history, in which sources can be checked against each other. Sometimes the same specific episodes are recorded in different independent sources. Thus Sennacherib's invasion of Judah in 701 B.C. is recounted in the Bible and in the Assyrian annals. The general agreement between both sources fixes the historicity of the event, and each version fills in lacunae of the other. Naturally the war communiques from two enemy camps are not going to have the same tone or point of view, but it is precisely the difference in origin that enables us to reconstruct what we call controlled history.

Occasionally, controlled history enables us to put into context, what had seemed to be an isolated phenomenon. As an example let us consider the return of the Jews from the Exile in the time of Cyrus the Great. From the biblical account one

might imagine it was an isolated act of grace by a sovereign
who was interested in the Jewish people and wanted to restore them to their home and revive their worship. All that
is in general true, but taken out of context, it gives a false
impression. Upon reading the inscribed Cylinder of Cyrus,
we see that such grace was his policy toward minorities and
cults in general. He prides himself on sending people back
to where their home had been and on reviving their religion
in its authentic temple. Therefore the return of the Jews was
simply an application of the policy of that enlightened monarch. The historian must not only seek to discover facts but
also to place facts in their proper perspective.

Now if we imagine the entire sweep of Near East history
from the beginning of time down to, let us say, Alexander
the Great, we have to reckon with a vast number of facts
intricately interrelated. To one man, a certain group of things
will have an intimate relationship. To another person with
different background and point of view, those same things
might seem totally unrelated. Usually, he who can see relationship in a group of events has got more to the heart of
the matter than a person who sees in them only isolated
phenomena; but ingenuity, without adequate judgment or
knowledge, all too often leads to false combinations of unrelated facts. From the facts can be derived a controlled history. However, before that can be achieved, it is necessary to
reduce the maze of facts to an intelligible whole by organizing what is important and suppressing what is not. To determine what is important presupposes a standard of values. It
would be presumptuous to set up a universal standard of
values. But, as a mature viewpoint, containing much if not
all of the truth, we might consider the following principle:
In any period the important facts are those which determine
subsequent history. In Hezekiah's reign it is likely that the
constructing of the Siloam Tunnel impressed the Jerusa-

lemites more than did Isaiah's Messianic prophecies. Yet the latter, which are infinitely the more important, can be correctly evaluated on the principle set forth above, from our point of vantage. It is this principle which, incidentally, explains why it is hard to evaluate current events and the recent past.

Non-written archeological material also requires methodical evaluation. A single object found in context will throw light on the entire context. For instance, a snake idol found in a temple strongly suggests some aspect of snake worship in that temple. So the individual object is not only of interest in itself, but when found in context, or when attributable to some definite context, throws light on the whole picture. An object that cannot be associated with any context, is not usable for historic purposes.

In addition to single objects, there are complete categories that may be found in context. The jewels of the royal tombs of Ur form a category of singular importance since they constitute the highest accomplishment of the Sumerians in fine art. Before the discovery of the royal tombs of Ur it was possible for the greatest historian of the ancient Near East to state that the Sumerians did not excel in any form of fine art and that if one compares their statuary with Egyptian statuary, he will find the Sumerian products primitive. The Ur excavations have shown that we must not generalize from the statuary. In the field of metallurgy the Sumerians are unsurpassed in antiquity, while in the arts of the goldsmith and gemcutter, the Sumerians are second to none in all history. Thus objects put in context and interpreted rightly, may have wide implications.

It is also possible to treat a category of objects and study them throughout a long history. Seal cylinders are quite numerous and constitute the most characteristic form of art in the cuneiform world. Those seals are small engraved cylinders (usually of stone) used to authenticate documents by impressing the seals on the soft clay. Such seals may be arranged according to type and period, and studied as a function of history, since, like all human products, they are a reflex of the historic process. First they should be studied *per se;* and then integrated into the whole picture of history.

The sum total of artifacts (by which is meant everything made by men from great edifices to tiny pots) may be regarded as a part of history. We must be selective because the material is so abundant. Thus it would be foolhardy to try to exhaust the evidence of ceramics in the Near East if we hope ever to study history as a whole; because the ceramics, if studied in detail, would take more than a lifetime. A knowledge of history enables the scholar to put specialized material into perspective and to evaluate it. A knowledge of varied specialized materials—written and archeological—enables the historian to control his subject by checking one type of evidence against the other. History without knowledge of source-detail degenerates into unfounded platitudes and false reconstructions; while concern with details without historic perspective becomes cataloguing, which, though important, is not history. One can take the evolution of the tomb in Egypt from simple to complex structures as an aspect or reflex of Egyptian history, with particular regard for religion and beliefs concerning the dead.[10] Just because something is specialized does not mean it is devoid of broader implications and human interest. The representation of Asiatics (particularly of the Semites) and African Negroes on Egyptian monuments could be studied and published as an illustrated catalogue; and in such a form it would be useful. However, if the physical types and the costumes are at the same time analyzed, the study becomes a key to the ethnology

[10] G. Reisner, *The Development of the Egyptian Tomb down to the Accession of Cheops,* Cambridge (Mass.), 1936.

of the times and to the migrations of peoples and their historic roles.

One of the most interesting aspects of the field is to take texts and combine them with art objects reflecting the same phenomenon. Thus there is a passage in 2 Samuel 2:14-16 that tells of a battle fought between twelve champions of one army and twelve of another army around the year 1000 B.C. The fashion in which the twenty-four contestants fought is described as follows: "And each grasped the head of his opponent, with his sword in the side of his opponent, and they fell down together." This description is so brief and refers to such a strange type of combat that none of the interpreters of Scripture were able to make sense of the text. At last some-one [11] pointed out that a relief from Tell Halaf in northwest Mesopotamia, shows two men engaged in exactly this type of combat; each grasping his opponent's head with one hand and with the other plunging a blade into the opponent's side. The relief illustrates the text graphically, and the text provides whatever commentary is necessary for understanding the relief.

There are a couple of general methods in preparing material objects for historical study. Of basic importance is stratigraphy, which means that in excavating, the archeologist distinguishes the strata as sharply as possible and carefully records the provenience of all objects within their strata. Successive settlements forming a mound were built one upon the other so that what lies below is earlier than what covers it.[12] If the objects of one stratum in one mound go with those of another stratum in another mound, a synchronism is established between those two strata. The sum total of such synchronisms enables us to set up the relative chronology of the

[11] Y. Yadin, "Let the Young Men, I Pray Thee, Arise and Play before Us," *Journal of the Palestine Oriental Society* 21, 1948, pp. 110-116.
[12] For an account of stratigraphic excavation, see my *The Living Past*, New York City, 1941.

ancient Near East,[13] which is of paramount importance for periods before the introduction of writing around 3000 B.C. The stratification of each mound provides the relative chronology of all the levels of that mound. The synchronisms between mounds make possible the establishment of comparative stratigraphy and a relative chronology for vast areas that formed a cultural continuum. Stratigraphy must, however, be used with caution, for the altitude at which an object is found does not necessarily determine its stratum. Something that dropt into a well belongs not to the level where it was found at the bottom of the well, but to the level from which it had been dropt. Hence archeologists must carefully note whether an object came from a pit of some sort so as to enable the historian to ascribe it to its proper context. The soil and debris excavated by ancients in digging a well and then put in a dump, will not belong to the level as found, but to the level from which the soil and debris were taken from the well pit. There are many such limitations to stratigraphy. Mastering them takes experience and reflection. The art of stratigraphic excavation is best learned in the archeological field, not from books and lectures. But our few remarks will suffice to indicate the nature of the problem and the snares to beware of.

The other general method of handling material objects is according to their type. Anyone who knows styles in clothing, appreciates the fact that there is a definite evolution that enables the expert to date any characteristic specimen. The approximate datability of all manufacture is within the power of the specialist. Sometimes it is possible to assign exact dates as in the case of automobile models which change from year to year. The evolution of any object follows a trend; and the typological arrangement of specimens will conform to their actual (or reverse) chronological order. If any two or more

---

[13] Cf. C. F. A. Schaeffer, *Stratigraphie comparée et chronologie de l'Asie occidentale,* London and Oxford, 1948.

individual specimens in the series are datable (even relatively), the order of the series can be determined as to direction so that the possibility of the order being in reverse can
be eliminated. Furthermore, any specimen between two dated
ones, can be interpolated in time between them. But like all
other methods, typology must not be used blindly, for it too
is subject to complications (like recurrent cycles in style) that
call for vigilance and common-sense.

Another method used by historians of religion, art and
literature is that of motif. There are certain things that tend
to crop up independently in different periods and areas. Sometimes we are able to understand the meaning of a historic
phenomenon upon recognizing the general motif into which
it fits. Yet this is often risky because while mankind in different periods and in different parts of the world have many
things in common, there are also profound divergences and
it is possible to read a false motif into source material, which
should be examined internally before we attempt to classify it.
Furthermore the seeking of universal motifs often results in
neglecting the differences which point to the evolutionary
process that characterizes historic development. Here again
common-sense and awareness of the facts will enable us to use
the motif-method profitably. In the Ugaritic tablets, a crown-
prince is destined to suckle the breasts of goddesses while a
sick king threatened with death makes his family wonder
whether a god can die. The motif of divine kingship explains
such phenomena immediately; for the king attained divinity
through claiming to have nursed at divine breasts, and the
death of kings caused perplexity because of the contradiction
between their pretended godhood and actual mortality.

Despite all the foregoing and other methods with which the
scholar should be acquainted, the material itself must dictate
the method. There is no such thing as taking a course, or
reading a book, on methodology and becoming thereby an

expert in the field. The expert must master and understand his material. The material will dictate the method to be used. The only advantage in learning other methods and what has been done in the field, is that it sometimes saves time and suggests things that are applicable to our new problems. We can apply established methods to new problems insofar as those methods are applicable but not beyond.

Although objectivity is essential for the historian, the reconstruction of history will always have a personal element. The capacity to see implications and relationships; the standard whereby certain elements are more important than others; and the ability to reconstruct an evolving continuous whole; demand individual creativeness on the part of the historian.

The emphases and omissions in this book are personal, for any other author would make a different choice of his own. The reader should also realize that this book will require additions and revision increasingly with the passing of time. This is true of many fields, but especially of the ancient Near East where discoveries are constantly adding so much new source material that the subject is now the most dynamic aspect of the study of man's past.[14]

---

[14] Addendum: Professor S. N. Kramer's discovery (*New York Times,* Sunday, Sept. 21, 1952, p. 28) of a fragment of Urnammu's Sumerian law code pushes back the date of attested codes to the first reign of the Third Dynasty of Ur. Moreover the preamble tells that Urnammu vanquished Namahni (a Lagash predecessor of Gudea), so that Gudea's reign falls during the Third Dynasty of Ur. Thus our statements as to Gudea's date (p. 66) and the oldest known law code (p. 69) already need revision.

## Chapter II

# IN THE BEGINNING

In speaking of beginnings, there are several different subjects we can have in mind. One is actual beginning as attested by material remains.[1] We can speak of prehistoric men who lived tens of thousands of years ago, such as those whose skeletons have been found in northern Palestine around the Carmel Ridge. We may speak of prehistoric migrations of people, probably from Central Asia, who introduced to the Near East the Egypto-Semitic languages. We may work back from the languages and talk about the relations between Indo-Europeans and Egypto-Semites. From archeological discoveries we can trace the evolution of arts and crafts. We can see how the knife, the arrow or pottery developed throughout the ages. From about 5000 to 3000 B.C. we have preliterate stratified towns, one on top of the other, each of which reflects organized society; for only an organized society can construct and maintain a complex social unit. In Mesopotamia we can trace the change between the earliest levels and those where Sumerian culture begins. That kind of evidence indicates to us that there was a population earlier than the first literate population, the Sumerians, of whom we have definite records.[2] In Babylonian mounds, a layer of silt separating two towns of sharply different cultures, indicates that a flood terminated

[1] See V. G. Childe, *New Light on the Most Ancient East,* London, 1934.
[2] Sumerian script was not devised for the Sumerian language, as incompatibilities between the script and language show. Accordingly there was an earlier literate people from whom the Sumerians borrowed their system of writing. However, we so far have no clearly discernible texts in the language of that earlier people.

the earlier settlement, and that the newcomers who resettled the place represented another civilization. (River floods are characteristic of Babylonia but not of Palestine. It is therefore not surprising that the Hebrew Deluge is, as we shall see, derived from Mesopotamian sources.)

It is also possible, by getting behind the texts which preserve the traditions of a more remote antiquity, and behind the materials of art and archeology, to trace the evolution of society in its main outlines. The texts and monuments reflect the early mode of hunting wild animals, the later mode of herding domesticated animals, then the settled agricultural life, and finally the development of commerce and industry. But the fact that people go into a new stage does not mean that the earlier stage disappears. We still have farming in America in spite of the fact that we also engage in commerce and industry. There is also extensive herding in certain areas. Hunting, of course, is now relegated almost entirely to the realm of sport in America but not so in the ancient Near East, where hunting sometimes appears as a means of subsistence in comparatively late periods (Genesis 25:27). With the development of writing about 3000 B.C. independently in both Mesopotamia and Egypt, we begin to enter upon the full light of history. What we can learn of times prior to that date is a subject in itself, which we may call prehistory but which does not concern us in our present investigation. It is rather another type of beginnings that concerns us: the beginnings as the people of the Near East saw them. Their views of the origin of the universe are manifestations of their intellectual growth and of their outlook on life.

Several accounts of the beginnings have come down to us. The best as far as wealth of material goes, are from Mesopotamia. But the Hebrew version is by far the most familiar and best organized. How did the world come to be as it is? This is the first question taken up and answered in Scripture. The

Hebrew answer is not the same as the latest scientific answer, but that is not our concern. Our concern at present is to understand how the Hebrews approached these problems and answered them. For the Hebrews, God created heaven and earth.[3] The next step was to introduce light into a world of darkness. After that, waters had to be separated into orderly arrangement, so that there were two sets of waters, those above and those below. Those above are the waters which provide us with rain, and are released for distribution on the earth by opening the windows of heaven. The waters below spring from wells and fountains and account for the rivers and seas. The next stage was to separate seas from dry land on the earth. Then comes vegetation in an orderly world; not chaotic vegetation, but an orderly vegetation in which each species produces seeds according to its own kind. Then come the luminaries of heaven: the sun, moon and stars, which are not only to give light as such, but also to mark seasons, ranging from the time of day and night, to months and years. Then come fish and fowl and beasts and finally, as the crowning accomplishment of creation, comes man in God's image to enjoy creation in a privileged way like no other creature (Genesis 1:1-28).

After this creation in six days, God rested on the seventh thus establishing the precedent for the day of rest, which remains the most useful and widespread and enjoyed of social institutions for the working man in practically all of the civilized world. Why we rest on the seventh day need not be answered in the same way by the modern critical historian, who is in a position to show on a comparative basis that the number seven permeated the thought of the ancient world.

[3] Simple translation does not convey all that the Hebrew text might signify to an ancient Hebrew. Pairs of antonyms often mean "everything" or "everyone" as in English "they came, great and small" = "everybody came." In Hebrew "heaven and earth" might be such a pair, signifying "everything, the universe."

Thus there is not only the seven-day week, but also the seven-year sabbatical cycle, and the jubilee year following seven sabbatical cycles. But, while we are able to explain "the seventh day" as a manifestation of the widespread "seven-motif," we are for present purposes interested in the biblical answer, according to which God's precedent sanctified the seventh day (which must therefore be kept hallowed as the day of rest by man and beast).

So far Scripture deals with the broadest considerations. At this point the focus is narrowed on man and the fundamental questions of man and society. Why was woman created and why is there the institution of marriage? Because Deity saw it was not good for man to be alone. He therefore created woman as a "help meet" for man; that is, a help suitable for man.[4] The type of marriage indicated is one whereby a man forsakes his parents[5] and cleaves unto his wife so that they become one flesh (Genesis 2:24).

The next crucial problem is why is man intelligent as distinct from the beasts of the field. Man is intelligent because (against the command of God) he obtained and ate magic fruit from the Tree of Knowledge, thus gaining knowledge that up to that time had been a monopoly of divinity, not intended for man. It is interesting to note that the knowledge imparted by the fruit of this tree is the "knowledge of good and evil," a much misunderstood phrase. The antonyms "good and evil" mean "everything" here.

The same expression in inverted order occurs in Egyptian, where "evil-good" means "everything."[6] The only reason it

---

[4] The process whereby the noun "help" plus the adjective "meet" has been transfigured into the compound noun "helpmate" is called popular etymology.

[5] Note that this is not the marriage typical of patriarchal society, where the bride comes to live with the groom's family. However, it would be going beyond the evidence to insist that the verse presupposes matriarchy.

[6] As I have pointed out in *Archiv Orientální* 18, 1950, p. 202, n. 7.

has not generally been applied to the Tree of Knowledge "good and evil" is that the traditional interpretation is so deeply entrenched.[7] Thus man obtained universal knowledge, and to that extent, shares with God a faculty that had been a divine prerogative.

Why are human beings, unlike animals, ashamed of nudity? Because man's newly won knowledge included a knowledge of decency, about which animals in their blissful ignorance know nothing. Why are snakes vile and why do snakes and men show hostility to one another? It is because the snake induced Eve, who in turn induced Adam, to eat of the forbidden fruit; and as a divine punishment for this, the snake must crawl on its belly, eat dust and bite at men's heels; with men, in retaliation, bruising snakes' heads. Why must men work for a living? This was Adam's punishment for his share in the transgression against divine will. And why does woman have disabilities such as being subject to her husband's authority, and to suffer pain in childbirth? This is her punishment for violating the divine decree. Why does not mankind live forever in a paradise? Mankind was driven out of paradise for all time because God saw that man could not be trusted to obey His will and to refrain from eating the magic fruit of another tree in the Garden of Eden which would give man immortality. God decided that man should not obtain immortality lest he become like the gods. Accordingly, if we examine the story in Genesis objectively, we see that, while many elements go into making up the whole picture, it is not so much an account of the "Fall of Man" but rather of the rise of man halfway to divinity. He obtained one of the two prerogatives or characteristics of the gods: intelligence; but

[7] Thus it is not included by A. M. Honeyman in his study of antonymic pairs under the title *"Merismus* in Biblical Hebrew," *Journal of Biblical Literature* 71, 1952, pp. 11-18.

he was checked by God from obtaining immortality, which would have made man quite divine.[8]

The next problems that confronted the Hebrews were such as: How did Adam and Eve give rise to the nations of the world? The Hebrew answer to such problems was that families and nations developed in a way that can be traced through genealogy: genealogy of actual people, from father to son, with certain individuals giving rise to groups and nations. How did society originate? Society originated, according to the Hebrews, by the contributions of individual historic characters. The first children of Adam and Eve were Cain and Abel, Cain being the farmer and Abel the herdsman, each representing different ways of life. The age-old hostility between the farmer and herdsman is thus traced back to the first farmer and the first herdsman. The herdsman Abel had what God liked better than what the farmer had to offer; meat is preferable to vegetables as an offering. God's preference reflects a Semitic standard of values whereby the austere nomadic pattern is the good life.[9] But Cain, the farmer, killed Abel, which may reflect the victory of stable societies depending upon agriculture over nomadic societies that depend on herding. Cain was the father of an Enoch associated with a city named Enoch: the first city in history according to Hebrew tradition. Later the genealogies take us to Lemech, who had two wives, Adah and Zillah. Adah gave birth to two sons. One was Jabal, who gets credit for founding the nomadic way of life; the other was Jubal, who instituted music, both on stringed instruments and on pipes. Zillah had two children who occupy a lower scale on the social ladder.

[8] The element of disobedience is present in the story but only circumstantially. To stress the "evil" and overlook the "good" in the text would have no justification, even on the part of exegetes who are not familiar with the inclusive meaning of antonymic pairs.

[9] The best statement in Scripture comes from late in Judean history (Jeremiah 35:1-19).

Her son was Tubal-Cain, who founded the art of metallurgy. Among nomadic Semites the smith has a status inferior to those who own and tend the herds. Zillah's daughter Naamah should, according to some scholars, be fit into the pattern as the founder of some way of life. It has been suggested that she is either the prototype of dancing or singing girls, and perhaps even of prostitutes. However, there is no textual evidence to support such a patternistic reconstruction. Another child of Adam and Eve was Seth, whose son was named Enosh, to whose time the worship of Yahwe is traced (Genesis 4:26). This tradition, to the extent that it relegates Yahwism to pre-Hebraic antiquity and ascribes Yahwism to non-Hebraic origins, is confirmed by early references to Yahwism outside the Hebrew sphere.[10]

There follows another set of genealogies, of heroes before the Flood. A few of them may be singled out because of particular interest. There is a second Enoch who "walked with God and he was not, for God had taken him" (Genesis 5:24). This is the first assumption of anyone, who instead of dying was taken aloft into heaven. Another character, Methuselah, famed for longevity, lived 969 years: not very much longer than some of his fellows in the genealogy; but because he lived a bit longer, his name is a household term for long life.[11] Then comes Noah, who is the father of Shem, Ham and Japheth; each son being the ancestor of a major division of mankind.

Man and creation proved to be a disappointment to God, so that God regretted His work and decided to punish the world. Some steps were taken like the reduction to 120 years, of man's hitherto phenomenally long life-span; but even that

[10] Yahwe occurs in Amorite names of Mesopotamia; and *yw* may stand for the same divine name in Ugarit. That Yahwe was known in Syria far north of Israel we shall see in Chapter XV.

[11] The longevity of ancient worthies harks back to an old tradition. The fantastically long lives of their Mesopotamian counterparts make these biblical life-spans look quite brief.

was not enough. Drastic punishment was called for, and God decided on a flood. Noah alone found grace because of his virtue, so God instructed him to build an ark according to exact specifications. He was told to take his family, including his sons and their wives, and pairs of all the animals of creation, plus supplies. He entered the ark at the appointed time and a flood destroyed all living, except those in the ark, which eventually landed on the mountains of Ararat in Armenia. Noah did not open the door of the ark until he was sure the earth was sufficiently dry. To determine this he sent out birds on three successive occasions; first a raven, then a dove and then again the dove. It was only when the latter did not return that he knew there was a place for birds to nest in a dry world and it was safe to come out. He therefore made his exit and sacrificed to God to show his gratitude. The sweet savor that rose was so pleasing to God that He promised never again to curse the land and the living because of man's innate evil. God realized by this time that man's evil was here to stay, and that the best would have to be made of a bad job. God promised man that the seasons would continue, that nature would not be upset, that there would be plowing time and harvest time. There would be cold and heat, summer and winter, day and night. Never in Semitic ideology is there any desire to strive for seasonal perfection, whereby the best time of the year should prevail all the time.[12] Each thing is wanted in its season and when the seasons are regular there is a feeling of security in a world run properly accordingly to rules by God. — Then came a blessing for Noah and a code was laid down. The main article in this code regards blood. Man's blood must not be shed. If it is shed it will be sought not only

[12] This is overlooked by those who assume that in the ancient Near East the normal advent of the dry season was received with weeping for a god of fertility who died yearly at that season and who came back to life yearly with the return of the rains. It must be borne in mind that rain out of season was as disturbing as drought out of season (1 Samuel 12:17-20).

from the hands of a man but even from an animal guilty of murder. Furthermore, since blood contains holy life, it must not be drunk but poured into the ground. This law, according to Hebrew tradition, is binding on all mankind. The obligations of Mosaic Law are binding only upon Jews; but God demands of both Jew and Gentile, obedience to the Noachian Code. As a final touch, God put in the sky the rainbow to remind man He had made this covenant and would never again destroy the world by flood.[13]

To proceed with the next questions: Why is it that nations are unequal? Specifically, why were non-Hebrew inhabitants of Canaan, who are called Canaanites, inferior to the Hebrews?—For aside from the Hebrews' disliking the Canaanites, the latter were subjugated by the Hebrews.—The answer of Scripture is that Noah, who after the Flood planted a vineyard and made wine, got drunk and allowed something to happen that he never would have, had he been sober. He was lying in a tent naked. Ham, quite by accident, came in and saw his father's nakedness, which is a sin, whether intentional or not. He went and informed his brothers, who walked in backwards and covered their father.[14] But when the father woke up, he blessed his two sons who had covered his nakedness and cursed Ham who had seen it. But even more than Ham is the latter's son Canaan cursed. It will be noted that the story puts the ancestor of the Egyptians (with whom the Hebrews shared a reciprocal antipathy) in a bad light. Furthermore, it removes the Canaanites from the Semitic family, in which they properly belong, and classifies them as Hamites. Thus the story is used to explain a number of relationships of

[13] Such causal explanations of origins (like the origin of the rainbow) are common in the Bible; they are called "etiological."

[14] In European art the scene is miscalled The Drunkenness of Noah. More correct would be The Nakedness of Noah, for his being drunk is only circumstantial to his nakedness. According to the account in Genesis (9:20-27), not the intoxication of the father but only the son's beholding his naked father was the offense.

basic importance to the Hebrews. Such biblical stories should
not be pulled out of context and regarded as isolated phenomena. There is a purpose in such narratives and it is our
business to get at the meaning to the best of our ability. Here
the problem is one which still concerns the best scholars of our
time: the differences among the ethnic groups of mankind.[15]

We now turn to Genesis 10, which remains a great historic
document. It is an attempt, containing considerable historicity, to put all the nations known to the Hebrews, into an
organic framework to show their interrelationships. There are
things of technical interest worth paying attention to. For
instance, two cities well-known from excavation are mentioned in verse 10: Babylon and Erech. But it is interesting
to note that two other cities, Accad and Calneh, have not
been discovered yet. Accad was the capital of the first Semitic
empire. Thus there are opportunities ahead to make major
discoveries in archeology in the Near East. In verse 11, Assur
(the envisaged ancestor of Assyria) is credited with the
building of Nineveh and Calah, Assyrian capitals which have
been excavated. But between them is Rehoboth-Ir about
which nothing else is known. The following verse, 12, names
Resen as "the great city" between Nineveh and Calah; the
identity of Resen is still shrouded in obscurity. While we must
always reckon with the possibility that the text is in error, we
must exercise caution for the simple reason that the trend of
archeological discovery is to confirm even points that the
consensus of opinion had rejected as false.[16]

---

[15] Compare one of the most influential books of the nineteenth century:
J. R. de Gobineau, *Essai sur l'inégalité des races humaines,* 1854 and
1884; 4th ed., Paris, 1916(?).

[16] The confirmatory trend of archeology is applicable not only to Sacred
Scripture but also to profane writing such as Herodotus, whose most
amazing "yarns" have in a number of instances turned out to be sober
truths. The absence of suitable mounds to account for lost cities near the
Tigris, may be due to the destructiveness of the River during the spring
floods, which I have seen overrun and devastate the countryside.

As we continue to read the genealogies, we note that the interest is focused more and more narrowly. The emphasis is now on Shem (verses 21-30), the ancestor of the Semites, including all the "sons of Eber" (verse 21) who embrace the Hebrews.

The next question (Genesis 11:1-9) is why does mankind have so many mutually unintelligible languages. The reason is that man in his haughtiness aspired to power through the building of a city with the Tower of Babel, whose top would reach the heavens. But God thwarted the plan by confounding human speech so that men no longer spoke the same language. Without a common language, men cannot engage in great cooperative enterprises; so the project was abandoned and men were scattered over the face of the earth with linguistic diversity.[17]

We now come to the final narrowing of the genealogies with the descendants of Eber (Genesis 11:16-26) down to Nahor, who begat Terah, who in turn begat Abram, the father of the Hebrew people, who are to occupy the center of the stage of human history, although they were encompassed by nations far greater than they. Terah in keeping with his patriarchal authority, moved his family, which included Abram and the latter's wife Sarai, from Ur of the Chaldees to Haran in northwest Mesopotamia, en route to Canaan. But Terah died in Haran, whereupon Abram assumed the role of patriarch.

This brings us to the full light of history around the year 1400 B.C. From now on the focus is on the evolution of Abram's seed in its relation to the God Who had chosen it as His people. However, the Bible does not narrate the experi-

---

[17] The greatest American handbook on linguistic science inadvertently takes the above biblical view of the main function of language; i.e., to make human cooperation possible. See L. Bloomfield, *Language*, Chicago, 1933, pp. 23-27.

ence of the Chosen People as though isolated, but instead within the framework of world history.

The Mesopotamian accounts of the origin of the universe and of human institutions are more complex than the Hebrew account. Some of the Mesopotamian complexity is due to the pluralistic attitude that goes with polytheism. But part of the complexity results from the fact that unlike Israel, which to some extent harmonized its traditions in the Bible, Mesopotamia never established one canonical recension of its traditions to the exclusion of all others. This is fortunate for the historian, whose ability to reconstruct the past is better when the sources are abundant and varied.

The chief creation account is called *Enuma Elish* "When on High," the first words of the text. It tells about the creation of gods who became embroiled in plots and strife. One of the deities, the sea-god Apsu, was so bothered by the noisy young upstart gods that he wanted to wipe them out. But his wife Tiamat, the sea goddess, was more moderate, and pleaded: "How could we destroy what we have created? Their way is grievous but let us act kindly!" (I :45-46).[18] Apsu's resolution brought upon him the hostility of the gods, headed by the wise Ea, who lulled Apsu to sleep by magic, and then attacked and slew him. This act of violence stirred Tiamat to rebel with the aid of the god Kingu. The revolt obliged the community of the gods to take action against Tiamat. To destroy her they created Marduk, who was beautiful and wise; so wise that he had four ears and four eyes the better to hear and see and accordingly to be more intelligent than other gods. Furthermore, to make him a king among gods, he was suckled by goddesses, in keeping with a motif whereby kings (regularly in Egypt, sometimes in Mesopotamia and often elsewhere as in Ugarit) claimed divinity through the

[18] See R. Labat, *Le poème babylonien de la création,* Paris, 1935.

fiction that they had suckled divine breasts.[19] Marduk fulfilled
his mission, slaying Tiamat and subduing her whole host of
minor deities. Then Marduk proceeded to create the universe
from Tiamat's corpse. Among his creations were three con-
stellations of stars for each month, to fix the days of the year.
The moon he created not only to shine by night but also to fix
the monthly cycle and to maintain a relationship with the sun.
Details of this sort bring out the sophistication and scientific
superiority of the Babylonians as against the Hebrews who
were satisfied with less astronomical data. Marduk then proceeded to form a man, who bears the non-Semitic name
"Lullu." [20] Marduk needed some material including blood for
creating man, and it was decided that a guilty god would have
to give up his life so that man could be created. Kingu was
chosen because he had incited and helped Tiamat in her revolt.
He was put to death and his blood was used for creating man.
Thus man was created out of divine stuff,[21] albeit from a
rebellious god.[22] The purpose in creating man was that he
might serve the gods. The underlying idea is clear enough:
There is no use being a god unless you have men to worship
you. Mankind was created to make life agreeable for the
pantheon; to perform work, to provide food and drink, and
to practice religion for the benefit of the gods. The gods were
so grateful that they awarded the great temple of Esagila to
Marduk in Babylon. They made a housewarming for him
there and offered him lavish praise.

Although the mythology of the Creation Epic stems from
Sumerian and perhaps earlier non-Semitic origins, the Babylonian recension which we have just outlined, has been recast

[19] Such notions may be quite functional. The acceptance of the divinity
of the king bolstered his authority and so contributed to law and order.

[20] This points to a non-Semitic origin of the Babylonian Creation Epic.

[21] Compare the biblical creation of man "in the image of God" (Genesis
1:27).

[22] From whom man derives his troublesome qualities?

in such a manner as to show that Babylon is the chief of cities and the center of empire; that its shrine Esagila is foremost among shrines; that Marduk of Babylon is the greatest of the gods, the creator of the world and the official god to worship above all others in the Babylonian Empire. It is interesting to note that when Assyria made its version of the Creation Epic, it transferred some of the glory of Marduk to Assur (the patron god of the capital Assur and of the Assyrian Empire) in order to reshape the Epic for its own political ends.

In addition to *Enuma Elish,* there are some lesser cuneiform creation accounts, to which we may refer briefly. One of them is a text which tells of the creation of cities, gods and man; the creation of the Tigris and Euphrates, the creation of plants and animals. According to another tablet, Ea creates out of clay the gods of the arts and crafts. Thus the creation is of gods, not of men, and it is gods that institute the arts, crafts and sciences.[23] Another tablet tells of the creation of a divine man and a divine woman for serving the gods and performing the occupations of society such as herding, irrigation and agriculture.[24] The divinity of the pair may have been occasioned by the importance of the first ancestors of mankind or by the fact that they had been made with divine blood.

The greatest literary accomplishment of Mesopotamia is the Gilgamesh Epic, which was translated in antiquity into other languages of the Cuneiform World. The best preserved versions are in Accadian, though the Epic has Sumerian and perhaps earlier non-Semitic antecedents. We have fragments of Hittite and Hurrian translations and the heroes of the Epic are frequently portrayed on works of art, such as seal cylinders, in ancient Mesopotamia.

[23] Contrast the Hebrew account where there is no theogony, and where crafts and sciences are traced back to men.

[24] The minor Babylonian creation stories are collected in Chapter II of A. Heidel, *The Babylonian Genesis,* 2nd ed., Chicago, 1951.

The Epic starts out with praise for the city of Erech, with its wonderful brickwork, fine city plan and magnificent walls. Gilgamesh, who is the tyrant of the city, is partly divine and partly human; for (like Achilles) his mother was a goddess. Gilgamesh was highhanded toward the populace; he forced young men to work and took girls for himself. At last the people of Erech cried out to the gods to rescue them. The gods accordingly designated one of their number to fashion a powerful creature out of clay, who was a bull from the waist down and human from the waist up, to oppose Gilgamesh and deflect him from his tyranny. Enkidu, as that creature was called, is placed in the fields where he lives among the animals, and is a lover of nature and an enemy of the hunter. He releases animals from traps and thwarts all the devices of the hunters so that wild life rejoiced but the hunters were dismayed. One particular hunter, on seeing Enkidu, realized why the hunters had not been catching any game. That hunter went home to his father to tell him of the sight he had beheld. The father sends the young hunter to Erech to fetch a girl named Shamhat who will alienate Enkidu from nature, introduce him to society and bring him to Erech where he will fulfill his mission by battling the tyrannical Gilgamesh. Shamhat has carnal relations with Enkidu, whereupon all of nature is alienated from him; the beasts no longer trust him, and he finds himself a changed but wiser creature. Enkidu comes back to the girl who tells him he is much too heroic a character to waste his time in the fields with the beasts and he should come to the big city where there is scope for his talents. She tells him of Erech where people wear festive garb, where every day is a holiday, and where he can meet Gilgamesh. Enkidu realizes there is no more turning back to nature and that he must to the big city, where, as he tells Shamhat, he intends to shout (referring to heroic challenges and the war-cry of victory).[25] But she warns him that he better not plan on shouting because Gilgamesh outclasses him. Then Shamhat introduces Enkidu to other aspects of civilization such as eating bread, which he finds difficult because he had been grazing on grass until that time. He also has trouble learning to drink from vessels, for he had hitherto been lapping water from streams. Finally he learns of some of the joys of civilization like anointing himself with oil and putting on clothes. After becoming familiar with such facets of civilization, Enkidu is ready to go to the city where Gilgamesh has been behaving outrageously toward the people. The two heroes meet and Enkidu challenges Gilgamesh, who had been apprised of Enkidu in dreams. The two fight on a monumental scale and so impressed each other with their might, that they decided not to wear each other out but instead to practice heroic virtue, by slaying evil dragons and enabling uprightness to triumph.

Their first victory was against the dragon Humbaba in the cedar forest. The elders of the city, and Enkidu, did their best to dissuade Gilgamesh from undertaking the perilous mission, but Gilgamesh, preferring fame to security, resolved to go through with it. He obtained the blessing and good advice of everyone including his divine mother Ninsun, who was troubled by the restless spirit of her son. With the help of Enkidu, Gilgamesh made the dangerous journey and located the dragon. By hurling, through magic, eight winds into the wicked dragon's mouth, our two heroes overcame and captured it. Humbaba begged for mercy but in vain. They cut off his head and won immortal fame.

After that, Gilgamesh, who was handsome, dressed up. He looked so attractive that the goddess Ishtar proposed marriage to him. She offered him rich marriage gifts but he pointed out that he was not prepared to give her food and

[25] Discussed below in Chapter VII.

drink and in general the standard of living to which a goddess
is accustomed. He then reminded her of her long and shameful marital history : She had once loved a horse, but when she
had tired of him, she treated him brutally and beat him to
make him run. She had once loved a shepherd but tired of
him and turned him into a wolf so that his own dogs drove
him away. Gilgamesh enumerated all the instances of Ishtar's
treachery to her mates, and rejected her proposal. His rebuff
infuriated her and she determined to avenge the affront. She
went to her father, the great god Anu, and asked permission
to have the Bull of Heaven placed at her disposal. The Bull
of Heaven was to be a human-headed bull of great strength
which she hoped would slay Gilgamesh. To extract permission
from her unwilling father, she made threats of violence. Anu,
in granting permission, reminds her that the slaying of a hero
will cause a seven-year famine. She had anticipated this dire
consequence and assured Anu that she had laid up a seven-
year supply of food.[26] Thereupon Anu commissions the goddess Aruru to make the Bull of Heaven. She obeys; but in
the combat that ensues, Gilgamesh and Enkidu kill the Bull
of Heaven.[27] Ishtar is dismayed at this and complains, but
Enkidu cuts off a leg of the Bull of Heaven and flings it at
Ishtar as a terrible insult.[28] She, in revenge, plans the death
of Enkidu; for such an indignity to a goddess could not go
unpunished. Pathetically Enkidu perishes and vainly does
Gilgamesh try to bring him back to life. He touches and talks
to him but gets no answer. Finally after watching his body

[26] Two different motifs are combined here. One is the motif of a seven-
year famine in sympathy for a slain hero; the other is the theme of antici-
pating a seven-year famine by laying up supplies. The first motif is matched
in Ugarit where such a cycle of famine years follows the slaying of Aqhat;
while the second is familiar from the biblical story of Joseph in Egypt.

[27] Fighting the Bull of Heaven is one of the most frequent themes in
Mesopotamian art, particularly on seal cylinders of the Accad Dynasty.

[28] That this symbolized, over a wide area, a serious affront, is demonstrated by its recurrence in Homer's Odyssey (see Chapter VII).

with pious devotion, he notices a worm on the corpse and realizes that death takes its victims beyond recall. The awful reality of death fills Gilgamesh with fear because, inasmuch as he is not completely divine, he too must die. Hence he becomes obsessed with the drive to obtain immortality.

Only one man had ever become immortal. That was the Babylonian "Noah," named Utnapishtim, who with his wife had become immortal after the Flood. Gilgamesh reasoned that the way to get eternal life, would be to go to the immortal Utnapishtim and find out the secret from him. He knew the road was difficult, beset with many obstacles, but Gilgamesh could not refrain from his quest. On the way he met a divine barmaid, who was used to tales of woe and had observed personal frustrations. She gave him sensible advice:

> "Gilgamesh, whither runnest thou?
>    The life which thou seekest thou wilt not find.
> When the gods created mankind,
>    They allotted death to mankind;
>       Life they retained in their own keeping.
> O Gilgamesh, let thy belly be full,
>    Day and night be thou merry!
> Make every day one of rejoicing,
>    Day and night, dance and play!
> Let thy clothes be clean,
>    Thy head washed
>       And thy self bathed in water.
> Cherish the little one holding thy hand
>    Let (thy) wife rejoice in thy bosom.
> This is the lot of [mankind]." (X:iii:1-14).[29]

But Gilgamesh cannot get himself to make the most of mortal reality and persists on his dangerous mission to far-off

[29] R. Campbell Thompson, *The Epic of Gilgamesh: Text, Transliteration and Notes;* Oxford, 1930, pp. 53-54.

Utnapishtim. When he at long last beholds the old man, he is surprised. Gilgamesh, who thought he was going to see a mighty hero different from other men, looks at him and says:

> "I look upon thee, Utnapishtim.
>   Thine appearance is not different
>     Thou art like me.
>   Yea, thou art not different
>     Thou art like me.
>   My heart had fancied thee as one perfect for
>       waging battle
>   [But] thou liest idly on thy back.
>   [Tell me!]
>   How didst thou enter the company of the gods
>     And obtain immortality?" (XI :2-7).

At this point Utnapishtim decides to tell him the whole story, which includes the flood epic of Babylonia. While the Hebrew and Babylonian creation accounts are radically different, their flood epics are quite similar and come from a common source.

Gilgamesh is told that Utnapishtim lived before the Flood in the city of Shuruppak. The gods had decided to destroy mankind. One god, Ea, was friendly to Utnapishtim and determined to give him the information necessary for saving him. Ea did not venture to talk to him directly but instead went to the reed hut of Utnapishtim and addressed the hut.[30] Utnapishtim was there to hear the message, which instructed him to disregard his possessions, to construct an ark according to exact specifications, to take the seed of all living aboard, to include his wife, and to secure adequate supplies and a crew. The Babylonian account is more detailed and realistic

---

[30] The device of addressing an inanimate object with a message meant to be heard by people, occurs also in 1 Kings 13:2, where a prophet, whose message is to be heard by Jeroboam and the public, addresses the altar.

than the biblical version, because the Mesopotamians were more advanced than the Hebrews in material civilization in general, and specifically in the arts of naval construction and operation. It is interesting to note that the wall of the reed hut was to be converted into the ark. This was a well-known technique in ancient Mesopotamia, where the reed wall of a house could be converted into a boat.[31]

The rains came and, as in the biblical narrative, the ark landed on a mountain. Utnapishtim sends out first a dove, then a swallow, and finally a raven before he determines, much like Noah, that the earth was dry. Again like Noah, he gets out and sacrifices to the gods, who hover over the sweet smelling sacrifice like flies. One particularly malicious god, Enlil, was angry because the flood secret had been divulged, and a man and his wife had been spared. Enlil wanted to destroy all life out of sheer malevolence. But Ea appeased him and counseled moderation. Ea mollified Enlil so successfully that Enlil put his hand on the forehead of the man and woman and conferred immortality upon them. Utnapishtim, as he closes his narration, reminds Gilgamesh that special circumstances had accounted for the conferring of immortality after the Flood, but that no such circumstances are at hand to secure a similar favor from the gods for Gilgamesh. The latter is dismayed by his shattered hopes.

Utnapishtim then asked Gilgamesh to try to stay awake for seven days and seven nights. Apparently the idea was that if a man aspires to immortality, he ought first to be able to overcome sleep. If one cannot fight off ordinary sleep, how can he hope to escape from the sleep of death? But Gilgamesh, unable to stay awake, falls asleep, whereupon Utnapishtim

[31] The consonantal text of Genesis 6:14 has *qnym*, which should be read *qanim* "reeds," not *qinnim* "nests" (which does not mean "compartments of a ship"). The Hebrew word for the "ark" occurs elsewhere only in the story of Moses, who as a baby was exposed in such a vessel, which is explicitly described as constructed of reeds (Exodus 2:3).

tells his wife to bake bread, a loaf each day, for Gilgamesh. She does so day after day until the seventh day, when he wakes up and claims he had only been dozing a little. But the loaves of bread, each in a different stage of mold, proved he had been asleep for a week; and the man who could not resist sleep is hardly a candidate for immortality.

Just before Gilgamesh is to leave Utnapishtim and his wife, the latter tells her husband to give Gilgamesh a parting gift: the secret of how to find the elixir of youth, which happens to be a plant at the bottom of the sea. By putting stones on one's feet and diving to the ocean floor, one could obtain the plant which restores the aged to vigorous youth. Gilgamesh gratefully goes off with Utnapishtim's boatman. The twain get the plant; but instead of eating it right away, Gilgamesh keeps it against the time when he will be old and decrepit, and when eating it will rejuvenate him. On the way back to Erech, Gilgamesh stops at a pool to refresh himself, leaves the plant there; and a snake steals it and eats it—which explains why the snake sloughs off its old skin, and thus, as it was believed, is rejuvenated in a new skin every year. Disconsolate, Gilgamesh goes into a bitter complaint, for he had gone through countless woes not for himself but for the serpent; and his quest had ended in utter failure.

Gilgamesh asks the boatman to go on to Erech with him. The two visit that great city and behold its wonderful brickwork, its fine city plan and its magnificent walls. Thus the Epic repeats the note on which it began. For, though men cannot win immortality, they can at least appreciate their earthly abode. The fact that it is not our lot to share eternal life with the distant Utnapishtim need not prevent us from enjoying the advantages of our native city.

There are numerous mythological texts dealing with similar and other problems. We may refer briefly to one that concerns the quest for immortality. It is about a wise hero called Adapa, who while fishing was infuriated by the South Wind which upset his boat. He retaliated by breaking the South Wind's wings and was consequently summoned before the gods. Ea instructed him to refuse the water of death and the food of death that the gods would offer him. But, as things turned out, he was offered the water of life and the food of life; yet, following Ea's bad advice, he refused them. Thus again is sounded the sad note of man's aspiring in vain to immortality, which the gods withhold as their own prerogative. Like the biblical Adam, Adapa acquired wisdom but not eternal life. The theme of the gods preventing mankind from attaining immortality is accordingly widespread throughout the Bible World.

# Chapter III

# EGYPT TO THE AMARNA AGE

OUR discussion of the biblical account brought us down to about 1400 B.C., by which time the Near East had experienced considerable development both in the Nile Valley and in Asia. Now we shall summarize the historical experience of the Near East down to that time, starting with Egypt.

Egypt had a long prehistory attested by stone implements, skeletal remains, and eventually pottery—much of it quite well made and attractive. There is evidence of a number of migrations. At an early date (perhaps well back in the fifth millennium) Hamito-Semites swept down from Asia into the Nile Valley, where they vanquished an earlier population. Egypt has always been exposed to infiltration from the north and south ends of the Nile Valley. Negroes came up from the south and constituted in the main the racial stock of Nubia in antiquity and of the Sudan today. Further north, however, the white immigrants predominated, with the result that the population came to be light brown and to speak the Egyptian language, which is related to the Semitic languages of Asia.

Inhabitable Egypt was the long river valley divided into districts called nomes, each with a capital city, where there was a temple dedicated to the local god. The division into nomes remained a factor in Egyptian history long after the country had attained unity. The nomes tended to be divided into two groups—those in the north and those in the south. The final development was the unification of Upper (= south) Egypt and Lower (= north) Egypt somewhat before 3000 B.C. A predynastic king named Narmer has left us a monument, on which he is shown wearing on one occasion the flat red crown of Lower Egypt and on another occasion the elongated white crown of Upper Egypt, indicating that he was in a position to claim sovereignty over both halves of the country. Shortly after his time, Menes, the first king of the first official dynasty, ruled over the two Egypts and he, according to the tradition of the country,[1] was credited with the achievement of uniting the two Egypts and with him begins the full light of actual Egyptian history.[2] His personal monuments and relics, inscribed with his name in hieroglyphs, have been found so that he is not a shadowy king known only from late tradition, but fully attested by contemporary evidence. By his time Egypt had already developed a well-defined and distinctive civilization with an art (and system of writing[3]) whose basic canons were in large measure established.[4]

Egypt had a strong love of tradition. Once a thing took hold there, it rarely died out. Other things could be added but this resulted in an accumulation of mixed traditions, because the Egyptians could learn new things more readily than forget old ones. Thus, along with the development of hieroglyphic writing was included an alphabet. Each consonant in the language could be represented by a separate hieroglyph, but the Egyptians were not systematic enough to see the advantages in writing in a purely alphabetic way. Instead they combined three different systems of writing: (1) the logographic,

[1] The authority for the accepted division of Egyptian rulers into dynasties is Manetho, an Egyptian who wrote a history of his nation in Greek during the third century B.C.

[2] The difference between Narmer's and Menes's work may have been that Narmer's unification was ephemeral, whereas Menes's endured.

[3] Egyptian hieroglyphic writing remained, to the end, a branch of the graphic arts.

[4] For Egyptian history, its sources and art, see J. H. Breasted, *A History of Egypt*, 3rd ed., New York, 1943; *Ancient Records of Egypt* I-V, Chicago, 1906-07; and J. Pijoán, *Summa Artis*, 2nd ed., III, Madrid, 1945. Also note Part I of A. Scharff and A. Moortgat, *Aegypten und Vorderasien im Altertum*, Munich, 1950.

whereby each sign stands for a word; (2) the syllabic, whereby each sign stands for a syllable; and (3) the alphabetic, whereby each sign stands for a single sound. Often a word is written in two or even in all three systems simultaneously plus a "determinative," which is a hieroglyph that places the word in a semantic category.[5] Script is not the only manifestation of the Egyptians' inability conveniently to forget during the process of accretion. In religion, gods were added but not dropt from the pantheon, with the result that the growing host of deities became an ungainly clutter. So too, myths were added to myths, with the sum total growing ever more complicated.

Early in the third millennium the Egyptians began to exploit the mineral resources of the Sinai Peninsula. It is characteristic of Egyptian history that whenever Egypt was strong, she left traces of her activities, including inscriptions, in Sinai. Thus, although compared with Mesopotamia, Egypt was relatively isolated, it had contacts with the outside world, not only at the north and south ends of the long Nile Valley, but also through conquest and trade with the continent of Asia, and with the islands and coasts of the Mediterranean and Red Seas.

After the first two Early Dynasties, the period of the Old Kingdom was ushered in by the Third Dynasty. The most important king of that Dynasty was Joser, whose adviser Imhotep was a remarkable man later to be deified and to come down in Egyptian history as a giant in the development of civilization. He was a physician, sage, counselor and the architect of the imposing Step Pyramid that still amazes the traveler at Saqqara, near Cairo. The king at the end of the Third or beginning of the Fourth Dynasty, Senefru,

---

[5] A determinative tells, so to speak, whether a consonantal combination like *ct* means "cut," "cute," or "cat."

had contacts with Syria and Palestine, so that already in the third millennium, Egyptian influence was felt in Canaan.

The Old Kingdom was in many ways the most noteworthy of all the periods of Egyptian history. It has left us the greatest monuments and the finest art of Egypt, as well as embraced the essential pattern that the contributions of Egyptian civilization were to follow down to the end. Already in this early period, there was the tendency to place Re, the Sun, as the foremost god in the Egyptian pantheon and in Old Kingdom times temples were built for the worship of Re. This ran against another current in Egypt, whereby the deities were local gods, rather than the personifications of natural, universal phenomena. Nomic deities are more numerous than those with claim to universality. The notable and early exception was the Sun, although it took over a thousand years for Egyptian solar worship to gain enough momentum to produce one of the most amazing revolutions in world history.

The fact that the gods varied from nome to nome did not mean that real religious differences existed between nome and nome. The underlying ideas were the same for all the nomes. Egyptians, depending on which was their nome, worshiped at different shrines and had gods with different attributes. The different gods might be represented each by a different animal; and each might have different festivals. But an Egyptian who changed his residence from one nome to another, had little difficulty, emotionally or intellectually, in getting used to the change. The differences between the cults were as a rule only externally varying expressions of the same religious character that prevailed from one end of Egypt to the other.

The Egyptians visualized the universe as divided into three parts; (1) the land of the gods was located in the east where the sun rises; (2) in the middle was the Nile Valley, the land of men; (3) to the west lay the land of the dead. Such was their universe. They were not particularly concerned with foreign lands, for which no Egyptian cared to leave Egypt; nor with foreign nations, which the Egyptians viewed with contempt. The common man was not interested in foreign contacts nor in conquests, however much his sovereign might embark upon them.[6]

Egyptians lived in a rich country, where they developed their own homogeneous civilization in spite of changes partly brought about by periodic infiltrations from the north or south. They were ideally situated to develop their own distinctive culture that far excelled anything that men had achieved anywhere else. The Egyptians knew this; whence their national pride and disdain for other civilizations and other people.

They believed in the existence of an other-worldly paradise —in fields where the dead could enter if they had lived meritorious lives in this world. In paradise no chores had to be done by the blessed, who enjoy plenty and happiness.

The king was considered divine, as was indicated in a country where vital projects of nationwide scope have to be correlated, particularly in irrigation. The whole length of the river valley must be under one "Nile Valley Authority"; and the best way to get the people to cooperate throughout the vast length of the land, was to have them respect the king as divine and follow his authority unquestioningly. The cult of the dead during Old Kingdom times was reserved for the king and eventually extended to the nobles (but not to the common people) and so the magnificent funerary structures and the elaborate rituals and sacrifices in them—all of which necessitated onerous taxation and forced labor—were just for the king and his immediate circle. The Pharaoh was a busy,

---

[6] The modern Egyptian Arab feels much the same way and rarely wants to go abroad. In this he is unlike the Lebanese Arab who gladly goes to the ends of the earth in quest of opportunity, much like his Phoenician predecessors.

enlightened administrator, who kept the country united by holding his governors in check.

In family life, woman had a peculiarly important position, for inheritance passed through the mother rather than through the father. Accordingly, the oldest daughter was normally the heir; and the chief protector of a person was not his own father but his mother's oldest brother. This system may well hark back to prehistoric times when only the obvious relationship between mother and child was recognized, but not the less apparent relationship between father and child.

A wisdom literature was growing up, whose authors warned the reader against vice; admonishing him to live the good life and to shun evil. But the evils that the sages refer to are described so graphically that we can see the corrupt social usages that evoked wisdom literature.

The royal circle maintained a standard of luxury that almost defies imagination, while the peasants, as always in Egypt, lived in abject poverty. Yet there was no caste system and it was possible for a talented lad of humble birth to attain the circle of officialdom by getting an education. The motive to learn to read and write was to qualify for government work. Any boy, by excelling first in his studies and then in government service, had just as much chance to rise to the prime-ministry as an American boy has to become President.

In spite of ideas like the divinity of kings and the cult of the dead,[7] the mentality of the Egyptians was basically materialistic and practical. Even the cult of the dead was quite materialistic. The body was mummified because corporeal ex-

---

[7] Superficially an Egyptian custom like writing letters to the dead might convey an impractical and spiritual outlook. But such a conclusion would be just as false as it would be to conclude that American messages addressed in the second person to the dead (such messages can be found nearly every day on the obituary page of the *New York Times* under the title "In Memoriam") indicate that the U. S. A. is an impractical, spiritual nation.

istence was the only existence acceptable to the Egyptian. Offerings of baking and of beer figure prominently because an afterlife without food and drink would be no life for an Egyptian.

Included among the practical arts, however misguided it may have been, was magic. Magic was designed, as it is all over the world, to produce practical effects; to restore or insure health, and to obtain things that otherwise seem out of reach. Naturally, magic was not used where the Egyptians could accomplish their ends scientifically. Only when science and rational technique broke down, would magic be invoked. For example, Egyptians might resort to magic in an attempt to cure a disease they did not understand; but they would never depend on magic for the construction of a pyramid, which they did understand.

Already in Old Kingdom times, sculptured portraits are often superb likenesses. This again was practical. The identity of the dead had to go on and this could best be achieved through an exact portrait likeness, which explains why such statues as the one known as Sheikh el-Beled,[8] are superb portraits of definite individuals; in that particular case, of a man of the upper classes, well-fed, sure of himself, used to exerting authority, self-satisfied. It is not an idealized portrait but one calculated to fulfill a purpose that called for faithful individuality.

Old Kingdom reliefs already show the canons that were to remain in Egyptian art to the end. The eye and shoulders had to be front-view. The feet and trunk, however, are in profile. This is a strange combination for us until we get used to it, but once we accept it as the standard, as the Egyptians

[8] The best comprehensive volume on the art of the ancient Near East is H. Schäfer and W. Andrae, *Die Kunst des alten Orients,* 3rd ed., Berlin, 1942. A selection of Egyptian masterpieces is available in H. Ranke, *Meisterwerke der ägyptischen Kunst,* Basel, 1948. See plate 53 for the Sheikh el-Beled.

did, it becomes quite acceptable. All art has its conventions; and Egyptian conventions in no way detract from the greatness of Egyptian art. Another difference between our art and Egyptian is that while we like to have only one moment represented in an artistic composition, the Egyptians felt free to combine a number of different moments in the same composition. One part of a scene may represent one stage of the action, while another part of the same scene represents a later stage. Thus in battle scenes of the Empire Period,[9] one and the same scene can show a number of operations ranging in time from the launching of an attack upon a city to leading off captives and booty after the victory.

The temples had only straight lines, upright and horizontal. The arch was already known; it was reserved for vaults in funerary buildings, but was not used in temples.[10]

After Joser and Senefru, we come to the great builders of the Fourth Dynasty, whose first king Cheops is the builder of the greatest of all pyramids, the first one at Giza containing 2,300,000 blocks. The average weight of the blocks is two and a half tons. The height of the pyramid is 481 feet; the base has sides 755 feet long. The margin of error in construction is for all intents and purposes nil. Precision, organized labor, planning, varied personnel (from drudges to masons and up to the master architect) and the backing of an entire economy were necessary for accomplishing the greatest of the Seven Wonders. And it may be worth noting that of all the Seven Wonders, the pyramids alone survive.

The governors were strong men who inherited their position. Other officials, too, increased their power as time went

[9] This is not limited to Egyptian art; it is also common in Mesopotamia and elsewhere.

[10] As my student, Mr. H. G. Stigers has explained to me, the reason is that the Egyptians did not know how to buttress walls sufficiently for taking the thrust of an arch. In thick-walled tombs, the thrust offers no problem.

on. After the great pyramid of Cheops, the subsequent Old
Kingdom pyramids progressively diminished in size, because
the resources of the kingdom were being exhausted and power
was passing from the Pharaohs to the governors and officials.
Decentralization was setting in. However, it was in this
period, when the process of disintegration had begun, that the
finest artistic work (as in painting) and the finest texts of the
Old Kingdom were produced, during the Fifth and Sixth
Dynasties. As is often the case, the arts flowered most, as
power began to decline. With the fall of the Sixth Dynasty,
the Old Kingdom comes to an end. Not only has the Old
Kingdom left the greatest monuments ever put up by men,
but it was an age that had seen the building of ships for sailing and exploring lands and seas; and, more than that, an age
that had seen the beginning of a concept of personal judgment
based on character and merit in this world.

The intermediate period that followed is not one of glory.
For the Eighth Dynasty we have little or no trace of activity
in the fine arts. No monuments were then erected by the
Pharaohs. There are texts of local governors, in which the
Pharaoh is disregarded, indicating that he had become more
or less a figurehead. The Ninth and Tenth Dynasties need
not delay us. For present purposes we may note in passing
that their center was Heracleopolis in the nome where the
crocodile was worshiped. The rulers are known as the
Heracleopolitans.

With the Eleventh Dynasty, however, the rulers of the
ancient city of Thebes asserted themselves, first locally, and
later uniting the two Egypts to inaugurate the Middle Kingdom. The ruling family formed a succession of kings, some
called Intef, and some called Mentuhotep. Expeditions were
resumed and a Mentuhotep put up a mortuary temple that
was the prototype of one of the greatest temples in the Nile
Valley; namely, the one built at Deir el-Bahri by Queen

Hatshepsut, whom we shall discuss later. Out of the Theban ruling family came a leader, around 1800 B.C., who founded the great Twelfth Dynasty. His name was Amenemhet I. He emerged from Thebes, got control of all of Egypt and checked the nomarchs (as the heads of the nomes are called). However, in his rise to power he had to depend on friendly nomarchs, so that feudalism was a foregone conclusion. The Twelfth Dynasty which marked the height of the classical age of the Middle Kingdom is characterized by feudalism. Yet the king was able to control the nomarchs so that the country could function efficiently as a whole, though at the same time local sensibilities and local initiative were not crushed. Because Thebes was in Upper Egypt, and therefore not in a central position, the capital was moved north, to a point south of Memphis in Middle Egypt, where control could be better kept over the northern and southern parts of the land. The king was able to exert authority through his treasury, for all taxes had to filter through from the nomes into a central treasury. Another unifying factor was the palace schools, where reading and writing were taught for the training of officials. The officials thus had contact with the royal circle and felt allegiance to the divine king. The masses were in abject poverty as usual. But again there was always the opportunity for the individual, regardless of the station in which he was born, to rise by showing his ability, to get an education and enter government service.

The local gods continued, but their cults, to survive, had to be associated with, or subordinated to, Re. For example, the god of Thebes, the royal city, was Amon who became so important that his priests were the most powerful in the land. Yet Amon was combined with Re into "Amon-Re," in order to fit in with the trend whereby gods had to be connected with Re in order that their cults might continue.

Egyptian religion developed a kind of Passion Play concerning Osiris, the god of the dead, showing his suffering, death and revival.[11] Each dead person was identified with Osiris on the assumption that the deceased would undergo, but emerge triumphant like Osiris from, a trial full of vicissitudes to qualify for the life eternal.

The fully developed concept of a personal judgment, whereby each man enters paradise if his character and life on earth warrant it, appears quite remarkable when we consider that centuries later there was still no such idea in Mesopotamia and Israel. The Babylonians and Assyrians never developed it. And in Israel, throughout nearly all of the Old Testament, the afterworld was considered a dreary underground place called Sheol, where the good and bad alike led an eventless existence. Indeed the later Jewish, Christian and Islamic concept of the afterlife, as one in which the individual is rewarded or punished depending on his earthly record, is more akin to Egyptian views than to those of the Old Testament.[12]

The aggressive and progressive Amenemhet I organized the realm and brought Egypt into its second era of splendor. A palace plot on his life convinced him that his throne was not secure, so he made his son, Sesostris I, coregent, a precedent that was followed throughout the Middle Kingdom. That is, each king at some point in his reign associated the crown prince with him so that when the father died, the son was already enthroned. (This was to happen in Hebrew history; e.g., when David made Solomon coregent before his own death.[13])

The most charming piece of Egyptian literature comes from this period. While Sesostris I was performing military

---

[11] Osiris died and rose from the dead once. The idea that he died and rose annually has no foundation in the ancient Egyptian sources.

[12] As we shall see in subsequent chapters, it is only toward the close of the Old Testament that the concept of personal salvation comes in.

[13] I Kings I:32-40.

service in the field, news came secretly of Amenemhet's death, whereupon Sesostris hastened to the capital to forestall trouble. There he made sure of the throne. One of Sesostris's courtiers was a man named Sinuhe, the hero of The Romance of Sinuhe. This story relates that when Sinuhe got wind of Amenemhet's death, he feared that evil consequences might befall him, as so often happens to courtiers in times of political change. Sinuhe therefore fled from the camp of his master and went stealthily from Egypt to Asia as a fugitive. In the desert, around the Isthmus of Suez, he was saved by hospitable Semitic bedouin. He had nearly died of thirst and they gave him to drink water and then cooked milk, like the modern bedouin who regale their guests with *leben*. Thence, Sinuhe wandered north into Canaan where he fell in with a sheikh, or local ruler, who respected him because of his Egyptian origin and his experience in Pharaonic circles. He offered him a frontier post to be defended against invading Semitic bedouin. Sinuhe accepted the position as well as the ruler's eldest daughter in marriage and soon attained wealth and success. The bedouin made attacks on him but he got the best of them. His orchards and vineyards yielded rich harvests of figs, olives and grapes. His sons had grown strong and were helping him. He had everything an Asiatic could want. But to an Egyptian, even an Asiatic paradise was bitter exile. All Sinuhe's prosperity was vain because of his longing to return to his native land. At last he got in touch with emissaries on diplomatic missions of Sesostris, and after many years of waiting and growing old, he received in writing from the Pharaoh a clean bill of health and a welcome home. Without any hesitation, he liquidated his Asiatic interests, turned his power over to his sons, and apparently felt no qualms about leaving the wife who had borne them. He put his affairs in order, as an upstanding administrator should, and wended his way back to Egypt, going through the frontier posts, and then boarding a Nile boat provided by the King. Sinuhe tells us glowingly about the wonderful service aboard the Egyptian boat, on which every member of the crew knew his job, and performed it smoothly. What a change from "barbaric" Asia! As he sailed up the Nile to the palace, his heart rejoiced, for he was glad to be back in his homeland, and on his way to the court where he belonged. The King received him well and summoned the Queen and royal children. When they came into the court and saw Sinuhe, about whom they had heard so much, they screamed on seeing him clad like an Asiatic. They could not believe that the exotic person before them was Sinuhe, but the King assured them it was he. Then Sinuhe was clad in fine linen, perfumed, shaved and given an estate and royal support. The King also gave him a funeral endowment and a statue covered with gold to perpetuate his existence in the world to come. Gratefully Sinuhe put behind him all the years of exile, and settled down to enjoy the rest of his life in honor, as a favorite in the court of his sovereign, with the prospect of proper burial, indispensable for securing immortality.

The Romance of Sinuhe is literature composed for enjoyment, without any religious or political motive. It is of some special interest to Bible students, because in the course of the narrative, conditions in Canaan are reflected. Sinuhe's geography includes Qedem ("East"), where bedouin were commonly seen. The land of the tent-dwelling Job (1:3) is also designated as Qedem ("East"). But from the Egyptian viewpoint, the text was literature written for the sake of entertainment. Papyri inscribed with the story have been found in tombs; they were placed there so that the dead might have good reading matter in the future world.[14]

[14] Magical and religious compositions such as the Book of the Dead were for the grim business of securing salvation. The Sinuhe story and other Middle Egyptian pieces of literature are the world's first secular literature composed for reading enjoyment.

The greatest conqueror of the Middle Kingdom was Sesostris III, who made the first real Egyptian invasion of Canaan. Among the towns he encountered there was Sekmem, which is either the biblical Shechem in Central Palestine or another Canaanite town of the same name.

Middle Kingdom art does not have the originality and genius of Old Kingdom masters. The figures now begin to get bigger. More effort was spent on size than artistic merit. However, the best portraits of this period are still excellent.

Another phenomenon of this period is prophecy. There is for example a prophet called Ipuwer; Neferrohu is the name of another. A prophet, according to the Egyptian pattern, appears before the king and gives him sad news. He tells him that because of evil, the land is going to suffer. An enemy will invade Egypt and inflict upon it all kinds of misery including the inversion of all social relationships, until a righteous king will arise as a savior, drive out the destructive invader and institute a godly order. Egyptian prophecy may have had an influence on Israelite prophecy, though Israel added further religious and ethical content.[15]

One of the literary masterpieces of the Middle Kingdom is The Song of the Harper, in which the minstrel appears before a banquet, where he sings to the guests that everything in life is vain, that we cannot take our possessions with us after death, and that the only thing to do is to eat, drink and be merry because the future holds nothing certain in store for us; nor have the dead ever come back to tell of the future life. This represents an inquiring, skeptical attitude of oriental origin, that may have eventually influenced (centuries later) the author of Ecclesiastes,[16] whose musings run the gamut of

[15] For extensive translations (with bibliography on the originals) of Egyptian literature, cf. J. A. Wilson's contributions to *Ancient Near Eastern Texts (Relating to the Old Testament)*, edited by J. B. Pritchard, Princeton, 1950.

[16] Some attribute the skeptical outlook in Ecclesiastes to Greek sources.

thoughts expressed by the Harper; although in good Hebrew fashion, the biblical Book concludes that after all is said and done, the best course is to fear God.[17]

As the Harper shows, there were Egyptians who doubted the make-believe future world, where the blessed eat, drink and play, with no work to do. Thinking people, even in Egypt, questioned the widely-accepted tenets of the cult of the dead. This should warn us against the temptation to generalize. Thus, while most ancient Egyptians were more concerned with the life beyond than are most modern Americans; some ancient Egyptians were more skeptical in such matters than are some modern Americans.

The splendor of the Middle Kingdom was not to last. It ended with usurpers seizing the throne one after the other. Finally, foreign invaders called the Hyksos entered the country from Asia, imposing their rule which was intolerable to the Egyptians. However, the Hyksos did introduce the horse-drawn chariot and modernized warfare to the degree that made possible the next step of Egyptian history: the Empire Period. The Hyksos ruled an empire, not merely an Egyptian kingdom. They chose as their capital the city of Avaris in the Delta from which to govern their holdings on two continents. A capital in Upper or Middle Egypt would not have been sufficiently central. That the Hyksos ruled not only over Egypt but also over some of Western Asia, paved the way for the Egyptian Empire that was to see Egypt's maximum expansion beyond her own natural borders. Since the capital of the Hyksos was in the far north, they were not in a position to control the far south; and it was from there that nationalism, as has always been the case, rose again, finally to drive

---

The Song of the Harper shows that notions such as "you can't take it with you" (etc.) need not have been borrowed from Greece.

[17] The Hebrew language has no word for "religion." The true religion is designated as "the fear of God (or Yahwe)."

out the invader and establish the New Kingdom (as the Empire Period is also called).

The Hyksos consisted of a mixed multitude, including many Semites along with other Asiatic elements. With their expulsion around the year 1570 B.C. by Ahmosis I (about 1570-45 B.C.) of Thebes, the founder of the Eighteenth Dynasty, the New Kingdom begins.

The Middle Kingdom had been an age of feudalism. The New Kingdom is an age of royal ownership of the land, as is depicted in Genesis 47:19-20, where the system is attributed to Joseph's planning. The people were nearly all serfs bound to the king who owned the land. The taxes included one-fifth of the crops which the serfs had to pay into the royal treasury. This too is attributed to Joseph's administration in Genesis 47:23-27. The Joseph story shows familiarity with New Kingdom government, national economy and society. The only tax exemptions were those of the priesthood, again specified in the Joseph story. The priests received their maintenance from the crown and, being tax exempt, were able to hold on to their lands.

The state was military and the Egyptians were now able to accomplish feats of warfare that they had never been able to do before. Both in tactics and in the strategic distribution of troops, new features were added. The world's first well-documented accounts of strategically conducted campaigns come from the New Kingdom. The new branch of the army was the chariotry, whose charioteers formed the uppermost military class. Members of the old nobility who wished to retain a privileged position sought their way into the circle of charioteers; because caring for horses and serving the king in his chariotry constituted the most important source of New Kingdom power.

There was no public opinion. Egypt was an absolute dictatorship. Accordingly, there had to be a strong king. If a dictator is inept, it is impossible to run the country satisfactorily. Thus, as long as there was a succession of strong Pharaohs, the New Kingdom was able to survive. When able leadership was lacking on the throne, the doom of the New Kingdom was sealed.

The old nobility, as we have mentioned, disappeared as such, but in its place comes an officialdom. The king always needed an able prime minister, who in turn needed able civil servants to administer the land. There was thus opportunity for talented common people. As was typical throughout Egyptian history, a young man able to show his merit and to rise first in school and then in civil service, could aspire to the highest positions. Accordingly, the rise of Joseph from an obscure lad to the highest position next to the king, fits in with the picture of Egypt as we know it from native sources.

The name Thutmes figures prominently in the Eighteenth Dynasty. Thutmes I invaded Syria and his records are consequently important for the study of Canaan. The complicated succession to the throne at this time, forms one of the most interesting chapters of history. There were three kings named Thutmes whose careers and succession to the throne were complicated by a woman: Queen Hatshepsut (about 1501-1480). She assumed not only queenship but kingship, and she even wore a false beard to simulate masculinity in posing for some of her monuments. The able woman sent expeditions abroad and built edifices at home. The man of her confidence was Senmut, the architect who built at Deir el-Bahri her funerary temple, which as we have observed, was copied after the older neighboring temple of Mentuhotep. The ambitious men in her family naturally hated her. Thutmes III (about 1502-1448), the ablest monarch of the Dynasty, was related to her by marriage as well as through other family ties. She suppressed him, obliging him to wait until she died before he could rule by himself and carry out his grandiose plans. When she died, male resentment expressed itself in defacing her monuments, erasing her name and trying to obliterate her memory from history.

Thutmes III invaded Canaan against a coalition headed by the King of Kadesh, a city by the Orontes River in central Syria. Thutmes III's account of the way he conducted his battle at Megiddo (around 1480), in the course of the war, is now classical. There were three routes by which he could go. The shortest, now known as Wadi Ara, happened to be the most dangerous because it is so narrow in places that men must march in single file. Accordingly, if the enemy had intelligence of his passage through the narrow wadi, they could attack him with relatively few troops and wipe out his forces. Against the advice of all his counselors, he insisted on taking this daring, shortest, and least expected route. The gamble turned out to be a complete success and he vanquished the coalition of kings near Megiddo. That city, however, shut its gates on those that were defeated so that the men who saved their own lives and got back into the city had to be hauled up over the wall. In those days, strongly walled cities were rarely captured. The Egyptians did not yet know the science of effective siege warfare, for the Assyrians were yet to invent such basic techniques as mining under city walls. Accordingly expedition after expedition was necessary to exercise control over Canaan, because the back of the opposition could not be broken. The walled cities provided refuge and perpetuated the resistance. In this particular case, although gifts were offered to Thutmes in recognition of his "conquest," Megiddo's gates remained closed to him. Moreover, the King of Kadesh escaped so that another battle had to be fought in the vicinity of Kadesh, where again Thutmes was victorious, though none of his victories had permanence for the reason already given.

Thutmes III introduced naval adjuncts to supplement his

land movements. His ships landed troops to help in the attack on North Syrian points.

Thutmes III reached the Euphrates River, which was the natural Syrian boundary of the Egyptian Empire at its greatest extent. On the other bank was the Mitanni Kingdom. The River surprised the Egyptians who had not realized that nature permitted a great stream to flow south, instead of north like the Nile. To the Egyptians (to whom "upstream" and "south" were identical), the Euphrates was the river that paradoxically flowed "upstream."

Biographies of generals that served under Thutmes III are interesting compositions of the period. One of them tells how an elephant broke loose and menaced the King near Carchemish on the Euphrates, until the general slashed off his trunk with a sword. The story incidentally shows that elephants were still known in the area.

Another of his generals, Thutiy by name, tells in his biography how he captured the Palestinian city of Joppa. He loaded donkeys with baskets on both sides of each animal, and in the baskets he hid men. These were gotten into the city stealthily as goods, and once they were behind the fortifications, the city of Joppa was captured. The tale is thus a forerunner of Ali Baba and the Forty Thieves. In any case, deception could lead to the capture of walled cities that were invulnerable to the force of arms. (Long afterward, David captured Jerusalem through deception, for he lacked the means of direct assault.) Accordingly, year after year the great conquering Pharaohs of the New Kingdom returned to Canaan, ravaged the countryside, carried off all the booty and tribute they could get, and kept the land within the Empire. Yet the conquest was never complete because of the impregnability of the walled cities.

It is interesting to note that two of Thutmes III's obelisks from Heliopolis are now in the English-speaking world. One is on the Thames embankment in London; the other is in Central Park, New York. They are reminders in our midst of Egypt's greatest conqueror.

Thutmes IV (around 1422-13) married Mutemuya, a Mitanni princess, and thereby inaugurated an era of close diplomatic contacts between Egypt and Asia. It is true that such princesses did not become the official queens in the royal harem, but nevertheless they were wives of the king and cemented friendships with Asiatic royalty. Mutemuya and Thutmes IV were the parents of Amenophis III (about 1413-1377), the first of the two Amenophises who ruled Egypt during the Amarna Age. The favorite wife of Amenophis III was Tiy, a commoner but an Egyptian. The queen at this time could not be anyone except an Egyptian. However, we observe a certain breaking down of old traditions, in that he married the daughter of a commoner. Amenophis III also married a number of princesses from Asia, one of them a Mitanni princess named Giluhepa. He also obtained in marriage for his son Amenophis IV (about 1377-58), another Mitanni princess named Taduhepa. The prestige of Egypt remained higher than that of any country of the day. Egypt would take princesses into the royal harem but would never give an Egyptian princess, or for that matter any Egyptian woman, in marriage to any of the Asiatics.

With Amenophis III and IV the political decline of the New Kingdom had begun. But in their time, internal and international developments combined to make the period one of the most fascinating in the pages of history. The Egyptian Empire had come into direct contact with the Cuneiform World. To understand the events, we must now turn back to Mesopotamia and follow its course down to the Amarna Age.

# Chapter IV

# MESOPOTAMIA TO THE AMARNA AGE

THE physical geography of Mesopotamia is important for understanding the history of the country.[1] The converging of the Tigris and Euphrates Rivers made it possible for a network of canals to be dug and maintained, giving the land a productivity unheard of in any other area.[2] Accordingly, enterprising invaders in early times were able to settle down and by their industry establish the agricultural basis for a stable, civilized society, and eventually to conquer and rule over a vast empire.

When history dawns in Mesopotamia, Semites and Sumerians are both in the land. But it is the Sumerians who predominate in warfare, politics and culture. It is they who have first left us numerous business records which give us a detailed insight into the economic life. They also produced a classical and religious literature which was translated into Semitic Accadian and then into other languages. As long as the Babylonians and Assyrians perpetuated a culture of their own, they regarded Sumerian as their classical language and studied it as such. There was no cultural hostility between the Sumerians and their Semitic contemporaries and successors. The Semitic inhabitants of Mesopotamia recognized their debt to Sumer and cherished its cultural heritage.

---

[1] Babylonia (as southern Mesopotamia is called) has been formed by silt brought down by the two rivers. The land is still in the course of expanding southward into the Persian Gulf. Many southern cities that are now far inland were under water in well-documented historic times.

[2] Herodotus, who describes both lands, found Mesopotamia more productive than Egypt in the fifth century B.C.

Sumer was divided politically into city states, each with its own cult. Thus the city of Ur was a center for the worship of the moon god Nanna (who was called Sin by the Semites). Nippur was the center of the cult of Enlil. Gods like Nanna and Enlil formed part of the pantheon known and revered throughout Mesopotamia. But some cities had cults dedicated to the worship of local gods. Thus Lagash was the center for the worship of Ningirsu, the patron god of the little city state, that in more than one period reached high levels of culture. By the happy accident of discovery, many outstanding records of Lagash—both written and artistic—are in our possession.

One of the rulers of early Lagash in the first half of the third millennium was Ur-Nanshe, who has left us a number of monuments including a relief of the royal family, on which the individuals are named. The sculpture is undeniably crude; but it is so "literal" in detail that it is a valuable and factual source of information. The last ruler of this early period was the remarkable Urukagina, who like other heads of Sumerian city states in the standard tradition, bore the title "Ensi." An *ensi* was not a king (for "king" is *lugal* in Sumerian), but the human agent of the city god appointed to look after the population as a shepherd takes care of his master's flocks. In other words the city god was viewed as the actual ruler; the *ensi* was merely his executor. Government in the name of gods is theocracy. The human executor was regarded as relaying and implementing the god's commands, which could be conveyed by the god directly to the *ensi* in a dream, or as an oracle through a priest.[3] As Urukagina rose in power, he

[3] The clearest description of the process is provided by two long inscribed cylinders of Gudea, a later ensi at Lagash, who relates in detail how he received and fulfilled the commands which the gods revealed to him. In a community where theocratic ideals are fostered, there is no difficulty in accepting the necessary assumptions and techniques, however exotic the latter may appear to the modern reader. Forms of theocracy appear in the Bible. The clearest example is perhaps the period of Samuel's ministry (1 Samuel 3-16). The simplest formulation is Samuel's "Yahwe, your

assumed more ambitious titles. Though he began as Ensi, he later became the King of Lagash and finally through conquest, he was able to call himself King of Lagash and Sumer. He is most famous, however, not for his conquests but for his reforms of which we have the written record. He reduced the fees extorted by a rapacious priesthood, and reduced prices in general, in the interest of the common man. The modern idea of a prosperity that consists of high prices and scarcity of goods is unknown in antiquity. Thus, in the Bible World, material prosperity implied abundant goods and low prices. The old idea is more down to earth than the modern concept; but obviously it is becoming harder and harder to have such a simple formula as world society becomes more and more complex.

Urukagina's reform is the first evidence we have of an attempt by a ruler to improve society, although it remains a possibility that some Sumerian mound may yet reveal an earlier one.

Near Lagash was situated the rival city of Umma. The rivalry often waxed to friction, which in turn sometimes burst into the flames of war. In Urukagina's time, Umma was ruled by an able conqueror named Lugalzaggisi, who vanquished Urukagina and destroyed Lagash. The catastrophe is lamented bitterly in a poem that has survived on clay. This type of composition is one of the forms of literature in the ancient Near East. The classic example in the Bible is the Book of Lamentations about the destruction of Jerusalem in 586 B.C.

Lugalzaggisi not only conquered all of Sumer but extended his conquests far beyond and laid the foundation for the first empire emanating from Mesopotamia. However, his success was of short duration because in his reign there arose the

---

God, is your king" (1 Samuel 12:12). Samuel's granting the people a human king could only be justified by God's order to do so (1 Samuel 8:22).

first Semitic conqueror in history: Sargon of Accad (around 2251-2196).[4] Since Sargon's establishment of Semitic supremacy, which was to be eclipsed only for short periods by the Sumerians, the Semites have remained the dominant ethnic element through the Assyro-Babylonian, Aramean and Arabic periods down to the present.

Sargon, according to legendary tradition, was born of obscure parents and was exposed as a baby in a basket set afloat on a stream. An irrigator found the child and took care of him. The goddess Ishtar loved him and facilitated his stellar rise to the throne. The tale has features typical of a number of stories about the birth and career of famous men. His being found in a basket on water recalls the story of Moses. Being the favorite of some deity is a frequent motif in the legendary biographies of ancient characters.

Kings in Sargon's Dynasty (about 2251-2071) sometimes put the star for divinity in front of their names showing that the idea of divine kingship had made its appearance in Mesopotamia. This had not previously been typical of Sumerian rulers, who governed *for* gods but not *as* gods.

Sargon calls himself King of the Universe, a claim that rested on his conquests extending from the Persian Gulf to the Mediterranean Sea, even up into Asia Minor. For Sargon's period, the meagre historic records must be supplemented by the epic and omen traditions which have preserved the record of events (often containing some historic truth) in his reign. The King of Battle epic tells of his exploits in Asia Minor. Quite popular among future Mesopotamian kings were omens, whereby observations of livers and other inwards of animals were interpreted as implying such and such, even

---

[4] The chronology, especially for dates prior to 1500 B.C., is undergoing drastic reduction and is not yet stabilized. The dates given here for Western Asia are those of E. Weidner, *Archiv fuer Orientforschung* 15, 1945-51, pp. 98-102.

as such and such had taken place during Sargon's career when a similar observation had been made.

Sargon's life came to a violent end through an upheaval in his own palace. Though he perished, his Accad Dynasty continued. Ever since his time, Babylonia could be referred to as "Sumer and Accad," Sumer being the more Sumerian south; and Accad, the more Semitic north.[5]

Sargon's greatest successor was Naram-Sin (about 2171-35), who conquered far and wide, and claimed divinity as well as rule over the four quarters of the world. His stone stela of victory is the most remarkable composition in the early history of art. Like so many masterpieces, it stands isolated as a peak, and was not equalled anywhere in the world for centuries to come.[6]

The seal cylinders of the Accad Dynasty are often large and well cut. They include a great number of mythological scenes, which in many cases can be correlated with texts of later date, though the seals prove the early existence of the myths in question. Accad glyptic art is much more vigorous and realistic than the earlier Sumerian glyptics; the musculature becomes more pronounced and the scenes are more convincing.

Under the impact of invaders from the mountains of the northeast, the Accad Dynasty collapsed. The principal invaders were from the land of Gutium. The Guti, as they are called, were looked upon as destructive barbarians. Their invasion was part of a recurrent pattern in Mesopotamian history: the hostility between the hardy men of the hills against the more civilized men of the plains. Wave after wave of mountaineers have descended on the plains, lured by agricultural and urban wealth, only to become plainsmen whose

[5] L. W. King, *A History of Sumer and Akkad,* London, 1916.
[6] C. Zervos, *L'Art de la Mésopotamie,* Paris, 1935, p. 164.

descendants would be menaced by further invaders from the highlands.

With the passing of the Accad Empire, Sumer and Accad split into their component city states, among which Lagash is outstanding culturally. Under the Ensi Gudea, after the Guti conquest,[7] the city rose to unprecedented heights of artistic achievement. Gudea speaks neither of aggressive wars nor of any human overlord. He apparently lived in an era when central authority was either weak or nonexistent, and when small city states could once more come into their own. His statues are the apex of Sumerian sculpture in the round. While the bodies are somewhat dwarflike, the faces are superb. His two great cylinders mark the zenith of Sumerian literature; and his literary compositions form the basis of the only up-to-date manual of the Sumerian language. In keeping with the best traditions of Sumer, he was an ensi concerned with piety and construction. He obtained by trade and peaceful expeditions the materials he needed for his greatest undertaking, the Eninnu temple of Ningirsu in Lagash.

Gudea's cylinders are leading sources for ideas and institutions in the Bible World. For instance, Gudea gives names to parts of, or furnishings in, Eninnu. Thus a pillar or a divine emblem will have a name given to, and inscribed on, it. This is in keeping with "Jachin" and "Boaz": the names ascribed to pillars in Solomon's temple (1 Kings 7:21).

Gudea's dreams were accepted as oracles delivered through a regular channel used by gods in giving instructions to men (as often in the Bible; see 1 Samuel 28:6). Dreams, to be sure, have meanings that need not be clear to ordinary people, not even to rulers of cultured cities.[8] An ensi might have to

---

[7] The Guti seem to have introduced a turban with a short, heavy brim. Gudea, who wears this type of headgear, must follow the time of its introduction to Mesopotamia.

[8] The biblical Hebrews never need interpreters to explain their dreams, although individual Hebrews (like Joseph or Daniel) may interpret dreams

go to priests or priestesses, skilled as interpreters, for the meaning. But once the dreams are interpreted, the ruler knows what the god wants, and if the ensi is virtuous, he proceeds to fulfill the divine wish. Gudea's dreams conveyed to him divine orders to build a temple. The implication of dreams figuring in the authentic records of Mesopotamian rulers, is important for biblical studies. Solomon's dreams (1 Kings 3:5-15; 9:2-9) need not be taken to be late additions to the biblical text on *a priori* grounds. For against the background of royal inscriptions from the Bible World, we know that dreams formed an integral part of kings' actual accounts of their own reigns. The difference between ancient and modern attitudes toward dreams obliges us to evaluate dreams in Scripture in proper historic context. To write off all dreams as apocryphal accretions, is unhistoric. The fact that a number of dreams in historic inscriptions might have been invented by the ancient rulers who claimed to have dreamed them, does not affect the case. Since dreams—even invented ones—could be accepted by the public as divinely inspired, they would be included in pronouncements and texts concerning current events.

The foreign yoke of Gutium was thrown off by Utuhegal (about 2041-34), a ruler of Erech. The expulsion of the invaders made possible a Sumerian revival that culminated about 2000 B.C. under the Third Dynasty of Ur (about 2028-1920), whose first king was Urnammu (about 2028-11). He united the land and extended his conquests beyond Sumer and Accad. His son, Shulgi (about 2010-1963), who reigned for almost half a century, not only claimed divine kingship

---

for foreigners. Were it not for texts like Gudea's, showing that gentile rulers admitted their need for interpreters, we might suspect the Hebrews of prejudice (for Gudea's dreams, like Pharaoh's, seem too obvious to require interpretation). It may be that the undeniable religious genius of the Hebrews included a greater and more popular exercise of psychic qualities than characterized the other people of the Bible World.

but had a religious cult established to adore him. The events of the Dynasty are known largely from the date formulae on the countless business documents of the period. Instead of numbering years, the Sumerians (and Accadians) named each year after some event of a military, religious or commemorative character. Thus the names of the years provide us with a list of military operations, ecclesiastical developments and building projects.

The tablets are frequently dated even to the month and day. The month is of considerable importance for the host of Third Dynasty tablets, whose provenience is unrecorded. Because each town had its own set of month names, it is usually possible to identify the town in which the tablet was written.

Most of the tablets deal with economic transactions regarding grain, fruit, vegetables, large and small cattle, slaves, employment, family life and the whole gamut of business contracts. Business dealings were concentrated in the town temple in keeping with the tendency for the temple to be the social and economic, as well as religious, center. No transaction was too small to be recorded. If an obscure shepherd had a single sheep assigned to him, it was recorded on a tablet. Accurate ledgers were kept for daily, monthly and yearly totals. Sumerian life was meticulously recorded, especially from the bookkeeper's standpoint.

The courts of law made decisions in keeping with the accepted standards and accumulated social experience of the land. Thus the law was more akin to the common law of the Anglo-Saxons, than the code law of continental Europe. The idea of codified law existed in the Bible World since Sumerian times. However, the codes were not followed by the people or the law courts, as we know from the numerous contracts and lawsuits. The contracts often violate the law codes promulgated in their respective periods; and the decisions of the judges regularly omit any reference to the codes. The real law was thus the common law, representing custom and public opinion. The concept of a written law whose statutes should be consulted for the definite answer to every conceivable dispute,[9] was a different institution, emanating not from the people or the courts but from the crown.[10] The first law code to be accepted [11] as permanently binding was the part of the Bible known as the Law of Moses. The latter did not win chronologically unbroken adherence until 621 B.C., an event we shall take up later. Among the nations of the Cuneiform World, none before the Medes and the Persians had in practice accepted the idea of absolute law.

Fragments of a law code in Sumerian have survived from a ruler named Lipit-Ishtar (about 1850-40). That earlier Sumerian law codes existed is quite probable. The first known code is, however, written in Babylonian and comes from Eshnunna. It shows that Hammurabi (about 1704-1662) was not the first to promulgate a code in the Semitic language of the land, even though Hammurabi's formulation is by far the best organized and most comprehensive of antiquity.

From time immemorial, but especially since the days of the Accad Dynasty, the Semites kept pouring into Mesopotamia from the desert which lies to the west. As the Semites grew more numerous, their Accadian language became the predominant speech, while Sumerian, though persisting as a classical written medium, was dying out as a spoken language. Although the Third Dynasty of Ur was a Sumerian revival,

[9] We adhere to this ideal, though common sense tells us that it is impossible. Changing conditions constantly render the best of law codes inadequate.

[10] To be sure, code law was studied, as we know from Neo-Babylonian copies of parts of Hammurabi's Code. However, code law remained essentially a theoretical subject, while the actual law practiced in the courts was at the discretion of judges who respected custom and opinion but did not cite codes.

[11] Earlier codes, such as Hammurabi's, claimed but did not win permanent validity.

the land of Sumer, as well as Accad, was Semitized; and even the names of the later kings of the Dynasty are Semitic. Thus Shu-Sin (about 1953-45) meaning "He of the Moon-god" and Ibbi-Sin (about 1944-20), generally taken to mean "The Moon-god has called," are Semitic. The latter monarch, who was the last of the Dynasty, was carried off in chains as his empire was destroyed. For the hapless king and his destroyed city, a lament, in the tradition of lamentation literature, has survived.

The breakdown in central authority resulted in the splitting up of Sumer and Accad into the older system of city states. The period is known as the Isin-Larsa Age, because the leading city states that emerged from the ruins of the Third Dynasty of Ur were Isin (about 1934-1709) and Larsa (about 1937-1675). By this time, the western Semites, known as Amorites, who were pouring in from the desert, had established the Semitic element as the definite majority. However, in cultural and official circles, the Sumerian pattern continued. Thus the law code of Lipit-Ishtar of Isin, to which we have referred, is written in Sumerian.

By now (nineteenth century B.C.) the influence of Mesopotamia was felt far and wide. Assyria, though politically independent of Sumer and Accad, adhered to the same cultural complex that included language, script, religion and art. There were differences between Assyria in the north and Babylonia in the south, but such differences were matters of variety not of kind. Assyrian merchants had penetrated Cappadocia, where they established communities that maintained trading relations with the Assyrian homeland. The Cappadocian tablets—as the abundant documents of those Old Assyrian colonists are called—constitute a major branch of Assyriology.

Virtually all of Mesopotamia fell into the hands of Amorite rulers during the Isin-Larsa Period. Assyria was governed by an Amorite king, Shamshi-Adad I (about 1727-1695):

an able monarch who established his sons as the rulers of a realm along the middle Euphrates. Their capital was Mari, where French archeologists unearthed about 20,000 tablets of military, administrative and diplomatic contents. One of the interesting features of the tablets is the clear picture of how Shamshi-Adad trained his sons for leadership, by giving them reasons as well as orders, so that they might understand as well as act.

The Mari Age was one of numerous kinglets entering the ever-shifting coalitions in the struggle to jockey for power or to avert ruin. The interrelated terrain of those kinglets included Canaan as far as northern Palestine. One of the city states in Accad was Babylon,[12] now ruled by its First Dynasty (around 1806-1507), whose greatest king, Hammurabi (about 1704-1662), was a junior contemporary of Shamshi-Adad. Both monarchs were fine civil administrators and military commanders. Of the two, Hammurabi emerged triumphant. By shifting adroitly from coalition to coalition, Hammurabi in the course of his long reign eliminated his rivals, one by one, until he achieved the unification of Babylonia and adjacent areas. Babylonian unity is reflected by the spread throughout the land of a single calendar, whose month names persisted to the end of Babylonian history, and live on in the religious calendar of the Jews, who adopted it during the Babylonian Exile.

Numerous business documents, lawsuits and letters attest the activity of the land during the First Dynasty of Babylon. The normal language is now the Semitic, Old Babylonian, though Sumerian ideograms and technical formulae appear commonly enough. The years are still dated by formulae, usually in Sumerian, alluding to events. Many tablets deal with Hammurabi's personal interest in the administrative details of his empire. His crowning achievement was the law

[12] L. W. King, *A History of Babylon*, London, 1919.

code, never to be to surpassed in scope or quality in the
ancient Near East. On the top of the stone stela is carved a
relief of Hammurabi receiving the law from the sun-god
Shamash. Thus the law was to be regarded as god-given. It
was this divine origin that made it in theory sacred, and not
subject to addition, diminution or revision. Like biblical law,
Hammurabi's Code thus claims divine authority. However,
Hammurabi's Code was not destined to have its claims take
permanent root in human history, whereas biblical law has
been accepted in an unbroken tradition since 621 B.C.

The society reflected in the law of Hammurabi is divided
into three classes: (1) an upper class, whose members have
the greatest rights but also the greatest responsibilities; (2)
an intermediate class; and (3) slaves.[13] Society was carefully
regulated. Prices were pegged at fixed levels. Fees varied
according to the social class of the client or patient. Laws for
all situations in society, ranging from marriage and the care
of children to river traffic regulations and a Veterans' Bill of
Rights, are worked out in detail and lucidly phrased in language devoid of obscure legalistic jargon. Hammurabi's stated
aim was to enable the average citizen with a legal problem
to go to the stela and have the appropriate section read to him
so that he would understand the law. Quite likely, Hammurabi's worthy aim is impossible to attain, but no one ever
came closer to reaching that goal.

Hammurabi's Code has a comprehensive literary form. The
prologue and epilogue are in poetry, whose form is parallelistic [14] and whose language is archaic. The laws in the middle,
however, are in prose, so that the whole composition has a
pattern, which we call ABA; A being poetry, B being prose.

[13] In Babylonian, the members of the three classes are called, in de-
scending order: *awilum, mushkenum* and *wardum.*

[14] In the pre-Greek Near East, poetry is not characterized by meter.
We must not be deceived by the illusion of meter that results from parallelistic repetition. See Chapter VII.

This has an important bearing upon other oriental compositions including the Bible. Thus the Book of Job starts out with a prose prologue; but the main body of the book is poetry with parallelism and archaic language; and the epilogue is in prose. Some scholars are inclined to detach the prologue and epilogue because they are in prose, whereas the rest of the book is in poetry. Such an argument fails to reckon with the literary composition as a whole, which, like Hammurabi's Code, has the architectural form ABA. Although in the Book of Job the prose and poetry are reversed, the architectural balance remains the same. Similarly the biblical Book of Daniel begins and ends in Hebrew, though the middle is in Aramaic. The possibility of an intentional ABA structure deserves earnest consideration and should deter us from hastily dissecting the text.

In the poetic sections of the Code stela, Hammurabi tells of the pious deeds he performed for the various city gods and their shrines. However, Marduk as the god of Babylon the capital, attained a preëminent position as the god of the empire. It is probable that the version of the Creation Epic (and other literary compositions) in which Marduk figures as the supreme god, came from the time that the First Dynasty of Babylon reached its zenith under Hammurabi.

As is normally the case in Mesopotamia, the First Dynasty of Babylon was not to endure long. Foreigners called Cassites invaded the land, and divided the rule of the land with Hammurabi's successors. The First Dynasty of Babylon ended with the fall of the capital around 1507 B.C. Then the Cassites ruled the country from Babylon for some centuries without adding lustre to the nation's history. Art went into decline and Cassite texts are relatively few, though there are some sculptured and inscribed boundary stones to indicate the limits of landgrants.

In Asia Minor, from about 1800 to 1200 B.C., the Hittites [15] were in power and have left many texts behind them. The Hittites contributed militarily to the destruction of Babylon that ended the First Dynasty there. The Hittites politically absorbed a varied population, including people that had long been in Anatolia. However, the official language, the ruling class and a number of cultural elements were Indo-European. Hittite documents are our earliest written records related to Sanskrit, Greek, Latin, English and the other languages with which we are familiar in the West. Being Indo-Europeans, the Hittites reared horses. The earlier Near East knew of the donkey (for both riding and drawing chariots) and, in the case of the nomads, knew also of the camel. The Indo-Europeans introduced to the Near East the horse for pulling chariots, thus revolutionizing the art of war and the economy of the area. The aristocracy of charioteers called *mariannu* spread from the Indo-Europeans throughout the civilized Near East in the second millennium B.C.

Another great cultural center that flourished throughout the second millennium B.C. was the Aegean and Minoan sphere,[16] including Crete. The civilization of that sphere spread, by trade and migration, to the Asiatic and Egyptian mainland, starting early in the millennium. By the Amarna Age, the immigrants formed an important segment of the population of Canaan. Aegeo-Minoan art is remarkable for its vivacity and it injected a notable degree of liveliness into the art of the Near East (including Egypt) of the Amarna Age.

[15] They probably came from Central Asia, which is the most likely home of the Indo-Europeans.
[16] The area is called Caphtor in the Bible and Ugaritic tablets.

# Chapter V

# THE AMARNA AGE

THE Amarna Age (when Amenophis III and IV ruled Egypt in the fifteenth and fourteenth centuries B.C.) derives its name from Tell el-Amarna, the capital built by Amenophis IV, where nearly four hundred extant documents of singular interest were discovered. The texts are written in Babylonian on clay. Since Babylonian cuneiform had become the medium for international correspondence, there was a school to train Egyptian scribes to write it in Tell el-Amarna.

The tablets are mostly letters exchanged between the Pharaohs and the rulers of Asia. The latter include the kings of Cassite Babylonia, Assyria, Mitanni and the Hittites; and especially the kinglets of Canaanite city states. The documents from Canaan have nothing to do with the Hebrew Conquest, for they come from the earlier period when the Hebrew Patriarchs flourished. There is but little in the Patriarchal narratives that can be expected to fit into the political or military history of the Near East, with the one great exception of Genesis 14. That chapter tells of a coalition of four kings against five, who fought near the Dead Sea. The invaders were from the Mesopotamian sphere. The forces are small, as is shown by Abraham's ability to defeat the victors, although his men numbered only 318 (Genesis 14:14). The incident fits into the Amarna Age, when Canaan was the scene of petty strife, foreign infiltration and nomadic bands. Typical of the period was small-scale Mesopotamian interference. Until the actual personages of Genesis 14 are encountered in other documents, we cannot be sure of the situation.

Meanwhile that chapter will remain the most tantalizing historic problem of the Bible.

Canaan was divided into two spheres of influence, Egyptian and Hittite.[1] Many a little city state tried to pit those major powers against each other in the hope of bettering its own position locally. Thus the real hostility in the land was among rival city states whose kinglets engaged in international intrigue and fought petty local wars. The belligerents would affect loyalty to a great power, such as Egypt, in the hope of getting assistance against local enemies. Roving bands of 'Apiru[2] infested the country and menaced the settled communities thus adding to the general insecurity.

Egypt was still capable of cultural achievement, and still enjoyed international prestige, but its actual power was a thing of the past.

The outstanding personality of the Amarna Age was Amenophis IV: a sensitive intellectual, married to the beautiful Queen Nefertiti. He was at the head of a group of religious revolutionaries dissatisfied with the crass and complicated polytheism of Egypt. His theology had developed among a circle of priests at Heliopolis, where the sun-god was worshiped. As the Amarna Letters show us, he neglected his empire so that Egypt lost its grip on Canaan. Instead he dedicated himself to a religious revolution whereby all the gods were suppressed except the Sun, called Aton (or Aton-Re),

[1] The Mitanni Empire was the leading power of Western Asia at the start of the Amarna Age but it was gradually eclipsed and finally destroyed by the Hittites.

[2] The 'Apiru (in Mesopotamian cuneiform Ha-pí-ru) have often been equated with the 'Ibrîm "Hebrews." Apiru appear all over Mesopotamia, Anatolia, Canaan and Egypt. They are not a specific nation, speaking one language, attached to one country, devoted to one religion, or what is most important in nationhood, sharing consciously a common destiny. The Hebrews, on the other hand, definitely constituted a nation. That the Hebrews originally included "all the sons of Eber" (Genesis 10:21, 24) should not obscure the fact that of the five sounds in 'apîr- only two occur in 'ibr-, so that we are dealing with two different words.

which was elevated to the position of the one and only god of the universe—thus culminating the trend toward solar mono-theism that had begun back in Old Kingdom times. The change was thoroughgoing. The state was revolutionized as well as religion. Art was revolutionized with the breaking down of old canons, and the introduction of new trends. Modernistic realism and distortion suddenly appear in the art of what had been the world's most conservative country. Up to this time the Egyptian written language remained that of the classical Middle Kingdom texts. With the Aton revolution came a break with the classical past, and new forms were allowed to penetrate the written language from the spoken, thus inaugurating the New Egyptian stage of the language.

So thoroughgoing was the Pharaoh's fanaticism that he changed his own name, because "Amenophis" contained the name of the god "Amen" (or "Amon"; the vowels are un-expressed in Egyptian writing). Instead he called himself "Ikhnaton" containing the name of the sun-god "Aton." The name of Amon and of other gods were eradicated from monu-ments, even where they only formed part of the names of royalty or commoners.[3]

Ikhnaton founded a new capital, Akhetaton ("The Horizon of Aton"), whose site is today called Tell el-Amarna. But neither his capital nor his religious revolution were to endure. The resentment stirred up through his religious persecution, particularly among the priests and devotees of the powerful Amon cult, was profound. Shortly after Ikhnaton's rather early death, a counterrevolution burst loose, destroying the fanatical reform of Ikhnaton. Akhetaton was for all time

[3] This trend has a minor counterpart in Hebrew tradition, where the name of Saul's son Eshbaal (1 Chronicles 8:33; 9:39) is changed to Ish-bosheth (2 Samuel 2:8, 10), where *bosheth* "shame" is substituted for the pagan deity Baal; and a closer parallel in the name of the Judean king Abijam (1 Kings 15:1, 7, 8), where the last element Yam "Sea-god" is changed to Yah (= Yahwe) so that the royal name is altered to Abijah in 2 Chronicles 13:1, 4.

abandoned. The Amon cult was restored in all its glory. Ikhnaton's memory was held in bitter hate. But the Amon counterrevolution could not wipe out all the traces of Ikhnaton's reform. The New Egyptian language was there to stay. And while the old canons of art were reinstated, the modernistic effects of Ikhnaton's school occasionally peer through later works in some of the details.

Ikhnaton is certainly to be ranked as a genius in the history of religion. Aton monotheism, although it had behind it the long history of Re theology and worship, owed much to the fanatical planning and implementation of the Pharaoh. The purity of the monotheism far exceeded that in biblical Hebrew circles for centuries to come. The hymns to Aton reach heights of beauty eclipsed only by much later Hebrew Psalms. Yet we must recognize that Ikhnaton's reform was stamped out so thoroughly that it had no influence on the subsequent history of religion. Ikhnaton's son-in-law Tutankhaton ("The Living Image of Aton") changed his name to Tutankhamon [4] ("The Living Image of Amon"). Aton monotheism was quickly and thoroughly obliterated from Egyptian life, including the royal circle. Accordingly, it is out of the question to assume that Moses (whose career falls in the next century, the thirteenth) could have shaped Hebrew monotheism on the inspiration of Ikhnaton's reform. Nor is chronology the only reason for dissociating Mosaic monotheism from Ikhnaton's. Typologically the two are unrelated. Aton was the sun disc, representing a single phenomenon in nature, and elevated to sole god of the universe through the suppression of the other deities of Egypt. Yahwe was never a specialized phenomenon of nature, such as the sun. As His name indicates, He is, the One Who "Calls into Being," or the Creator. [5]

[4] The minor Pharaoh who has won modern fame because of his rich and virtually unrifled tomb discovered by archeologists.

[5] Such is the meaning of "Yahwe" in Hebrew. However, the name may be an expansion of a shorter form (cf. Yo-, Yeho-, Yah and -Yahu, which

Babylonia under the Cassites had more pretension than power. It could claim to be the successor of Sumer and Accad, and of the Hammurabi Age, but genuine cultural attainment and military prowess were lacking. The Cassite king of Babylonia would send his daughters and other ladies of his family as gifts to the Pharaoh; but in vain would he beg for the daughter of the Pharaoh or even for any Egyptian woman— beautiful albeit picked from the common people—to be sent as the Pharaoh's daughter to save face for the Cassite. The latter also repeatedly begs for gold because Egypt, unlike Mesopotamia, was rich in the precious metal. The stated purpose for seeking the gold was for the adornment of temples and similar cultic embellishment.

Assyria was a rising power, soon to be ruled by Assuruballit (about 1362-27), who made encroachments on Babylon and Mitanni.[6]

The Mitanni Kingdom was the leading power in Asia during the early part of the Amarna Age. We have already mentioned its close alliances through marriage with the Pharaonic House. The Mitanni King Dushratta sought the brotherly love of the Pharaoh, but he wanted that love to be expressed in terms of gold.

In Anatolia the Hittites were rising at the expense of Mitanni and Egypt. Although relations in the diplomatic correspondence are cordial, the Hittites were making encroachments in Syria to the detriment of Egypt. North Canaan fell into the Hittite sphere of influence and the little kingdoms of the area became vassal states. A tablet from Ugarit records

---

also occur). The fatherhood of God strongly suggests a connection between His name and the first element of Iu-piter "Jupiter" (i.e., Yu, the Father). Thus His name may hark back to Nostratic (as the common denominator of Indo-European and Egypto-Semitic is called).

[6] For Assyrian history and its sources, see A. T. Olmstead, *History of Assyria*, New York, 1923; and D. D. Luckenbill, *Ancient Records of Assyria and Babylonia* I-II, Chicago, 1926-27.

the tribute sent by Niqmed, King of Ugarit, to his master, Suppiluliuma (around 1395-55), King of the Hittites.

Canaan is a country chopped up by mountain ranges and, in the north, also by rivers. The geographical barriers worked against the unity of the land, which was fragmentized along the coast and inland into little city states that might join into coalitions against a common enemy but otherwise remained rivals. However, the fact that the influence of Egypt from the south, of the Cuneiform World from the north, and of Caphtor from the west, converged in Canaan, preconditioned Palestine as the land in which the Hebrews could grow and make contributions of momentous effect on world history. Canaan was the crossroads of all the great cultures of the day so that the Hebrews had the richest possible international background on which to draw before adding the contributions of their own distinctive Semitic genius.

While the Amarna Letters do not give us any evidence about the Hebrews as a people, they do provide important data on the language of Canaan, which the Hebrews adopted as their own. In the Letters, Babylonian words are sometimes translated into Canaanite, showing that what was later known as Hebrew, was already spoken in the country. Inasmuch as those Canaanite words are written in the Babylonian syllabary, the vowels are indicated. This is of considerable linguistic interest because the inscriptions of the Hebrews, Phoenicians, Moabites and other Canaanites are written in a consonantal alphabet so that scholars have to infer what the vowels might have been by working back from later tradition and by theoretical deductions from comparative linguistics.

The Amarna Age is richly documented from several other sources, notably the texts from Ugarit (which illuminate the origins of Hebrew literature) and Nuzu (which clarify the social institutions of the Hebrew Patriarchs). In the following chapters we shall investigate those sources.

# Chapter VI

# UGARIT

THE newest evidence to come to light from the Amarna Age is the cuneiform literature from the north Syrian port of Ugarit. The texts are written by stylus on clay in the fashion of the Mesopotamian scribes; but the system of spelling is alphabetic: each sign stands for a single sound, which is a Canaanite contribution. As we have noted above, the Egyptians had already invented alphabetic values, but since the ancient Egyptians never got themselves to use alphabetic signs without syllabic signs, logograms and determinatives, they did not reap the benefits of pure alphabetism. Pure alphabetism goes back to Canaan, where one of the groups (the Phoenicians) passed it on to Greece. Copies of the ABC taught in the Ugaritic schools have been published; their fixed order of the letters is the one from which our own English ABC is ultimately derived.[1]

The Ugaritic language belongs to the northwest branch of Semitic, along with Hebrew, the other Canaanite dialects and Aramaic. In spite of its recent discovery (since 1929), it is now ranked among the leading Semitic languages and is taught in dozens of universities, colleges and seminaries.

The literature of Ugarit is mostly mythological and concerns the pagan gods of Canaan, including those such as the male Baal and female Asherah, whose worship is forbidden in the Hebrew Bible. El, whom the Bible identifies with Yahwe, appears as the head of Ugaritic pantheon. The Ugaritic tablets confront us with so many striking literary parallels to the

[1] See *Orientalia* 19, 1950, pp. 374-376.

Hebrew Bible, that it is universally recognized that the two literatures are variants of one Canaanite tradition. To the Hebrew writers, however, the mythology is often little more than a literary background on which to draw for poetic imagery. Just as John Milton was a good Christian in spite of his profuse allusions to pagan mythology, the Hebrew poets were monotheists who worshiped Yahwe and Yahwe alone.

The prose as well as poetic documents from Ugarit enable us to describe the society and ideas of the times in considerable detail. The king was considered divine by dint of being suckled by the goddesses Anath and Asherah. The king's duty was to exercise justice and benevolence in the land. His virtuous deeds include help to the widow, fatherless and other unfortunates.

The army is rather prominent in the numerous administrative documents that have been found in the archives of Ugarit. It consisted of infantry, including bowmen and slingers. The pride of the army was, however, the chariotry.

The chiefs of the army and the priesthood were sometimes selected from the tribes of the ruling class, including the king's own family. By planting members of trusted families in the priesthood and army, the king could exercise better control over the realm. Some of the priests were assigned on regular duty with the army. This is because of a theocratic ideal that permeated society. Not only in Ugarit, but also among the Mesopotamians and Hebrews, the army on occasion would have on its staff, in the field, a seer or priest to give oracles. Thus not only were wars embarked upon in accordance with divine will as revealed by oracles, but even tactics in the midst of military campaigns were frequently undertaken only after the will of the god(s) had been consulted.

Taxation, conscription and other government functions were exercised through three channels: tribes, towns and

professional guilds. The tribe, the oldest of these classifica-
tions, still functioned in Ugarit.[2] However, as throughout
Near East history, the town was encroaching upon tribal
organization, so that in many cases men were no longer
known as members of such and such a tribe but rather as
citizens of such and such a town.[3] Furthermore, the guilds of
various professions, and of the arts and crafts, were organized
to such a degree that a guild member could be related to the
state, not through tribe or town, but through the guild.[4]

The family had at its head a man who possessed one or
more wives. The children owed filial obligations to their
parents in return for which they had inheritance rights. A
model son was one who looked after his father's needs, such
as the performance of religious rites, washing his father's
mud-stained clothes, plastering his father's roof against leaks,
and holding up his father when the latter was in his cups.[5]
The ideal daughter was one who looked after the food supply,
fetched water and was gifted with the art of divination. She
was thus possessed of both domestic and psychic qualities.

The oldest son of the favorite wife would normally inherit
the chief share. However, the father had considerable latitude
in such matters. One man of Ugarit wrote a will whereby his
future widow had full charge of the estate, which she could
bequeath to the son that treated her best. Thus the father puts
the widow in a position whereby she controls the purse
strings, so as to place a premium of good filial conduct toward
her by the children, after he is no longer alive to provide for

[2] Indeed, in the Near East today, tribalism is still an important element
in society, government and economy.
[3] The agricultural population was dealt with through the provincial
towns.
[4] The guilds represented the latest and most advanced aspect of society,
for industry and art follow agricultural development which in turn represents a more advanced stage than nomadism.
[5] The desirability of children for holding up drunken parents is also
reflected in Isaiah 51:17-18.

her. So while the widow did not have the right to dispose of the estate to an outsider, she did have the power to select the heir from among the children.

Of course, slavery existed. However, the plight of the slaves was not always hopeless. We have one document which tells of how a man in consideration for twenty shekels of silver married off one of his slave girls so that as far as we know, she became the mistress of her own home.

Education was complicated because it consisted of scribal training in a cosmopolitan community where not only Ugaritic, but also Babylonian, Hurrian, Sumerian and still other languages were in use. As in all ancient communities, education was not popular but professional. Only scribes learned to read and write. In order to facilitate scribal education in so polyglot a community, bilingual and trilingual vocabularies were prepared for training in the intricate problems of translation.

The literary texts include legends primarily about men, and myths dealing entirely with gods. One of the legends is about a king called Keret, who feared that his line might die out because his wife had left him. He prayed to the god El, who tells him how to regain his wife who will bear him eight sons, the youngest of whom will be suckled at divine breasts so as to qualify to rule after him. Among the children will also be a daughter (whose name means "Eighth" =) "Octavia," who though the eighth will be elevated to the place of first-born. These facts constitute interesting literary themes. The announcing of children yet to be born is a recurring feature in the Bible, starting with Hagar, who receives an annunciation from an angel predicting the birth of Ishmael. This repeated characteristic of Hebrew literature thus harks back to an ancient tradition. Also the idea of a younger child eclipsing the older one(s), is a recurrent theme in Scripture, which we shall have occasion to discuss, particularly in the Patriarchal

Period. More specifically, it is interesting to note that the elevation of an eighth child over his elder siblings is paralleled in the account of David, whom Samuel anoints as king after looking over and rejecting the seven older brothers (1 Samuel 16:6-13). In the Legend of Keret it is not the oldest son who succeeds to the throne (at least as far as the story goes) but apparently the youngest who by virtue and good conduct achieves seniority as so often in biblical literature.

Another legend concerns Aqhat, the son of the heroic king Daniel, who ruled his people justly and protected the widow and fatherless. Daniel had only a daughter as the story opens, but he longed for a son. He therefore prayed to the gods and performed the necessary rituals, so that he was blessed by the birth of a model son Aqhat. To celebrate that event, he summons songstresses to sing joyously for seven days. The songstresses are called the Kosharot, who appear also in Psalm 68:7, where they celebrate the happy occasion of prisoners being released by God. Like so many passages in the Bible, this one was not understood until the discoveries at Ugarit.

The god of arts and crafts, Kothar-and-Hasis, who hails from Caphtor, fashions a wondrous bow for Aqhat, who uses it effectively in the hunt. The impetuous goddess Anath covets the bow, which Aqhat refuses to give her, in spite of her promises not only to make him wealthy but even immortal. His persistent refusal impels her to go to her father El, from whom, by threats of violence, she wrings permission to assassinate Aqhat and thereby get his bow. Even though it may have been her intention to bring him back to life (—the defective state of the tablets precludes certainty), Aqhat is slain so that the area is cursed with a seven-year drought by Daniel who retrieves for burial his son's remains from the crop of an eagle.

One of the epithets of Daniel is "The Man of Repha," referring to his tribe. Some scholars have taken the references to people called the "Rephaim" (in Genesis 14:5 etc.) as mythological because the word also means "shades of the dead." However that the name was borne by real people in the Amarna Age is not only indicated by the Legend of Aqhat and the biblical account of the Patriarchs, but also by occurrences of the name in administrative texts from Ugarit[6] where legend and myth are out of the question. To be sure, there are some tablets that contain references to divine chariot-riding Rephaim, who may be "shades of the dead" associated legendarily[7] with Daniel. Their attachment to the Legend may have been facilitated by verbal identity; resemblance in the sound of names often accounts for the association of elements that would otherwise not be placed together.

Most of the mythological texts concern the god Baal and his beloved Anath. Baal seized kingship by vanquishing the sea-god Yamm and then petitioned for a palace needed for living up to his newly won position. The fact that Kothar-and-Hasis from Caphtor fashioned the palace shows that Caphtor was already recognized in Canaan as the center par excellence for arts and crafts. The saga of Baal's palace is a mythological forerunner of the historical account of building Yahwe's Temple in Solomon's reign. After Baal wins his palace, he is challenged by Mot, the god of death, who kills him. On another occasion Baal killed Mot for seven years. Since Mot remains dead for seven years, this cannot be seasonal conflict. The significance of the fighting between Fertile Baal and Lethal Mot, leading to the death of one or the other for seven years, can have nothing to do with the seasons, but might possibly tie in with the Sabbatical Cycle of seven years appearing in the Bible. In any event, we know from Hebrew[8]

---

[6] See *Ugaritic Handbook* texts 91:7; 119:24; 300:rev. 14.
[7] Texts 121 to 124. For a mythological reference, see 62:45.
[8] 2 Samuel 24:13.

and Egyptian [9] sources that seven years of famine was the most feared scourge that could befall a nation. All of the Canaanites accepted the dry summer as an inescapable aspect of nature and wished only to get rain in its season. Moreover, the dry summer, far from being sterile, is precisely the season when many prized fruits ripen to the joy of the populace. What the Canaanites feared was a succession of famine years due to drought, locusts or other sources of calamity. It is possible that the Hebrews let the earth lie fallow in the seventh year of the Sabbatical Cycle in the hope that it would induce the next cycle to be fertile in accordance with an assumed principle of alternation. The problem was so important to the Ugaritans, that it transcended the myths and cult of Baal. Indeed the main Ugaritic text (number 52) touching on the problem is a myth wherein the spirit of privation is banished and the great god El begets auspicious deities for whom a cycle of abundant food and drink is inaugurated. The theme of "seven" permeates the text. Baal is not even mentioned, which shows that the question went beyond Baalism.

That Ugaritic is the greatest literary discovery from antiquity since the decipherment of the Egyptian hieroglyphs and Mesopotamian cuneiform is generally recognized. That it lies closer than any other literature to the Hebrew Bible is also well known. This does not mean that the ethical and moral heights reached in the Bible are to be found in Ugarit. The analogies are literary rather than spiritual. Indeed the Hebrew view is to a great extent a conscious reaction against the Canaanite milieu. This is illustrated by the fact that beastiality, far from being looked at askance in Ugarit, was practiced by the adored Baal, who copulates with a heifer as is celebrated in the religious texts (67:v:17-22).[10] If it be

---

[9] See J. Wilson, *Ancient Near Eastern Texts*, p. 31.

[10] Apparently no moral issue was made of beastiality in Ugarit. Or to state it differently, beastiality had no significance in Ugaritic criminology. In Israel (whose attitude we inherit), however, it was a heinous crime. I

argued [11] that Baal assumes the shape of a bull for the act, the same cannot be said for his priests who reenacted his mythological career, cultically. The Bible, in forbidding beastiality, expressly states that it was an abomination wherewith the Canaanites had defiled themselves (Leviticus 18:24). Other illustrations of the consciousness of the Hebrews' reaction against Canaanite usage can be found in the Bible and corroborated in Ugarit. The impact of Ugarit on biblical studies is growing constantly as new organic parallels are being pointed out by many scholars on three continents. That our sketch is so brief here is not due to any dearth of evidence or doubt as to the certainty and magnitude of the subject but to the facts (1) that the conclusions can be stated with confidence though briefly, and (2) that a full treatment is impossible because the parallels are multiplying with such rapidity that any account aiming at finality would be antiquated by the time it got through press. It is therefore more fruitful to turn to an important but unexplored aspect of the subject: the interrelation between Ugaritic and the Homeric Epics in the next chapter.

---

would suggest that in sociological studies, it would be worth-while to differentiate terminologically between features that are significant within the pattern of the society under investigation, and features that are not significant within that pattern. For reasons stated in *Ugaritic Literature* (p. 8), I have proposed that a significant feature be called a "socieme." Thus beastiality in Ugarit (where no issue was made of it) was nonsociemic; whereas in Israel or America (where it is a punishable crime), it is sociemic.

[11] So A. Kapelrud, *Baal in the Ras Shamra Texts,* Copenhagen, 1952, p. 20, n. 7.

# Chapter VII

# HOMER AND THE ANCIENT EAST

THAT the Bible must be understood in its ancient Near East context is generally recognized. But also the origins of Greek culture lie to an appreciable extent in the ancient Near East. Research along these lines is still in its infancy. While the extent of Greek indebtedness to the East cannot yet be measured with accuracy, that the indebtedness is there cannot be doubted.

There are two main channels whereby the ancient Near East penetrated the Greek World prior to the Homeric Era. One channel was overland, via the Hittites who were members of the Cuneiform World and were familiar with Accadian literature in Hittite translation. To be sure they developed their own literature and it is safe to predict that Hittite texts will, as research advances, prove to be more and more a connecting link between the earlier East and the later Greeks.

The second channel was by sea. By sailing on the Mediterranean, Greeks and the coastal peoples of Asia maintained steady contacts. It is for this reason that the strongest contacts between Homer and the East are to be found at Ugarit,[1] which was culturally linked to the Greeks both by sea and by being in the Cuneiform World.[2]

That contact existed between the Homeric World and Sidon is stated in the Iliad (6:290), for the Trojan Queen

---

[1] It is always possible that future discoveries in Phoenicia, Cyprus or on the coast of Asia Minor, will provide still stronger contacts with Homer. But we can only base our discussion on the material now available.

[2] For the probable Caphtorian influence on both Semites and Greeks, see the Appendix.

Hecuba wears embroidered robes from that Phoenician city. Since Sidon lies within the horizon of Ugarit,[3] the connection between Homer and Ugarit rests on textual evidence.

That general concepts are shared between Homer and the ancient Near East does not prove much, though it is of some interest. Thus Zeus's epithet of "Father of Men" (Iliad 1:544; 11:182; 22:167) is the same as El's at Ugarit. The full Homeric epithet for Zeus is "Father of Men and of Gods," which is at least implied in Ugarit where El "The Father of Man" is also the consort of Asherah who bore the "seventy[4] gods."

In the following discussion there are many such points which have a general character so that individually they prove little or nothing. Collectively, they have a cumulative value; but without supporting evidence, they would add up to something less than a proof. However, the specific and striking parallels in the paragraphs below establish the case for the relationship between Homer and the earlier East. The reader should therefore first view the evidence as a whole. Then, if he wishes to test individual points, he should remember that the cogency of the thesis rests on the parallels of a specific nature and not on those of a general character which are given only to round out the picture.

There is a common atmosphere shared between Homer and Ugarit as is attested in a number of typical situations. For example, Calypso asks Hermes why he came and then offers him refreshments (Odyssey 5:87-91). Similarly, El greets Asherah thus:

> "Why has Lady Asherah of the Sea come?
> Why came the Creatress of the Gods?

[3] See *Ugaritic Handbook,* p. 264, no. 1715.
[4] The number is a literary cliché for a large brood; it is not to be taken literally.

Art thou hungry?
  Then have a [morsel]!
Or art thou thirsty?
  Then have a [drink]!
Eat or drink!
Eat bread from the tables
  Drink wine from the goblets
From a cup of gold the blood of vines!"
(51:IV:31-38).

This parallel looks general enough but it takes on a more specific character when combined with other passages. The Ugaritic emphasis on serving wine in a golden cup is shared with Homer; e.g., "bearing in his right hand honey-hearted wine in a cup of gold" (Od. 15:148-149). The frequent Homeric epithet "honey-hearted" (as also in Od. 13:53, etc.), or its variant "honey-sweet" (Od. 14:78), for wine recalls the frequent parallelism between "wine" and "honey" in Ugaritic (Keret:72, 165). Moreover the mixing of wine is common to Homer (Od. 7:179, 183, etc.) and Ugarit (Anath:I:17; etc.). The theme of entertaining guests brings up still another parallel: In Ugarit the word for "soul" includes the idea of "appetite." The Homeric "when he had dined and satisfied his soul [= appetite] with food" (Od. 5:95) is paralleled in Ugarit where the guest's "soul" is satisfied with food and drink (127:11; etc.).

While such general parallels to Homeric expressions are most abundant in Ugarit, there are also some in other Near East texts. For example, the Homeric notion that gods may assume the guise of human strangers in order to check on men's behavior (Od. 17:483-487) is paralleled in the Bible, where divine beings in human form are entertained by Abraham and then proceed to Sodom, where they observe firsthand the iniquity of the people there (Genesis 18:1—19:25).

"Good at the (war-) cry" is a Homeric epithet, applied in Od. 15:14, 67 to Menelaus. The war-cry is a heroic feature that appears in ancient Near East sources. Thus in the Romance of Sinuhe, the hero Sinuhe slays his foe and then stands upon him and yells. Also, when Enkidu tells Shamhat that he intends to shout in Erech, he means that he will vanquish Gilgamesh. That is why Shamhat informs him that Gilgamesh is the stronger so that Enkidu should not be sanguine.

Elements of everyday life often appear in the epics. In such an instance in Homer, the oriental parallel may come from business documents rather than literature. The offending guests (in the words of Eurymachus) try to appease Odysseus by promising: "We shall each bring you the worth of twenty oxen and pay you back in bronze and gold until your heart is warmed" (Od. 22:57-59). In Mesopotamian business documents such as the Nuzu tablets, there are standard equivalents of fixed sums stated in terms of animals or metal.[5] Furthermore, "until one's heart is warmed" has a Neo-Babylonian parallel in the business formula "his heart is good" = "he is paid in full to his complete satisfaction."

Idiomatic clichés are shared by Ugarit and Homer. The Homeric "not yet was the word fully uttered" (Il. 10:540; Od. 16:11, etc.)—when such and such happened—is not only paralleled in Ugarit but also clarifies a grammatical obscurity in the Ugaritic texts. A repeated formula "from his mouth the word verily/not went forth" (1 Aqht:113, 141)—when such and such happened—has been erroneously translated with "verily" instead of "not," for both meanings can be expressed by the prefix *l-* before verbs in Ugaritic. However, the Homeric parallel provides the meaning for the Ugaritic, which improves the interpretation, because "the word had not (yet) gone out of his mouth" is more vivid than "verily had

[5] See *Orientalia* 5, 1936, p. 312.

gone out"; and in a lush literature like Ugaritic, vividness is more in character than restraint. A further cliché shared by Homer and Ugarit is "another thing will I tell you" (Il. 1:297; Od. 16:299; 17:548; etc.; Ugaritic text 51:I:20; etc.).

Concern for someone is expressed as far back as Gudea (Cylinder A:19:24) by the simile "like a cow that looks toward her calf." However in both Homer and Ugarit the simile is specifically applied before violent and vengeful action. We may thus compare "as a bitch stands over her tender whelps growling when she sees a man she does not know and is eager to fight, so his heart growled within him in his wrath at their evil deeds" (Od. 20:14-16) with

"As with the heart of a cow toward her calf,
As with the heart of a ewe toward her lamb,
So is the heart of Anath toward Baal" (49:II:6-9)

said of Anath before she wreaked vengeance on Mot for Baal.

A literary device characteristic of the entire area under consideration is the one whereby one or more digits in a number are increased by 1 for climactic effect. Thus Homer describes loudness "as when 9,000 warriors or 10,000 cry in battle" (Il. 5:860-861). Compare Ugaritic "he took 66 towns, yea 77 cities; 80, Baal—90, Baal—" (51:VII:9-12). Here we may also point to a Hittite parallel "77 I slew; 88 I slew"[6] although Hebrew, Accadian and other oriental examples are common, too.

Social attitudes often span Homer and the Semitic East. Neither Homer (Il. 1:348-363) nor the bards of Ugarit (Krt:30) saw any shame in great heroes weeping copiously.

The Homeric shame of one's corpse being devoured by dogs (Il. 22:75-76) or vultures (Od. 22:30) on the surface

[6] See *Ugaritic Handbook*, p. 39, n. 3.

seems universal to us, who share the tradition of decent
burial. However, consideration of Zoroastrian customs, which
call for the exposing of the dead to be devoured by vultures,
and which prohibit burial as a pollution of the land disabuses
us of the illusion of universal accord in such matters. Hence
it is not altogether idle to recall that (among other biblical
examples) the abominable Jezebel's corpse was devoured by
dogs (1 Kings 21:23; 2 Kings 9:36). Also the curse of one's
body being eaten by the fowl of heaven is common in the Bible
(Genesis 40:19). In the Ugaritic Legend of Aqhat, the hero
is slain for the sake of his wondrous bow and is devoured by
a vulture to climax the tragedy. (While the relationship, if
any, is distorted, it is at least interesting to note that in
Od. 22:30 the penalty for slaying a man with bow and arrow
is that of being devoured by vultures.)

All through the Odyssey, wisdom and guile are equated.
The hero Odysseus himself is "he of many wiles." Od.
13:294-299 shows that wisdom and guile are identified to the
credit of the goddess Athene no less than the mortal Odysseus.
This standard of values pervades the patriarchal narratives in
Genesis (particularly as concerns Jacob and Laban) and still
persists among the bedouin. To be sure, many people in
America today actually accept the identification; but our
mores are officially against it, which was not the case with the
milieu of Jacob or of Odysseus.

That guile even on the part of God was thinkable in Israel
down to at least Ahab's time is reflected in 1 Kings 12:23,
where a true prophet of Yahwe, Micaiah, states that Yahwe
had sent deceptive dreams. Similarly Zeus sends a false dream
to Agamemnon (Il. 2:1-15). Not only is this of interest for
the history of ideas, but it brings up an important question of
literary style. The dream is related with verbal variation in
Il. 2:23-34 and again in :60-70. Compare also a similar repeti-

tion with differences in :157-165 and :173-181. Among many examples of this phenomenon is Priam's message concerning the ransom of Hector's body in Il. 24:144-158 repeated in a slightly longer version in :171-187. Nowhere throughout ancient literature (Homeric, cuneiform, Hebrew, etc.) did the authors feel the need to reproduce a text with verbal exactness. The reproduction of the sense in the approximate wording was all they aimed at. Dr. G. D. Young has given abundant Ugaritic examples of this phenomenon with reference to the whole gamut of ancient literature and so there is no need to give further illustrations here.[7]

The structure of ancient Near East poetry differs considerably from that of Homer. In the ancient Near East, what makes poetic form is parallelistic repetition. The following is a Ugaritic example but the poetic structure of the whole ancient Near East follows the same pattern:

"The mountains will bring thee much silver
The hills, the choicest of gold" (51:V:77-78).

The parallelism is in thought rather than in syllables or stresses. There is no meter in ancient Near East poetry, as Young has convincingly demonstrated in the study just referred to. Homer, on the other hand, is metrical, each line composed of six feet.

The position of Ugarit as the known ancient Near Eastern culture closest to the Homeric World is brought out by a clear parallel: Dogs are accepted in the Homeric household; thus they are in Priam's palace (see especially Il. 22:69), while Argos is the pet dog of Odysseus (Od. 17:291-319). The Semites have a general aversion to dogs, which they regarded as useful for watching sheep, but not fit for admission to the

---

[7] "Ugaritic Prosody," *Journal of Near Eastern Studies,* 9, 1950, pp. 124-133.

home.[8] Therefore dogs do not figure as pets in the Old Testament or cuneiform literature. The great exception is Ugarit, where in the Legend of Keret ( :123, 226; 125 :2, 100), dogs are present in the royal residences of Kings Pebel and Keret.

Situations which in themselves are common enough, may constitute organic parallels because of the emphasis on those situations as worthy of saga. Hephaistus's making armor for Achilles (Il. 18 :478-613) is paralleled by Kothar-and-Hasis's making the bow for Aqhat (2 Aqhat :V :12-13; cf. :VI :24). Thetis, coming for Achilles's armor finds Hephaistus at his bellows working on other artistic creations (Il. 18 :372-379) much as the delegation approaching Kothar-and-Hasis to construct Baal's palace finds the divine artisan busy at his bellows on other works of cunning craftsmanship (51 :I :24-44).

Telemachus, after ordering his mother to return to feminine affairs, tells her "the bow shall be for all men but most of all for me" (Od. 21 :352-353). Aqhat brought on his own doom by telling the goddess Anath that the bow is for men and not for females (2 Aqhat :VI :39-40). Aqhat thus refused to give her the bow though she tried to persuade him by offering him immortality (2 Aqhat :VI :26-30); even as Calypso offered immortality to Odysseus, who, like Aqhat, refused it (Od. 23 :335-337).

Among the abominations hated by Baal is the "abuse of handmaids" at banquets. The word for "abuse" is *tdmm*, which is often mistranslated as "murmuring," though Dr. I. Yasin has found the correct Arabic cognate that confirms the meaning "abuse." [9] The same conclusion is indicated by

---

[8] This is still true in the Arab World. It is interesting to note (at least in northeast Iraq, where I observed it, but probably over a wide area) that an exception is made in the case of the salugi, which is not considered a dog in Arabic terminology.

[9] *The Lexical Relation between Ugaritic and Arabic*, New York, 1952, p. 148, no. 71.

Homer, who singles out the abuse of one's host's handmaids at banquets as a most grievous offense committed by Penelope's suitors in Odysseus's halls (Od. 20: 318-319 and 22:37). Another Ugaritic obscurity is clarified by a Homeric parallel: In Keret (:128, 285) it has been a question as to whether one of the gifts offered by Pebel to Keret should be translated "charioteers of horses and a chariot" or "three horses and a chariot," because the same consonants express "three" and "charioteer" in the related Hebrew language. But that "three" is correct is indicated by the Homeric "three horses and a well-polished chariot" (Od. 4:590-591) specified as a lavish gift, quite as in Ugaritic.

In Homer as in Ugarit,[10] horses were used only to draw chariots. "Charioteers (and infantry)" (Il. 11:529, 720, 745; 12:66, etc.) should not be translated "horsemen" as is sometimes done in the widely-used Loeb Classics edition (e.g., for Il. 11:529), for there was no cavalry in the Homeric World. Besides the charioteers, there are spearmen, bowmen and slingers (Il. 13:716) in the Homeric armies as in the Ugaritic.[11] The Trojan soldiers were grouped in fifties (Il. 8:563) precisely as the Hebrews (2 Kings 2:16-17; Isaiah 3:3; etc.). Moreover there may have been a predilection for grouping companies in fifties (Od. 20:49). The fair distribution of spoils among the troops is attributed to the precedent of Odysseus (Od. 9:40-42, 548-549) in Homer just as it is ascribed to David's precedent in Israel (1 Samuel 30:23-25).

When Telemachus insists that he has come of age and knows everything, he says "I know all things, the good and the evil" (Od. 20:309-310). Here the pair of antonyms indi-

---

[10] There are no references to horses in the myths of Ugarit but only in the Legends of Aqhat (in the so-called Rephaim texts = numbers 121-124) and Keret (and of course in certain prose texts). The translation of *lsmm* (49:VI:21) as "horses" should be abandoned. The myths reflect a culture before the introduction of the horse. The legends are of later origin.

[11] *Ugaritic Literature*, p. 124.

cate totality and mean "everything," exactly as Egyptian "evil-good" and Hebrew "good and evil" in such passages as the so-called "Fall of Man" in Genesis.[12]

Now we may consider a more striking and specific parallel between Homer and the ancient Near East. In the Gilgamesh Epic, Enkidu sealed his fate through affronting Ishtar by hurling a bull's leg at her. In Homer (Od. 20:299) Ctesippus commits a terrible affront by hurling a bull's foot (mistranslated "hoof" in the Loeb Classics edition). The deed is avenged in Homer (Od. 22:287-291) even as in the Gilgamesh Epic. Surely the singling out for epic celebration of so specialized a phenomenon is not fortuitous. A cultural common denominator must be assumed.

The curse that a herdsman be attacked or devoured by his own dogs (Od. 21:362-365) is reminiscent of Ishtar's cruelty whereby she changed a shepherd into a wolf so his own dogs menaced him.

The speech of Xanthus (Il. 19:404-417), the horse of Achilles, is of a piece with the talking of Balaam's ass in the Bible (Numbers 22:28-30). The ability of Balaam's ass to see things (verse 27) invisible to Balaam, is matched by Athene's invisibility to Telemachus, while the dogs perceive her (Od. 16:159-163).

Jacob's besting an angel in physical combat (Genesis 32:29) is paralleled in Homer's account of woes inflicted by men on gods (Il. 5:382-404).

The heroes mentioned in the Catalogue of the Ships (Il. 2) are to be compared with the catalogue of David's heroes (2 Samuel 23:8-39). Both lists are of a similar character and may well rest on authentic originals with the result that such catalogues have more historicity than the saga that flanks them.

Definitions of a good woman have considerable variety.

---

[12] See above, Chapter II.

One of the repeated virtues of womanhood in Homer is skill at fine handiwork (Od. 16:158; 24:128). This is matched in the account of the model woman in Proverbs 31:10-31, which is unique in the literature of the ancient Near East and may be of Mediterranean rather than inland Judean origin.

The idea that there is "a proper time for each thing upon the earth" (Od. 19:592-593) is expressed more fully in Ecclesiastes (3:1-8). However, the early date of the Homeric formulation shows how risky it is to view the ideas in Ecclesiastes as necessarily of very late origin; indeed his ideas are in most cases very old.

Another common bond between the Homeric World and the ancient Near East is the regular custom of sending messengers in pairs; thus Il. 1:320 ff. (etc.), 2 Kings 5:23 (etc.) and at every turn in Ugaritic.

Inasmuch as many of the above parallels are new, it is more important that they be pointed out than that dogmatic conclusions should replace source material at this early stage.

If our thesis that Homer and the ancient Near East have a common denominator is correct, we have a right to expect Near East texts to clear up points in the Homeric Epics. I have no doubt that there will be many such points. As a foretaste, I offer but one little illustration. In Hebrew the combination "yesterday + day-before-yesterday" is a regular idiom for "formerly." There is no doubt that the same idiom occurs in Homer (e.g., Il. 2:303), where we should translate "formerly" and not "it was as yesterday or the day before" (as is done in the Loeb Classics and elsewhere).

Scholarship is about to enter upon an era when the great classics of Greece and the treasures of the ancient Near East will illuminate each other as never before.

# Chapter VIII

# THE PATRIARCHAL AGE

FROM the Amarna Age comes a group of documents which has revolutionized our knowledge of the Patriarchal Period. The texts were unearthed at the town of Nuzu[1] in northeastern Mesopotamia and they provide us with a more complete picture of the community, than we have for any other town of antiquity. The tablets come from private archives and are written in a clumsy Babylonian, because the native speech of the people was Hurrian. Those Babylonian texts have a number of Hurrian loanwords that are a source for reconstructing the partially-deciphered language of the Hurrians.

Among the Nuzu texts is a series of tablets recording the lawsuit filed by the citizens against the mayor, who was guilty of complicity with a kidnaping ring, of accepting bribes, and stealing wood and misappropriating workers from public projects for his own purposes, and of shady dealings with a woman of the community. The interesting thing is that the people were able to appeal to the courts of law and present their case against the mayor himself and bring him to justice.

Most of the archives, however, are private documents pertaining to personal and family affairs. Some tablets are about the Hapiru, who enter into servitude, not *en masse* like the Israelites in Egypt, but individually contract to remain enslaved for life in the house of some wealthy person in the community. Their goal was simply economic security, for

---

[1] For accounts of life in Nuzu, see E. Chiera, *They Wrote on Clay,* Chicago, 1938; and my *The Living Past,* pp. 156-178.

being a permanent slave in a wealthy household guaranteed food, clothing and shelter for life, whereas freedom was often precarious for the poor. The Hapiru show no trace of Hebrew names or Hebrew religion.

Most of the archives dealing with private affairs hinge on the institution of adoption. Inasmuch as land could not be sold legally, sale of land had to be masked as adoption. In other words, a man would ostensibly adopt a son in order to pass on property to him, and the "son" would in exchange give the adopter a "filial gift." Thus land would be sold under the guise of adoption. A rich man might be the adopted son of hundreds of less fortunate neighbors, whose lands he thus snapped up. Playing such a game of make-believe adoption certainly fooled no one in Nuzu; but, being within the law, it was acceptable. Since the archives of Nuzu extend over a period of four to five generations, it is possible to trace the fortunes of various families, as well as of individuals, amassed mainly through acquiring land by fictive adoptions.[2]

There are also real adoptions in Nuzu, especially in the case of people without a son, who adopt one in order to keep the continuity of the family and estate, to perform filial service during the lifetime of the parents and the mourning rites after their death. Even a slave might be adopted as a son in Nuzu. However, there is normally a clause stating that if, after an adopted son comes into the family, a real son is born to the parents, the real son shall become the chief heir and the adopted son shall be relegated to a secondary position in the family. Very sacred is the possession of the household gods. Hence when a man is adopted, there may be the proviso that, if a real son is born to become the chief heir, the adopted

---

[2] The prohibition against alienating land outside the family held also in ancient Israel, whose law (Leviticus 25:8-17) calls for the return of land to the original owners every fiftieth (= jubilee) year.

son shall not have title to the gods of the father. Perhaps possessing the gods was in some way connected with being head of the family.

. Adoption is sometimes tied in with marriage in Nuzu. A father without sons may adopt his son-in-law thus at least making the grandchildren his by blood.

The purpose of marriage in these documents is not companionship but the producing of an heir. As a result, if a woman who is bought as a wife does not produce an heir, she may be obliged by clauses in her marriage contract to supply her husband with another woman to provide him with an heir. The wife's position could be protected by a clause to keep the second woman in a servile status to her. The children of the second woman could be protected by a clause forbidding the wife to expel them.

The analogies, to be pointed out presently, between the society of Nuzu and of the Hebrew Patriarchs, are so numerous and striking that scholars are agreed that the patriarchal narratives in Genesis portray a genuine social picture. We shall soon look into the various aspects of the narratives and see that some of the reputed anachronisms and legendary features are correct historically. But we may best begin the discussion with the all important problem of the chronology.

The three generations of the Patriarchal Age are represented by Abraham, Isaac and Jacob. Jacob, as an old man went to Egypt when it was called the land of Ramses (Genesis 47:11). The country could only be so called in the Ramesside Age, which began late in the fourteenth century B.C. It need not disturb us that this does not leave much time for Israel's Bondage in Egypt, which was terminated under Moses around the third quarter of the thirteenth century B.C. When Jacob came to Egypt, Joseph was a high official and presumably not young. Moses was the greatgrandson of Levi, the older brother of Joseph. If Joseph lived to an old age [3] as he is reputed to have, it would be quite possible for him to have been alive when Moses was born. This is the more likely since Joseph lived to see his own greatgrandchildren (Genesis 50:23), who in the natural order of things would be younger than Moses. Thus the gap between the coming of Israel to Egypt and the birth of Moses, who led the Exodus, could be spanned by a single lifetime.

If Jacob was aged late in the fourteenth century, his grand-father Abraham would have been born in the latter part of the fifteenth century and hence flourished during the Amarna Age.

The above conclusions are clearly indicated by the biblical genealogies (and other data of varied nature [4]) but not by the biblical figures in terms of actual years, which point to a far longer span of time.[5] Both the genealogies and the year reckonings cannot be correct at the same time, and it is neces-sary for us to evaluate the evidence. Among the tribal Semites, such as Arab nomads down to the present day, there is a great feeling for genealogy and it is not unusual for an Arab to be able accurately to recite the names of his ancestors back for ten or fifteen generations covering several hundred years. Yet that nomadic Arab will not know how old he is. Tribal Semites have no birth certificates, and while they memorize genealogies, they keep no track of birthdays. Accordingly, when we choose between the two conflicting chronological schemes of the Patriarchal Period, we are forced by the nature

---

[3] As J. Wilson (*Ancient Near Eastern Texts*, p. 414, n. 33) points out, Joseph's age of 110 (Genesis 50:26) is the ideal Egyptian figure for a full life.

[4] E.g., the fact that two midwives could handle the obstetrical needs of all the Hebrews (Exodus 1:15-21) points to a passage of time too brief for much numerical increase in the population.

[5] According to Genesis 15:13, it is predicted to Abraham that his de-scendants will be afflicted in a foreign land 400 years. In Exodus 12:40, 41 the stay of the Hebrews in Egypt is given as 430 years.

of that type of Semitic society to lean on the genealogies and not on the reckoning in terms of years.[6]

With the person of Abraham we enter into the actual historic phase of the Hebrew people. His family in Mesopotamia is Aramean.[7] He migrated in nomadic fashion from northwest Mesopotamia to the land of Canaan, where he had contacts with Shechem, the only city in that part of Central Palestine at that time. A famine in Canaan obliged him to sojourn in Egypt but he came back to Palestine when conditions there had improved.

In Genesis 14:13 he is called "Abram the Hebrew" marking a clean break with his Aramean past. He had already collected a group of followers so that he was able to muster 318 men in the field and, as small wandering sheikhs went, hold his own in reputable fashion. He met a Canaanite priest of El Elyon "God the Most High," whom Abram, and subsequent Hebrew tradition, identified with Yahwe.

Since Abram had no child of his own, he adopted his slave Eliezer as his heir (Genesis 15:2-3) but, as in the Nuzu tablets, with the proviso that if a real son should be born, the real son would be the heir (Genesis 15:4). The text does not use any word meaning "adopt(ion)" but the interpretation of the passage is no longer in any doubt since the Nuzu tablets have come to light.[8]

In the patriarchal narratives (Genesis 14:5) it is stated that among the inhabitants of Palestine are the Rephaim; whose mention is often misconstrued as a mythological illusion. However, as we have observed, the references to the

[6] We are led to the same conclusion also if we hold that biblical numerals down to the United Monarchy reflect schematic numbers taken over from the epic tradition (see the Appendix).

[7] Note Deuteronomy 26:5. Abraham's kinsmen who stayed on in Mesopotamia are called Arameans (Genesis 25:20; 28:5; 31:20, 24) and speak Aramaic (Genesis 31:47).

[8] The Nuzu evidence is collected in my article "Biblical Customs and the Nuzu Tablets," *Biblical Archeologist* 3, 1940, pp. 1-12.

Rephaim in Ugaritic administrative documents show that real people bore that name in Canaan of the Amarna Age.

Inasmuch as Sarai, the wife of Abram, was childless, she gave Hagar as a concubine to Abram for the purpose of producing an heir (Genesis 16:2). This is not an isolated instance of unfeminine generosity, but in accordance with the laws and customs of the times as we know from the Nuzu and other cuneiform tablets. It is interesting to note that Hagar later receives an annunciation that she is to bear a child (Genesis 16:11). As noted above, such annunciations are typical of Canaanite literature and we find them in the Ugaritic documents as well as the Bible. The angel predicting Ishmael's birth tells Hagar that the lad will be "a wild ass of a man" (Genesis 16:12). This is not an insult but a compliment because the wild ass was then to be found in the desert and it was the choicest beast of the hunt.

Abram entered into an eternal covenant with God, whereby, on the one hand God agreed to be the God of Abram and his descendants and, on the other hand Abram and his descendants agreed to be God's own people; and whereby the land of Canaan would be forever associated with this people and with this God; in token whereof, the family of Abram would for all time practice the rite of circumcision. To commemorate the covenant, Abram's name was changed to Abraham, and Sarai's name to Sarah. Ishmael was thirteen years old when he was circumcised and since he is recognized as the father of the Arabs, they still practice circumcision at about thirteen years of age, and not at the age of eight days, as the Jews do following the precedent of their ancestor Isaac, the son of Abraham.

In due time Sarah, the chief wife, bears a son Isaac, whose name means "laughs." The Bible explains it as referring to either the laughter of Abraham (Genesis 17:17) or Sarah (Genesis 18:12) because they were so advanced in years that it seemed ridiculous for them to expect a child. Scholars have been more inclined to explain the name as referring to the laughter of God, which is plausible in that God (expressed or understood) figures frequently in Hebrew names. Formerly, scholars thought the divine laughter was that of terrifying scorn (Psalms 2:4). But now that the Ugaritic texts refer to the good natured laughter of El, scholars are beginning to feel the laughter implied by the name Isaac is kindly. In the Homeric poems the laughter of the gods is jovial, not scornful. So comparative evidence, outside as well as inside Canaan, points to God's kindly laughter, which is better suited for a congenial personal name.

The closeness of men to gods in this period is a social [9] phenomenon for which we of today must develop a feeling, if we are to understand the biblical texts. In our society if a man claims to have divine visions, he would at worst be committed to an insane asylum, or at best be regarded as queer. In Hebrew society, it was not abnormal for people to experience theophanies, that is to see divine manifestations, and converse with the apparition. Nor would it be odd to attribute divinity to strangers, whose behavior might be appropriate to angels on divine missions. From the biblical viewpoint, it was nothing supernatural for three divine beings, in the form of men, to visit Abraham, who entertained them in good bedouin fashion with water for washing before a meal of bread, milk curds and meat (Genesis 18:1-8). [10] Far from being over-awed, Sarah engaged in some feminine eavesdropping and is reported to have been amused at the annunciation of her son

[9] To what extent the patriarchal institutions are those of actual life, and to what extent they reflect epic tradition, can now be outlined by the Nuzu (for real society) and Ugaritic (for epic) parallels respectively. Cf. the Appendix.

[10] Like the bedouin today, Abraham waited on his guests instead of eating with them. The best sources for understanding the society of the Patriarchs are: (1) bedouin life among the Arabs, and (2) cuneiform texts (especially from Nuzu) pertaining to law and custom.

(verse 12). Certainly such a reaction would be unthinkable among a people who regarded divine manifestations as supernatural. For the ancient Hebrews, the human and divine intermingled freely. Abraham was intimate enough with Yahwe to bargain with him and influence His policies. Abraham's reverence does not prevent him from dealing with God as a personal friend. They discuss a problem, finish speaking and part (Genesis 18:23-33) until their next meeting, without any unnatural event or circumstance, from the Hebrew point of view. It is not easy for every modern reader to understand the atmosphere of Hebrew society. Background is necessary, but the most important single element in obtaining the background is to read and reread the biblical text until it becomes familiar and real. Nearly always, we can know that we understand a biblical passage correctly, when its literal [11] meaning fits smoothly into the general context.

Abraham's bargaining with God was on behalf of the people of Sodom and Gomorrah, which God had decided to destroy on account of the cities' evil. Abraham persuaded God to reduce from fifty to ten, the number of righteous men that would have to be found there, for God to abandon His plan to demolish the cities. Two angels (Genesis 19) proceeded to Sodom where Abraham's nephew Lot received them well but where the mob of townsmen behaved abominably without respect either for strangers or for sexual decency. Sodom and Gomorrah were therefore destroyed, but only after Lot and his family were given a chance to escape. Through their own folly, his wife and sons-in-law perished, leaving Lot and his two daughters as the only survivors. To forestall the extermination of their family, the daughters got their father drunk on successive nights when he unwittingly impregnated them.

[11] It cannot be overemphasized that the discoveries of archeology tend to justify the literal meaning of the text as against scholarly and traditional interpretation. This holds not only for the Bible but for ancient texts in general.

The elder gave birth to the ancestor of the Moabites; the younger, to the ancestor of the Ammonites (Genesis 19:31-38). Such narratives have a purpose. On the one hand, the story brings out the kinship of Israel with the Transjordanian nations of Moab and Ammon. On the other hand, it also reflects the dislike that the Israelites had for those nations; whence the desire to trace them to a scandalous origin.

Abraham and Isaac are said to have had dealings with Abimelech of Gerar, a king of the Philistines.[12] This is generally regarded as an anachronism, because it is held that the Philistines first migrated from Caphtor to Canaan around 1200 B.C. However, the fact is that the wave of Sea People, which included Philistines, around 1200 B.C. was only a late migration in a long series of migrations that had established the Philistines (and related Caphtor folk) in Canaan before 1500 B.C. By the Amarna Age, their settlements had become linguistically Canaanitized so that interpreters are never needed to facilitate relations between Semitic Hebrews and Indo-European Philistines. To be sure, the Philistines left linguistic traces behind them. Indeed the name of "Palestine" (which means "Philistia") recalls their role in Canaan. The rulers of the five major Philistine cities[13] are each called in the Hebrew Bible, a *seren*—the native Philistine term. Furthermore, the warlike Philistines introduced the helmet to Palestine, so that their word *koba*ᶜ [14] appears in the Hebrew Bible and persists in modern Hebrew as the ordinary word for "hat." In some regards, the Philistines resisted Semitization; the Philistines, of all the nations in Canaan, are singled out in

---

[12] Genesis 20 and 26; note 26:1, 8, 18.

[13] Gaza, Ascalon, Ashdod, Gath and Ekron.

[14] The initial Philistine sound was intermediate between Semitic *k* and *q;* hence the word is written either *qoba*ᶜ (1 Samuel 17:38) or *koba*ᶜ (1 Samuel 17:5) in the Bible. In Ugarit, *Ḥkpt* (a synonym for "Caphtor") is once written *Ḥqkpt,* showing that the Semitic scribe vacillated between *q* and *k* in representing the same foreign sound.

the Old Testament as "the uncircumcized." In material civilization they excelled the other inhabitants of Canaan, specifically in the arts and crafts. Their pottery has been found not only on the Philistine plain of southern Palestine, and in central Palestine at points like Ginti-Carmel,[15] but even in the cities of Beth-shan and Jericho in the Jordan [16] Valley going back to about 1500 B.C.[17] As late as the time of Saul, about 1000 B.C., the Philistines held a monopoly on metal work in Palestine, and thereby were able to keep the Hebrews disarmed. That the Caphtorians were already recognized in Canaan as the masters par excellence of the arts and crafts, including metallurgy, is reflected by the fact that the divine artisan (Kothar-and-Hasis) in the Ugaritic pantheon comes from Caphtor, where his workshop is located. In the light of this many-sided evidence, the presence of Philistines in Canaan during the time of Abraham, is not anachronistic. Furthermore, the general historicity of the incident is favored by the fact that the social institutions exhibited, are not those of later Hebrew times. Biblical law forbids the marriage of all half-brothers-and-sisters (Deuternomy 27:22). When, however, Abraham in self defense had stated that Sarah was his sister, and Abimelech had discovered that she was in reality Abraham's wife, Abraham defended himself by assert-

---

[15] Modern Jett. Ginti is the same word that appears as the name of the Philistine city Gath. Amarna Letter 289:18-20 tells of men from Ginti-Carmel sent to garrison Beth-shan, which remained in Philistine hands after the collapse of Egyptian power until the rise of the Hebrew monarchy about 1000 B.C.

[16] "Jordan" is probably the Cretan word for "river" (cf. the "Iardanos" in Crete mentioned by Homer). That "Jordan" is a common noun meaning "river" is evident from such expressions as "this Jordan" (Joshua 4:22) and "the Jordan of Jericho" (Numbers 26:3, 63) and from the fact that the Mandeans apply "Jordans" to rivers in general.

[17] For some of the evidence, see F.-M. Abel, La géographie de la Palestine II, Paris, 1938, p. 358. For the archeological evidence I have profited from discussions with A. G. Barrois, author of the best handbook on biblical archeology: Manuel d'archéologie biblique, Paris; vol. I, 1939; II (in press).

ing that she was not only his wife but also his half-sister: the daughter of his father but not of his mother. Regardless of the veracity of Abraham's claim, the incident demonstrates that in patriarchal society it was permissible for children of the same father to marry provided that they were born of different mothers. Thus the Bible account was not revamped to make it conform to the later Hebrew legislation that became binding on the Jews.

In accordance with divine promise,[18] Isaac was born to Sarah and Abraham. Once Isaac was born, Sarah resented the presence of Hagar's son Ishmael. Custom did not favor Sarah's wish to expel Hagar and her child, as is suggested by the prohibition in the Nuzu tablets.[19] Sarah's request that Abraham drive them out to prevent Ishmael from inheriting along with Isaac therefore required a divine dispensation to justify Abraham's acquiescence (Genesis 21:1-14).

The "sacrifice" of Isaac (Genesis 22:1-13) is of interest in that it reflects a transition from human sacrifice to the vicarious sacrifice of some animal. Since Isaac was the first-born of Sarah, he would have to be sacrificed according to the old principle of giving to the gods the firstborn. Thus at the dawn of Hebrew history, the barbaric custom of sacrificing the firstborn child was eliminated, though the redemption of the firstborn, whereby parents buy back their firstborn from God, attests the existence of the earlier savage custom.[20]

We may also note that in Genesis 22:3 when Abraham took Isaac to be sacrificed, the caravan included an ass and

---

[18] From the Hebrew viewpoint, childbirth required not only biological conditions but also divine will. The Hebrews shared this attitude with their pagan neighbors; e.g., in Ugarit, where the Legends of Aqhat and Keret bring out the same point.

[19] Be it noted, however, that according to the Sumerian Code of Lipit-Ishtar (section 25), the expulsion would be legal in exchange for the freedom which Hagar and Ishmael thereby won.

[20] That human sacrifice was practiced by neighbors of the Hebrews, and even by isolated Judean kings, will be pointed out below.

the two errand lads of Abraham. This fits in exactly with the picture in Ugaritic literature, where missions move on donkey back and where two lads are regularly in attendance.

Later, Abraham, to bury his dead, wants to buy a parcel of land near the city of Hebron. The lot, which included the Cave of Machpelah, belonged to a "Hittite" named Ephron. Abraham dealt with Ephron and the latter's fellow "Hittites," all of whom speak Hebrew. As far as we can tell there was nothing Indo-European about those "Hittites." Ephron's people are "Hittite" even as all Canaan was sometimes called "Hattu" in Assyrian annals and "Heth" in the Old Testament. Thus Canaanites who were not related to the Hebrew clans are in some instances called Hittites. Abraham's purchase shows us something of the business methods of the times; the sale was conducted in public, and the price, weighed out in silver. The genteel restraint and the simulated desire of the seller to give away the land, deceive no one except perhaps the uninitiated modern reader.

Abraham did not want his son to marry a Canaanite, so he sent Eliezer to Paddan Aram (as the Haran region of north Mesopotamia is called) to secure a bride for Isaac. With ten camels and adequate personnel, Eliezer heads the caravan towards his master's Aramean kinsmen. The mention of camels here and elsewhere in the patriarchal narratives is often considered anachronistic. However, the correctness of the Bible is supported by the representation of camel-riding on seal cylinders of precisely this period from North Mesopotamia.[21]

Although Bethuel (the father of the prospective bride Rebecca) was alive, Rebecca's brother Laban figures as the head of the family and does most of the talking and negotiating with Eliezer about the marriage. This is to be connected

[21] The best of several illustrations is in the journal *Iraq* 6, 1939, plate II, 9.

with fratriarchal elements in family life, which are particularly common in the Nuzu tablets but are also present to some extent in Hebrew society. After Rebecca personally consents to go with Eliezer to Canaan, where she is to wed her kinsman whom she had never seen, the caravan returns with its mission successfully accomplished.

A gift she had received from Eliezer was a nose ring of gold weighing a *beqa'*. Stone weights marked *"beqa' "* have been found in Palestinian excavations.[22] While this is not of great importance in interpreting the text, it illustrates quite clearly the way archeology can supply exact meanings of hitherto vague words.

Laban had recognized Yahwe as the God of Abraham's household to judge from Laban's greeting Eliezer with "Come, thou blessed one of Yahwe!" (Genesis 24:31). As we shall see later, the Mesopotamian and Canaanite branches of the family had different ancestral gods.

The children resulting from the marriage of Isaac and Rebecca were the twins Esau and Jacob, Esau coming into the world first and therefore the firstborn. It is said that he was *admoni* "ruddy" (Genesis 25:25), which again has a purpose. Whether or not he was particularly ruddy is of little importance. The etiological character of the statement is the interesting thing: Esau's connection with the nation of Edom prompted the story that the lad was *admoni* at birth; for the Semitic ear, "Edom" and *admoni* are derived from the same root.

Jacob purchased from Esau the "birthright," which means the title to the position of firstborn. This is no longer a peculiar incident without parallel. In the Nuzu tablets, inheritance prospects are negotiable much as stocks and bonds are today. One Nuzu tablet records how a man in need of food

[22] Weighing about 6.1 grams.

sold his inheritance portion to his own brother [23] in exchange for livestock, even as the hungry Esau had sold his to Jacob for a "mess of potage." [24]

A famine sent Isaac to the same King Abimelech of the Philistines, at Gerar. There Isaac tried his hand successfully at a season of farming, and his yield was a hundredfold (Genesis 26:12), a statement worth recording because bedouin are as a rule poor farmers. Isaac's experiment is the early sign of a nomad beginning to settle down. The recurrent pattern, still going on in the Near East, is that nomads are attracted to the sown, where they plant crops (not very successfully at first) to supplement the means of subsistence they get from their flocks. This generally brings them into a semi-nomadic mode of life. Eventually they lay more emphasis on agriculture than on grazing so that they finally become peasants living in villages (though still possessing flocks). Isaac marks the transition to the intermediate semi-nomadic stage.

Esau married two "Hittite" (i.e., native Canaanite) girls to the chagrin of his parents. The name of the one is Judith, daughter of Beeri, which is quite Semitic; that of the other is Basemath, daughter of Elon, again Semitic. [25] To appease his parents who were quite disappointed in his marriages with strange women, he married a kinswoman, the daughter of Ishmael. [26]

[23] Since both the biblical and Nuzu examples are sales of a birthright from brother to brother, we cannot as yet be sure that it could be sold to a total stranger.

[24] The Hebrew text specifies the dish as lentils.

[25] Genesis 26:34; the variants in 36:2 are also Semitic.

[26] For the variant tradition of her name, compare Genesis 28:8-9 with 36:3. The fact that the Bible contains such variants shows how welcome extrabiblical sources are for the establishment of objective, controlled history. The wives' variant names contain elements in common, partly transposed. The problem of restoring the original text lies within the province of the philologian; in practice however, the results are often unconvincing, especially when there are a number of complications, with the result that the problem becomes as futile as an attempt to unscramble an omelette.

Before Isaac dies it is his wish to confer a blessing on his favorite and elder son Esau. Through deception, Jacob obtains the blessing, but still the blessing stands as binding. In patriarchal society, in which the bedouin equation of "intelligence" and "trickery" was accepted,[27] a man nevertheless felt obliged to abide by his word, though it might be to his disadvantage and had been extorted from him under false pretenses. A Nuzu tablet tells of a man repeating in court the blessing his father had given him on the death bed, willing to him a wife. Since the terms of such a blessing could be upheld by a court, it is in keeping with the times that an oral blessing on a father's deathbed was legally binding. However, unlike the Nuzu tablets which deal primarily with material things, the patriarchal narratives are more concerned with future leadership.

Repeatedly throughout the patriarchal account, but especially in Jacob's career, a premium is placed on a kind of cleverness, which if practiced in our society, would be condemned as cheating. The Bible does not confront us with a static code but rather with a historic evolution, whereby religion and morals grow from humble beginnings to the loftiest heights. The miracle of Israel is that it grew and gave an ever increasing message to the world; not one that remained static from Abraham's time on.

The mother, Rebecca, fearing that Esau would take revenge and kill Jacob, tells her favorite Jacob to flee to her people in Mesopotamia, and asks the rhetorical question: "Why should I be bereft of the two of you in a single day?" (Genesis 27:45). The implication is that the laws of blood revenge would have it that if Esau in his anger killed Jacob, the tribe in turn would have to kill Esau so that the mother

---

[27] Thus in Arabic, *shaṭâra* means either. Yet the danger of drawing sweeping conclusions in distinguishing bedouin from ourselves will be evident if we note that a similar range of meaning is inherent in English "shrewd" and "smart."

would lose both of them.[28] Jacob heeded her advice and
fled. On the way Jacob beheld a theophany, wherein God reaffirmed His covenant. On waking up Jacob was filled with
awe, but in no way mystified, by the experience. He anointed
with oil the stone that lay under his head during the theophany; for the Deity, That in some way resided in it, could
thus be gratified. The place, previously known as Luz, was
renamed Bethel ("House of God") by Jacob. (Such topo-
graphical equations are of considerable value in historical
geography.) Jacob furthermore vowed that if Yahwe, Who
had appeared to him, would guard him on his journey and
supply him with food and clothing, and bring him back
safely, Jacob would keep Him as his God. (Thus the relationship between man and God was still on a contractual basis,
and the individual man could still lay down conditions which
would affect that relationship.[29]) Jacob furthermore vowed
that he would pay God tithes on all God would give him
(Genesis 28:10-22). The theophany, and Jacob's response
to it, thus confirm the covenant, justify the sanctuary at
Bethel, and set the precedent for the paying of tithes.

After reaching his mother's people in Mesopotamia, Jacob
agrees to serve his uncle Laban for seven years for the hand
of Rachel. Entering into a contract whereby a man pays in
labor for his wife is again attested in the Nuzu tablets. But
there is much more to the affair than that. No sons of Laban
are mentioned and Jacob enters into this bargain for the
purpose of being heir of the household, not only as the son-
in-law of Laban but as his adopted son, as we shall demon-
strate in due course. Laban deceives Jacob and palms Leah
instead of Rachel off on him. So far Laban has gotten the
better of Jacob, and in this period (as we have noted) getting

[28] Compare 2 Samuel 14:5-7.
[29] The freedom of the individual man in such matters became more and
more curtailed as Israel grew from nomadism to nationhood.

the better of the other fellow was a sign of intelligence. But the last trick was yet to be played. After laboring another seven years, Jacob gets the hand of Rachel, the woman he wanted, and agrees to work for Laban another seven years to acquire flocks of his own. Meanwhile, sons had been born to Laban. Twenty years after the entry of Jacob into Laban's household, we first hear of Laban's sons (Genesis 31:1, 41), who are now young men, and whose presence changed the picture because, as we have pointed out, according to the social usages of the time, a real son (not an adopted son) of Laban would become the chief heir. The impression of the social milieu is much like that reflected in the Nuzu tablets, in considerable detail. Thus both Leah and Rachel each bring a handmaid as a marriage gift from their father. The paternal wedding gift of a handmaid to his daughter, is again attested in the Nuzu tablets. We shall presently note other detailed resemblances between the Nuzu tablets and the patriarchal accounts. Some of the phenomena are known from other cuneiform records but no set of known texts offer as many parallels to the patriarchal narratives as do the Nuzu tablets.

The most ingenious bit of cheating that Jacob went in for was his use of maternal impression on the yet-unborn of the flocks, which he and Laban had agreed to divide according to coloration. This piece of trickery ended with Jacob's becoming wealthy to the dissatisfaction of Laban's sons. Then Laban's daughters, siding with their husband, agree that home is no place for them. Since Jacob's inheritance prospects had deteriorated, Rachel and Leah agree that they no longer have any portion in the house of their father. Laban had gone off to shear his flocks, so Jacob took advantage of the occasion to escape with his wives, children and flocks. Rachel without telling her husband, steals Laban's household gods, which, as we know from the Nuzu tablets, were to go to a real son and not the adopted son. Rachel's motive was the securing of some prized advantage in family affairs, for her husband and children. Since they were bound for Canaan and were leaving Mesopotamia for good, it is not likely that the gods conveyed valuable property rights. The possession of the gods may rather have betokened clan leadership and spiritual power to an extent that made possessing them of paramount importance.

When Laban overtakes them, he expresses his claim that the daughters and their children, and the flocks, indeed everything belongs to him and that Jacob should have asked his permission before leaving. But what bothers Laban most is the theft of his gods. Obviously Laban is in the legal right, for his claims go uncontested.[30] Laban searches in vain for the *teraphim,* as the household gods are called. Rachel had hidden them under her saddle and courtesy prevented her father from forcing her off, so the theft remained unexposed. Laban's position was correct to the extent that as long as he (Laban) lived, Jacob as his adopted son belonged to him; and not only Jacob alone but together with his wives and children and all his possessions. Yet in a magnanimous forgiving way, Laban allows Jacob's household to depart. Jacob and Laban exchange blessings and make a treaty and all Laban requires of him is to swear he will treat his girls well and not to marry other women. They furthermore set up a monolith and swear that neither will transgress the boundary to harm the other. Their respective ancestral gods—"the God of Abraham" and "the god of Nahor"—were invoked to judge between them. Jacob also swore by "the Fear of his father Isaac," God's special epithet with reference to Isaac. The devotion to the god of one's father is a feature of Hebrew religion that stemmed from the pre-Hebraic East. The covenant between Jacob and Laban was solemnized by a sacrificial

[30] The simplest explanation is that Jacob, not as Laban's son-in-law but adopted son, was under Laban's jurisdiction.

feast and on the morrow they parted company and each went with his followers toward his native land.

En route to the land of Canaan, Jacob effects a reconciliation with Esau, who graciously pardons his brother. Jacob bows down to the earth seven times before his brother (Genesis 33:3); the sevenfold prostration is a widespread custom attested also in epistles from Amarna and Ugarit.

Jacob proceeds with his wives and children to Shechem, where he buys some land from the Beni-Hamor, the tribe that dwelt there. However, because one of that tribe seduced Dinah, the daughter of Jacob, her brothers Simeon and Levi, resort to treachery against the inhabitants which displeases Jacob, the more so since he has few supporters and is a stranger who can ill afford to have enemies. But again this episode, particularly the treachery of Simeon and Levi, is purposeful; and we must remember it to understand part of the blessing that Jacob is eventually to make on his deathbed.

In Genesis 35:2-3 we read "And Jacob said to his household and to all with him, 'Remove the foreign gods which are in your midst and purify yourselves and change your garments, that we may arise and go to Bethel, where I may make an altar to the God Who answered me in the day of my distress and was with me on the road I walked.' " Whereupon Jacob and his household bury their gods under a tree near the city of Shechem (Genesis 35:4), which clearly shows that foreign idols were still in the midst of the people, although Jacob recognized that his allegiance was not to them but to Yahwe, Who claimed his sole devotion by being with him when he was in trouble, and bringing him back safely to the land of Canaan. Thus, while the covenant between God and Israel was established and recognized, pagan survivals clung on, and, as we shall see, did not end until the destruction of Jerusalem in 586 B.C., when Judaism was purged of its idolatrous vestiges. The contractual nature of the relation between

God and His people stems from the Patriarchal Period and remains a cornerstone of biblical religion throughout both Testaments.

The narrative in Genesis continues with the birth of Benjamin, the second and last child of Rachel, for she died in bearing him. The family was moving from Bethel to Ephrathah, which is in the vicinity of Bethlehem. She was buried with a monolith to mark the grave. A little tomb, still frequented by pilgrims, now stands on the traditional site of Rachel's resting place.

Genesis 35 :22 records Reuben's scandalous affair with his father's concubine Bilhah with characteristic Hebrew conciseness; for the Bible, while not suppressing scandal from history, does not lavish time and words on sex and cheap gossip. The incident is not reported casually or to gratify idle curiosity. To the contrary, the incident is necessary for understanding Jacob's last blessing to his sons, the tribal fathers, that lies ahead in Genesis 49 (note verse 4). The more we study the Bible, the more we respect the importance of the details, if we are to piece together the story of Israel's experience.

# Chapter IX

# ISRAEL AND THE RAMESSIDE AGE

WITH Genesis 37 we come to the saga of Joseph, which is one of the most appealing narratives in world literature; for in it are blended the spirits of Israel and Egypt.

Joseph, the son of Rachel, is the favorite of his father. He is accordingly hated by his half-brothers; the more so because of his conceit. He has two dreams which are really duplicates of one another, as is typical in ancient Near East literature. In one dream he saw the family binding each a sheaf in the field; and everyone's sheaf got in circle around Joseph's sheaf and bowed down to it. In his second dream, the sun, moon and eleven stars bowed down to him. On this occasion, as regularly when the Hebrews were confronted with dreams, no interpretation is necessary; the meaning of the dream is obvious to them. Without more ado, Jacob scolds Joseph and asks rhetorically: "Must I, your mother and your brothers come to bow down to you unto the earth?" (Genesis 37:10). The offended brothers succeeded in expressing their resentment more drastically. They laid hands on him and sold him as a slave but deceived their father into believing Joseph had been devoured by a wild beast. Jacob, disconsolate on losing his favorite son, sums up his grief thus: "I shall go down mourning into Sheol to my son" (Genesis 37:35); indicating that there was as yet no concept of a heaven among the Hebrews but simply a belief in an underworld where everyone went to spend a dreary, inactive eternity.

The cycle of Joseph is a success story. Many ills befall him but everything turns out well in the long run because God is with him and a kindly Providence sees to it that he overcomes every obstacle and rises in station. He is sold as a slave into the house of Potiphar, an Egyptian official, but before long he is made the major-domo in Potiphar's house.

With Genesis 38, the narrative changes abruptly, interrupting the story of Joseph. There are two reasons why this chapter may have been injected. Firstly, the incident it relates is necessary for the genealogies of the fathers in Israel. Secondly, the Joseph story is told with exquisite artistry, including the element of suspense which is frequently introduced. In this particular case, where an entirely different tale is interposed, may it not be that the biblical author or editor purposely inserted this long chapter into the Joseph story for suspense? For, while Joseph is left behind as a slave in Potiphar's house, we must go through all of Chapter 38 before we get back to the fate of the hero, Joseph.

In Genesis 38, Judah, the son of Jacob, goes to an Adullamite friend of his, to live with him. This shows that toward the end of the Patriarchal Period, the Hebrews, in spite of their apparent clannishness, did not live to themselves but mingled freely with the natives of the land. Furthermore, Judah married a Canaanite woman who bore him three sons: Er, Onan and Shelah. A girl named Tamar was obtained as a wife for the firstborn, Er, who died without progeny, so that Tamar was automatically married to the next brother, Onan. Her second marriage was automatic because no children had been born of the first union, and according to the Hebrew law of levirate marriage,[1] it becomes incumbent upon the deceased's next of kin (usually the next brother in line) to marry the widow of a childless man in Israel, so that the first

[1] Levirate marriage goes back to crass beginnings, when a woman purchased in marriage belonged permanently to the family of the man that bought her. Nuzu marriage contracts sometimes specify that the woman purchased by a man for his son, shall, if later widowed, pass on to a second, and if necessary to a third, fourth (etc.) son of the purchaser.

child of the second union may be reckoned as the son of the deceased to carry on the latter's name in Israel. Onan selfishly did not want to raise a child for his dead brother so he practiced birth control, which was displeasing in the eyes of God, Who killed him for it.

The next son Shelah, still a minor, was too young to become Tamar's mate immediately; yet the law of levirate marriage entitled her to have him automatically upon his growing up. Pending his maturity, Tamar was sent away to wait in the home of her father. But when she heard that Shelah, who was still being withheld from her, had reached maturity, she resorted to a drastic subterfuge to obtain her right to be the mother of the family's heir. Her father-in-law Judah was coming to attend the shearing of his flocks. Tamar, seizing the opportunity, put off the clothes of her widowhood, and disguised as a veiled prostitute. Sitting by the wayside, she attracted the attention of her father-in-law Judah, who did not realize who she really was. Inasmuch as he did not have the hire with which to pay her, he left as security, at her request, his three articles of identification,[2] including his personal seal and staff. After this incident, Tamar took off her disguise, donned her widow's weeds and returned to the house of her father. Judah, wishing to pay his debt and redeem his security, sent a kid as payment for what he owed her. However, no prostitute could be found in the locality. Presently news of Tamar's pregnancy was spread abroad. Judah, not knowing that he was the father of her child, indignantly insisted that she be ousted from her father's house and burned alive for her sins. For even though she was residing with her father, she was legally Judah's daughter-in-law, belonging to his family and subject to his patriarchal jurisdic-

[2] In the Ugaritic myths, the gods each have three articles of personal identification. Since Judah's three were probably the standard articles possessed by every solid citizen, whereas the Ugaritic gods each have a different three, the parallel is subject to qualification.

tion. Her father had to comply and ousted her to be punished but Tamar turned the tables on Judah by showing the three incriminating articles of identification and declaring that their owner had impregnated her. She, after all, had been wronged by Judah, who deprived her of her rightful husband Shelah. Since she was prevented from bearing the heir to the latter, she made the best of her plight by tricking Judah into siring the heir out of her. The fact that she was in the right and he in the wrong, is confessed by Judah, who admits "She is more in the right than I" (verse 26). The twins that were born, far from being illegitimate, included the ancestor of King David and his Messianic Line (Genesis 38:29; Ruth 4:18-22; Matthew 1:1, 3, 6, 16). The fact that Judah and Tamar were father- and daughter-in-law would offend ancient Near Easterners less than might appear on the surface. In the Hittite Law Code, not only the deceased's brothers, but also his father, could marry the widow.

The twin boys were Zerah and Perez. Zerah, though the firstborn, was eclipsed by the younger Perez. The superiority of the latter was evident from quaint obstetrical circumstances attending the birth (Genesis 38:27-30). The motif of the younger eclipsing the elder, and the narration of it being worthy of saga, are, as we have observed, characteristic of Canaanite literature, both biblical and Ugaritic.

Now to come back to the narrative of Joseph in Chapter 39. He rises to the top of his master's household but due to the machinations of Potiphar's wife,[3] he falls out of grace and is sent to the king's jail, but even there he rises in station, so that when the king's cupbearer and baker fall out of favor and are sent to prison (Genesis 40), it is Joseph who is commissioned to look after them. The cupbearer has a dream in which

---

[3] Compare the Egyptian Tale of the Two Brothers for the theme of a married woman who attempts to seduce a virtuous youth and, on failing, maligns him.

he sees a vine with three branches and grapes growing. He squeezes the grapes into a cup, which he puts into the Pharaoh's hand. He is troubled by this dream, which Joseph interprets for him thus : The three branches mean three days, whereupon the Pharaoh will forgive and restore him to his former office. As a reward, Joseph asks the cupbearer to recommend him to Pharaoh and thus rescue him from prison.

The baker dreamt there were three baskets on his head; in the topmost there was baking for the Pharaoh, but birds descended and ate it. Encouraged by the favorable interpretation of the cupbearer's dream, the baker turns to Joseph who gives him a gloomy prediction : In three days the Pharaoh will remove the baker's head and hang his corpse, so that the birds will devour his flesh.

Both interpretations come true, but the lucky cupbearer forgets to help Joseph, who therefore has to wait two years for the Pharaoh to have a dream that will require Joseph's talents to explain, and so raise him from an inmate of a prison to the highest position under the Pharaoh.

In Genesis 41 :14 we read how Joseph was prepared for his first royal audience. He shaved and changed his clothes. The Semites did not shave themselves clean, but Egyptians did. At every turn the biblical author shows knowledge of Egyptian conditions.

Pharaoh characteristically has his dreams in duplicate and Joseph explains that this is merely to show that God had determined to fulfill the message of the dream quickly (Genesis 41 :32). The dreams are so familiar (Genesis 41 :1-7) that they need not be repeated here. The upshot was that, as Joseph realized, the dreams portended seven years of plenty followed by seven years of famine. Joseph wisely suggested that the government should gather and store grain during the seven years of plenty in anticipation of the seven years of

famine.[4] Joseph also advised that a competent director be put
in charge of the national program, with officials to assist in
collecting a fifth of the produce of the land so that the gran-
aries would be sufficiently filled before the bad years began.
Pharaoh decides that no man is better qualified for the job
than Joseph himself. So he appoints Joseph to the highest
position in Egypt (except for the Pharaoh himself) as major-
domo of the palace, and food administrator of all the land; in
token whereof His Majesty gives his signet ring to Joseph,
clothes him in robes of honor and places a golden necklace
on him. This is characteristically Egyptian and we compare
Sinuhe's elevation in rank together with royal gifts of robes
and other honors. The whole Joseph narrative is to be understood against the Egyptian background. Thus the word
shouted before the chariot of the Prime Minister Joseph is
*ab rek* (Genesis 41:43), which is Egyptian (composed of *ab*
"heart" and *rek* "to thee") meaning "pay attention!". The
narrative also contains genuine Egyptian proper names and
titles. While cuneiform documents are in general more important than Egyptian records for illuminating most of the
Hebrew Bible, the reverse is true for the section of Genesis and Exodus covering from Joseph to the Exodus.

Joseph marries the daughter of a priest of Heliopolis—the
city is called "On" in Hebrew, after the native Egyptian name
—and she bears him the firstborn Manasseh, and Ephraim
the younger.

Famine forces Joseph's brothers down to Egypt to secure
food. Semites coming to Egypt for food in famine years were
familiar enough throughout Egyptian history. For Canaan
depended on precarious rain, while Egypt could always count

---

[4] Although there is nothing mythological in the Joseph story the motif
of seven-year cycles both of plenty and of famine runs through Near East
mythology. As we have already observed, the Gilgamesh Epic even contains the element of laying up a seven-year supply in anticipation of the
famine.

on the Nile. The Semites of Asia knew this and turned to the bread-basket of Egypt when starvation faced them in Canaan.

The story proceeds with characteristic suspense and *dénouement*. Joseph recognizes his brothers, but they do not recognize him. He accuses them of espionage. They protest their innocence and relate that they are a family of twelve sons, the youngest of whom had been left behind with their father in Canaan. They add that one of their brothers is no more. Joseph declares that their veracity will be tested by their producing the brother left at home. The reader will find the intricate but charming story in Genesis 42-45. The way Joseph worries his brothers over a long period, and yet surreptitiously supplies the needs of their family, has an unmistakable resemblance to the Egyptian classic called The Eloquent Peasant, where the peasant is kept worried, so as to amuse his peers, who, though teasing him, see to it that his family is looked after.

At long last the whole family, including the aged Patriarch Israel,[5] come to Egypt, as the relatives of the famous Joseph (Genesis 46). Together with Joseph's children the family numbered seventy souls (verse 27), in keeping with epic tradition. The newcomers were settled in the Goshen region of the Delta, where they raised flocks as their ancestors had done.

The Pharaoh treated them well. One incident (regardless of its historicity) is a tradition reflecting an important trait of the nomadic Semites. Pharaoh asked Jacob his age. The reply was the unrealistic "130 years; few and evil have been the days of the years of my life, nor have they attained the days of the years of the lives of my fathers" (Genesis 47:9). If this is compared with the painstaking and specific genealogy in Genesis 46:8-27, it will be seen that, while the genealogies were transmitted with care, the Hebrews had not yet

[5] Jacob was renamed Israel (Genesis 32:29).

begun to reckon realistically with time in terms of years. An understanding of the facts explains how a document, so reliable in so many ways, can ascribe to Jacob the unreasonable life span of 147 years (Genesis 47:28).

Stripping the above events of unhistoric romance, we date the historic migration of the Israelites to Egypt in the early part of the thirteenth century B.C. The reference to the Land of Ramses (as Egypt is called in Genesis 47:11) fits in perfectly and need not be an anachronism.

The account goes on to tell how through Joseph's planning, the silver, the livestock, the very persons and the land of the people were step by step converted into royal property. The priests alone, through government support, saved their land. The people, now royal peasants, were to cultivate the king's land and pay one-fifth the yield to the crown. The biblical author is not concerned with the social implications of the national economy ascribed to Joseph's administration. For the author (who was no Amos), Joseph was a clever man who served his sovereign brilliantly. There is no merit in our demanding the later ethical standard of the Prophets, in early Hebrew history and tradition.

Jacob expressed a wish to be buried in Canaan, not in a foreign land. He falls ill and calls for Joseph and the latter's two sons. For the aged Patriarch's blessing, Joseph properly stations Manasseh at Jacob's right and the younger Ephraim at his left, but the old man crossed his hands so that the right touched the younger, and the left the older. Here again is the theme of the younger child eclipsing the elder; a theme worthy of Canaanite saga in both the Bible and Ugarit. The historic fact that the tribe of Ephraim was more important than that of Manasseh, is thus explained etiologically by a circumstance in Jacob's blessing.

Then follows the blessing of the tribes in which twelve actual sons are singled out as the ancestors of the future tribes

(Genesis 49). Reuben, destined to disappear from history relatively early, has his misfortunes attributed to his misbehavior with his father's concubine. Simeon and Levi,[6] who also come to grief, are reproached with their treachery at Shechem. But Judah, who is not an older son, is designated as a leader over his brothers, reflecting the emergence of Judah under the House of David.

After the blessing of the tribes, the last wish of Jacob is to be buried in the cave of Machpelah, that Abraham had purchased from Ephron. Subsequent to Jacob's death and his burial in Palestine, the brothers still feel that Joseph may seek revenge on them for what they did to him years before. So they invent the white lie that their father had expressed a wish to them before he died, that Joseph should forgive them. Joseph gladly does so. This telling a falsehood was not considered reprehensible when it was prompted by self defense; we have noted other examples of such deception in the patriarchal cycle.

Genesis ends with Joseph requesting that his bones be moved to the Promised Land and with the statement that when he died, he was mummified and placed in a sarcophagus in Egypt.

We now return to the events of Egyptian history. After the death of Ikhnaton, his widow Nefertiti offered to wed a son of Suppiluliuma, the great Hittite monarch. Suppiluliuma wrote back for confirmation, for never had Egypt accepted a foreign prince as the husband of an Egyptian queen. Since Egypt was weak and the Hittites were strong, the match would have been tantamount to making the Hittite prince the Pharaoh. Yet confirmation was received from Nefertiti, and Suppiluliuma sent his son. But Egyptian opposition was

---

[6] The Levites, however, by being scattered throughout the tribal territories as a sacerdotal class, have survived down to the present among the Jews.

organized and the prince was slain on his way into Egypt, which was a sufficient cause for war. Tutankhaton, husband of Ikhnaton's third daughter, succeeded to the throne and went to Thebes; his name, as we have stated, was changed to Tutankhamon (around 1358-49), in keeping with the anti-Aton reaction. But the situation was so bad that, in order to save Egypt from Hittite domination and from internal disintegration, a leader arose in the person of General Haremhab (about 1345-18), who founded the Nineteenth Dynasty, saved Egypt from the Hittites and established the basis for peace. Egypt was able to salvage its hold on Palestine during the period.

In spite of the Amon Counterrevolution, Ikhnaton's reform left some permanent effects on Egypt. For the intellectuals, all the gods were merely manifestations of one true god. Thus in the much later composition of the Wisdom of Amenemope, "the god" is often referred to. To be sure, it is not unparalleled in pagan cultures [7] to have a trend toward monotheism in the midst of a polytheistic milieu. Along with religion, there remained as always the practice of magic on a popular plane.

Egypt was not to produce a fourth flowering of her splendid native civilization. There had been the Old, Middle and New Kingdoms with their cultural brilliance; but now the end had come. Later revivals are insignificant compared with the three great periods now passed.

Ramses I (about 1318-7) is the first king of the Nineteenth Dynasty to embark on gigantic building operations, including huge temples and colossal statues, that eventually exhausted the resources of the land. His successor Seti I (about 1317-01) invaded Palestine against both the bedouin and the Hittites. Though the Hittites had conquered Mitanni and gotten North Syria into their sphere, Egypt maintained its domina-

---

[7] Many pagan Greek authors often speak of "the god" in the singular.

tion over southern Canaan. Ramses II (about 1301-1234) put up vigorous opposition to the Hittites. His well documented battles, particularly the one at Kadesh (around 1296), culminated in treaties and a century of peace with the Hittites. It was about 1280 that Hattusil III, King of the Hittites, and Ramses II made treaties in keeping with the peace allegedly established of old by the Egyptian god Re and the Hittite god Teshub. The kings made nonaggression and mutual assistance pacts; and cordial relations continued between members of the royal families. Thus the Egyptian Queen Naptera corresponded affectionately with the Hittite Queen Puduhepa. Around 1267 B.C., the Hittite king sent his eldest daughter with gifts to become the Queen of Egypt by wedding Ramses II. This might superficially convey the impression that Egypt won a diplomatic triumph in the match. Historic perspective, however, points in the opposite direction. Never before had an Asiatic been accepted as the official queen in the land of the Pharaohs.

The end of the reign of Ramses II marks approximately the period of the Exodus. As we have noted, the entire span of the Hebrew Bondage could have been bridged by the latter part of Joseph's career and Moses's prime.

Moses had contacts with the Semitic World east of Suez; notably with a priest of Midian whose daughter he married. In Asia, Moses also received a theophany, in which God recalled the covenant, and ordered Moses back to Egypt to save his brethren from their distress.

The Exodus and the incidents leading up to it, have authentic Egyptian elements. The Hebrew taskmasters, for instance, go to Pharaoh and say: "Behold, thy slaves [i.e., we] are beaten" (Exodus 5:16). The expression is not idiomatic in Hebrew but it rings true for Egypt, where beating was not so much a matter of brutality as it was a normal expression of relationship between men of unequal status in their daily work. Collecting taxes, educating scribes, or getting any work done without beating was rare in Egypt.

The Exodus of Israel and the celebrating of the first Passover are familiar enough (Exodus 12-14). We need only note at this time that God is recognized as the supreme but not the only god. The query in the Song of the Sea "Who is like unto Thee among the gods, O Yahwe?" (Exodus 15:11) implies that God is beyond compare but not the only deity. Also in the Ten Commandments (Exodus 20:2-17) it is said "Thou shalt not have other gods before Me. . . . Thou shalt not bow down to them or worship them because I, Yahwe, thy God, am a jealous God." The existence of other gods is still admitted but their worship is forbidden. God in His jealousy is the only God for Israel and tolerates no rival.

The period of the wandering in the desert before the entrance to the Promised Land via Transjordan is given the round number of forty years, which, in accordance with Hebrew idiom, need not be taken exactly, and in this case was probably shorter than that figure. Our thirteenth century chronology is supported by the explorations of Nelson Glueck, showing that Transjordan was not occupied between the seventeenth and thirteenth centuries B.C. The story of the wandering in Transjordan before the entry into Palestine tells us of armed resistance offered by the kings of the area. Since the land was desolate down to the thirteenth century, there could have been no such resistance prior to that century.

After wandering, and overcoming military and other obstacles in the south and in Transjordan, Joshua (the successor of Moses) and the people, accompanied by the Holy Ark,[8] crossed the River Jordan and entered a land "flowing with milk and honey." Palestine was a land of milk and honey only from the standpoint of people entering from the east.

---

[8] Arab tribes, even in late historic times, have carried a sacred cult object with them on their wanderings and into battle.

It is almost impossible to describe the beauty and richness of the land after you have been in the desert, but from the standpoint of people from really fertile areas like the Nile Valley or ancient Babylonia, Palestine was hardly a land of outstanding productivity, even in Joshua's time when soil erosion and the denudation of forests had not reduced the country to the wretched state it was in prior to the modern revival.

The Hebrew tribes had escaped from a weakened Egypt. They entered Canaan at a time when the world had no strong empires. The absence of great powers was a necessary factor in Israel's Conquest of Canaan and rise to nationhood, which could only have happened in a prolonged period when small states had a chance to come into being and evolve their own way of life.

Joshua's conquest was rapid. Jericho fell; then the neighboring city of Ai, and numerous other towns throughout Palestine. Between campaigns Joshua (8 :30-35) constructed a shrine on Mount "Ebal" near Shechem, with some of the people standing for the ceremony on Mount Ebal and others on the opposite Mount Gerizim. It is stated that no iron was used in constructing the shrine and its altar. This reflects the conservatism of religion; for though the Iron Age had begun, the innovations of the Age were characteristically shunned. The Samaritans are right in their claim that the Bible has been tampered with to suppress the priority of their Gerizim shrine. The orthodox Judeo-Christian view that Moses had Jerusalem in mind as the center of worship is weakened by the fact that nowhere is Jerusalem mentioned in the Pentateuch. The phrase used is noncommittally "the place which God shall choose" (Deuteronomy 12 :5). The Samaritans, who insist that "the place" is Gerizim, and not Jerusalem, have a better argument in that the altar erected "near" Gerizim (actually on Gerizim, for the Hebrew text has been

altered as several Hebrew manuscripts and ancient translations show) was the only one built in accordance with the
specific orders of Moses (cf. Deuteronomy 27:4 where the
Samaritan Pentateuch reads "Gerizim" versus Masoretic
"Ebal"). This is the correct view of the Samaritans, but history has made heretics of them and conferred orthodoxy on
Judaism.

Joshua had to face a large coalition of local kings in Palestine but at almost every turn he was successful. There was a
great deal of vitality in the Hebrew tribes, united in a common effort. One Canaanite group, the Gibeonites, that realized it could not stand against the Hebrew invaders, by a
ruse extracted a treaty from Joshua (9:3-15) and the Israelites. Even though the promise of protection was obtained
through guile, the Hebrews in accordance with the standards
of the time felt obliged to respect that treaty.

Joshua then turned against the coalition of five Amorite
kings. The cities they ruled included Jerusalem, Hebron and
Lachish. Now it is interesting to note that the word "Amorite" covers people of different tribal origins because Jerusalem
was in the hands of the Jebusites. Yet "Amorite" is the term
used to cover all of them (Joshua 10:5).

The biblical text quotes some of its written sources. At this
point (Joshua 10:13) we read that additional material can be
found in the Book of Jashar, now lost—a fate that has befallen
also other early sources named in the Bible. If we had those
lost books, the extent of Israel's literature would be considerably bigger than the Bible.

The impressive conquest of Joshua extended down to the
border of Goshen, the Delta land from which the Hebrews
had escaped. Most of the captured cities were not destroyed.
In fact, Hazor is singled out as the only city burned out of
quite a number captured in the north. The Hebrews did not

come to destroy but to occupy the land and keep it in as good condition as possible.[9]

Joshua then proceeded to parcel out the land to the twelve tribes some of whom settled in Transjordan though the majority remained west of the Jordan. The number "twelve" given to the tribes involves quite a bit of manipulation throughout biblical history, and yet that number is adhered to even though the facts in specific situations are against it. The reason for the insistence on the twelveness of the tribes [10] is that the tribes had a function within the nation as a whole. The function meant, as we shall see later in Solomon's time, discharging national obligations governmentally, militarily and religiously; each tribe, one month per year. Hence the twelveness of the tribes is a deepseated institution pervading Hebrew history.

Joshua had warred against thirty-one kings in Palestine. This large number of kings in so small a country, was possible only because they were kings of little city states. Joshua's Conquest achieved a peace that lasted for a number of years so that the tribes could settle down to normal life.

With the death of Joshua, there begins the Period of the Judges, when disorganized tribalism rather than united nationhood prevailed. However, it is also in that period that we see the beginning of a development from tribalism back to nationhood. The tribes had to reconquer much of the territory their armies had once occupied (as well as acquire new areas) for the simple reason that the strongest of the walled cities could not be taken by the means at the Hebrews' disposal.

The tribal Hebrews were not as advanced technologically as the longer settled groups in Canaan, especially those that

[9] The few exceptions (e.g., Jericho, Ai and Hazor) do not invalidate the general rule. Yet we must not overstate the case, for W. F. Albright has found burned strata of the age at Bethel and Tell Beit Mirsim.

[10] Not only in Israel but among other tribal confederacies in the Bible World and outside it.

had horse-drawn iron chariots. We read that Judah was
selected by oracle to proceed against certain Canaanites. Judah
invited Simeon to share its fortunes. Together they conquered
the cities of Gaza, Ascalon and Ekron, but they could not
occupy the plains, where the native population had iron
chariots, against which the Hebrew tribesmen were helpless.

The Jebusites at this time were living side by side with the
tribe of Benjamin. There was no mass destruction or driving
out of the Canaanites at any time in biblical history. If Israel
was strong in a given area, it reduced the local population to
servitude (as "gatherers of wood and drawers of water" in
Joshua 9:21, 23, 27) ; but the Canaanites were not wiped out.
The presence of so many Canaanites dwelling with the Hebrews meant Canaanite influence—even in religion—on the
Hebrews. The Bible explains God's purpose in sparing the
Canaanites as calculated to keep Israel strong by the constant
necessity of fighting. Furthermore, when the Canaanites inflicted disaster on the Hebrews, the calamity at least caused
contriteness and purged the Hebrews of their apostacy and
led them back to the orthodox worship of God, Who alone
could save them. Thus all such factors were reckoned within
the simple philosophy of history expressed in the Bible.

The Conquest was probably under way during the invasion
of Merneptah, the Pharaoh who ruled from about 1234 to
1220 B.C. Merneptah's texts, as is typical of those times, contain Canaanite words, which were familiar in Egypt because
of the long and intimate contact with the peoples of Canaan,
including the Hebrews. In his stela celebrating a victory in
Canaan, Merneptah mentions that "Israel" is destroyed;
hence Israel must have been in the country at that time. The
"destruction" of Israel is a hackneyed exaggeration of a type
that fills Egyptian, Mesopotamian and other royal annals.
The "Spring of Me(r)neptah" is mentioned in Scripture as
can be seen by examining Joshua 15:9 and 18:15.

In the reign of Ramses III (about 1197-65) a great wave of Sea People from Crete and the Grecian isles and coasts threatened not only Palestine but Egypt itself. Ramses III saved his country from invasion, although in Palestine the augmenting of Philistine ranks with fresh blood from Caphtor meant the subjection of the Hebrews to the Philistines during the Period of the Judges.

Within Egypt, the Amon cult was so strong in wealth and political power, that the holdings of the god Amon became a state within a state. Ramses III, the last of the Pharaohs with any strength to strike in Palestine for some time to come, was murdered by a plot in his own harem. The trial of the criminals has been preserved for us and it is interesting to note that the testimony of the dead Ramses through an oracle was accepted as legal evidence in the court and was instrumental in bringing the culprits to justice. The dead king requested support for his son who succeeded him, so that the oracle not only aided justice but also strengthened the government of the new Pharaoh.

## Chapter X

# FROM TRIBALISM TO NATIONHOOD

TYPICAL of the Period of the Judges is local tribal resistance to local enemies, and on occasion the union of a few tribes in a common cause.

Without a foe to face, the leadership lay dormant. But once an enemy appeared, a ruler or "judge" would arise to lead a segment of the Hebrews into battle. One such "judge" was Othniel, on whom the spirit of the Lord descended [1] so that he vanquished the foe, and characteristically established the peace for "forty" years. Then Eglon, King of Moab, afflicted Israel and invaded western Palestine but another judge arose, Ehud, who assassinated Eglon and gave the land peace for "eighty" years, again a multiple of forty. Shamgar (whose name is Hurrian and whose mother "Anath" was named after the Canaanite goddess) slew six hundred Philistines single-handed as the story goes. While such round numbers are not to be taken literally, this does not mean that all the other elements are unhistorical.

The tribes were confronted with a succession of enemies from many quarters, but the most formidable of the foes was King Jabin from the northern city of Hazor. His general Sisera, who could throw nine hundred iron chariots into the field, terrorized the northern tribes. A savior arose in the person of Deborah, a prophetess and a judge of her people. She chose a man, Barak, as her general. But inasmuch as he was

[1] Prior to the accession of King Solomon, Hebrew leadership was inspired, not hereditary.

uninspired and insisted that she come along into the fray, the glory for the victory went to a woman according to Deborah's own prophecy. The woman was not Deborah, but Jael, as the story later brings out. According to the prose account in Judges 4 the battle was fought and Sisera, who fled to a nomad's tent was craftily slain by Jael, and the Israelites gradually gained strength against Jabin until ultimately they eliminated him.

There is also a poetic account of the same historic events [2] in Judges 5, containing the famous Song of Deborah of genuine antiquity.[3] The God of Sinai is pictured as coming out of His holy mountain and using all of nature, especially the storm, to route the enemies of His people. He emerges from Edom amidst earthquake and storm, to bring salvation to His tribes. The poem describes how the highways of the land had become so insecure that people had to go by devious means along the byways until Deborah arose to restore security. The Israelites were so disarmed that among thousands there was not a single weapon. Not all the tribes responded to the call, but many of them did and are praised in the poem. Those that remained aloof are jeered at. As the poem tells us, even the stars in their courses took part in the battle and the dismay of the enemy was enhanced by a cloudburst filling the River Kishon (which might have been an insignificant stream just before it became a raging torrent). The town of Meroz is singled out for particular contempt in that its people did not participate in the battle. Sisera's mother, who is waiting in

---

[2] It is not unusual for history to be recorded in both prose and poetic versions almost simultaneously. In the New Kingdom, Pharaohs sometimes celebrated their compositions in three versions: poetry, prose and pictures.

[3] Semitic tribesmen are quick to celebrate important local events in poetry and song. Such compositions may be handed down for many generations with little significant change.

vain for her son to come back with spoil taken from Israel, is also the object of scorn.[4]

Deborah's career marks a milestone in the transition from individual tribalism to united nationhood.

Among the enemies of the Hebrews in this period were the Midianites: camel-riding nomads, who would make raids particularly at harvest time, stealing and destroying crops and making the people of the sown so miserable, that they would seek refuge in caves. The hero that arose on one occasion to redeem his people from Midianite oppression, was Gideon, who in his zeal for God destroyed an altar of Baal and the adjacent Asherah,[5] belonging to his father. The local populace were indignant but his father defended him from them, pointing out that gods can take care of themselves; and if Baal be a real god, he will avenge himself.

Gideon, who belonged to the tribe of Manasseh,[6] also assembled the other northern tribes of Asher, Zebulon and Naphtali to rid the Hebrews of their Midianite foes. Rivalry resulted so that Ephraim was offended. Gideon appeased the Ephraimite tribesmen by flattering them on their capture of the two Midianite chiefs, Zeeb and Oreb. According to Judges 7:25, the heads of those chiefs were cut off and sent on as evidence and trophies of the success. Naturally it is difficult to transport whole corpses around; so to count the foe or establish his identity, the head was cut off, for the sake of convenience and shipped to headquarters. This was a routine procedure all through the ancient Near East. There was an-

---

[4] There is another side to the poet's description of the enemy's mother back home. This may be the same feature that in Homer's Iliad is developed into the touching scenes where the heroic enemy Hector is at home in Troy with his mother, wife or other relatives.

[5] In the Bible, an "Asherah" is an idol or symbol of the Canaanite mother-goddess Asherah.

[6] Gideon claims to be from the poorest clan in Manasseh and the youngest in his family (Judges 6:15). The elevation of the lowly and of juniors to leadership is a frequent theme.

other way of counting the slain foe in order to facilitate
statistics and avoid too much bulk; that is by cutting off a
palm (really the whole hand from the wrist down) of the
victim's arm. In Ugarit, Mesopotamia and Egypt, cutting off
either palms or heads, and even heaping them up in triumph,
is referred to repeatedly. Also in art, heads and/or hands are
depicted to symbolize victory in battle. When Gideon proceeded to march against two other chiefs named Zebah and
Zalmunna, he came to a town where he asked for supplies and
help. The townsmen asked him sarcastically: "Is the palm
of Zebah and Zalmunna already in your hand that we should
give bread to your army?" (Judges 8:6). The meaning need
not be "Are you now leading them by their hand as captives?"
More likely it is "Have you already slain them with their
amputated palms as proof?" The word for "palm" is *kaf* (as
distinct from the "hand" of the victor, which is *yad*), precisely as in the Ugaritic tablets, where the same word designates the "palms" to commemorate Anath's victory. Gideon
saw the cogency of their argument, but told them that after
capturing the two chiefs he would come back and punish them
with physical torture for their lack of cooperation in his hour
of need. On his victorious return he carried out his threat.

The movement toward hereditary kingship was already
making itself felt in Hebrew society. Gideon was offered
hereditary rule but he refused it, expressing his reaction in
the standard formula of theocracy that God alone was the
ruler, and not men. However, when he died, his seventy[7]
sons, who were dividing the rule, fell out with their half-
brother Abimelech born to Gideon by a concubine from
Shechem. Abimelech was able to muster the citizenry of
Shechem behind him because of his mother's connections;
and, through treachery, butchered all his brothers except the

[7] This number is the familiar epic cliché. Compare "the seventy sons of
Asherah" in Ugaritic literature.

youngest, Jotham, who escaped and prophesied Abimelech's downfall, which in fact followed.

Next, the Transjordanian nation of Ammon molested Israel. The Hebrew chiefs in the Gilead region of Trans-jordan decided that the first man who would arise to fight the Ammonites, would be made the leader of Gilead. The Gilead-ite Jephthah (the son of a prostitute) whose half-brothers expelled him from his father's house, was chosen as the leader because of his ability and initiative. (Note the inspirational—rather than hereditary or aristocratic—nature of leadership throughout the Period of the Judges.) His message to the enemy is interesting in the annals of the history of religion: "Is it not that you should inherit what your god, Chemosh, has caused you to inherit? But we shall inherit all which Yahwe, our God, has driven out from before us" (Judges 11:24). Thus Jephthah did not deny that the enemy had its national god, just as Israel had Yahwe. Since Israel wor-shiped officially only Yahwe, Israel's religion was in a sense monotheistic, but not monotheistic in the sense that it was later to become, when the very existence of other gods was laughed at as ridiculous.

Jephthah was successful and again the tribe of Ephraim was angry because it had been left out of things. Because of insults that Ephraim heaped on Jephthah, the latter warred on Ephraim and won. Intertribal war was one of the mani-festations of disunity that weakened Israel in the Period of the Judges. During the war on Ephraim, Jephthah's forces were able to detect Ephraimite fugitives by their dialectal pronunciation of *shibboleth* as *sibboleth:* a valuable fact for the Hebraist concerned with early dialectal differentiation.

The enemy that next appears in the Book of Judges is the one destined to become the most serious of all: the Philistines. The hero to combat them is Samson, whose entertaining nar-rative is replete with folklore. Of greater historicity in detail is the story of Micah, a well-to-do Hebrew citizen, who makes for himself an idol, with ephod [8] and teraphim [9] with a view to setting up a private chapel for himself. So simple it was for a wealthy individual to establish his own cultic center! His own son was available to serve as a priest because in those days, priests did not have to come from a special class.[10] However, he was later delighted upon securing a genuine Levite to take over as his priest. Shortly thereafter, the tribe of Dan, located precariously on the Philistine border in the south,[11] and unable to get land of its own, sent spies to go north in search of a place where the population was weak enough to be conquered and so make room for the Danites to settle. On the way, they happened to come across Micah's household, where the Levite was serving as priest. They secured a favorable oracle from the Levite; and later when the Danite army came north, the Danites forced the Levite to accompany them with his ephod, idols and other cultic equipment of his master. The proposition was appealing to the Levite, in that he would be priest not for just a family but for an entire tribe. Micah's objections were silenced by Danite desperadoes, who convinced him that, right or wrong, they were not to be trifled with. The Danites proceeded (with their newly acquired Levite and cultic equipment [12]) to the tranquil and unsuspecting town of Laish that was enjoying peace within the Sidonian [13] sphere of influence in extreme northern Palestine.

[8] A cult object used for securing oracles.

[9] Household gods.

[10] The ideal of limiting priests to the tribe of Levi was not rigidly observed until much later. Even King David appointed sons of his own as priests.

[11] The fresh influx of Philistines around 1200 may have been the cause of Dan's dislocation.

[12] The reason a band of warriors in the midst of a military campaign required a cultically equipped priest, was that oracles were needed not only to know whether or not wars should be launched, but even whether or not tactical steps should be taken in the course of a war.

[13] "The Sidonians" are not necessarily the people of Sidon; the term can also refer to the south Phoenicians including, for example, those of Tyre.

They easily conquered Laish and changed its name to Dan, which became the northernmost town in Israel. The story not only shows us how tribes might move at this time, but also the religious usages and the way new cults might be set up. The incident explains the origin of the Danite cult that became quite important after the northern Kingdom of Israel was established.

There follows the story of an atrocious crime in Gibeah of Benjamin, where a concubine belonging to a Hebrew was abused and killed. The Hebrews stirred up the tribes to concerted action by dismembering the woman's corpse into twelve parts, sending one part to each of the tribes to rouse them to avenge the injustice that had been perpetrated. So strong a sense of right and wrong prevailed among the tribes that they united against Benjamin and almost wiped it out. However, there followed a feeling of remorse, in that a tribe was on the verge of extinction [14] in Israel. To provide wives for the decimated Benjaminites, girls were secured from the town of Jabesh-gilead, and the men of Benjamin were instructed to capture them as brides during a religious festival at Shiloh. Thus the extermination of the tribe was averted. The episode is the last in the Book of Judges, which adds only one revealing verse: "In those days, there was no king in Israel. Everybody did what was right in his own eyes" (Judges 21:25). Such freedom is not far removed from anarchy.

Shiloh at that time was an important sanctuary and Eli was priest there. However, the corruption of his household, particularly of his two sons, was so bad that reform was in order. The reformer was to be Samuel, who effected the

---

[14] The desire to prevent the extinction of groups—even disliked groups —is widespread. The Flood story thus records the urge to perpetuate unclean as well as clean animals. In our own time, the sentimentality in preventing the extinction of any species (human, animal or plant) is a manifestation of the same phenomenon.

transition from disunited tribalism to the establishment of a united monarchy.

The Philistines were menacing the Hebrews and inflicted so many losses upon them that as a last resort the Hebrews took the ark of Yahwe with them into battle. From the biblical viewpoint, so corrupt were the Hebrew leaders and people that God allowed His ark to fall into the hands of the Philistines. The catastrophe impressed upon the people the necessity of union and kingship, because only through kingship (despite the tyranny that goes with it) could the nation be united for concerted action on any emergency that might arise. Samuel was theoretically opposed to establishing a kingdom, because he adhered to the theocratic ideal, whereby God alone is king. Yet he had to yield to circumstances and to the insistence of the people, with the revealed permission of God, which was required to legitimize any step taken in a theocracy such as Israel was. On principle, the kingdom was not relished; as God's reluctant authorization and Samuel's reluctant consent show. But times had changed and the innovation, however distasteful, was a necessity. Samuel, the maker of kings, chose Saul—a tall, imposing man—although of the small tribe of Benjamin [15]—as king over the nation.

The Philistine disarmament of the Hebrews was in itself a great obstacle to be overcome. Saul had thus not only the task of uniting disunited tribes, but of facing without adequate weapons a well-armed foe. The test came when the Philistines demanded that the people of Jabesh-gilead submit to the brutal humiliation of having one eye struck out: a punishment now attested also as a curse in Ugaritic. Saul, who was plowing behind a yoke of oxen when the news of Jabesh-gilead came, slaughtered the animals, cut them up, sent the

[15] Again the theme of elevating the lowly, although here it is also possible that Samuel chose as king a man from a small tribe so that the secular government might not become too strong vis-à-vis the religious forces, whose leader Samuel was.

pieces throughout Israel with the ultimatum that any man
who withheld himself would have his cattle cut up the same
way. (The device is essentially the same as that of the cutting
up of the abused concubine. The shocking thing in the case
of the concubine was that it happened to be a human being
rather than an animal that was dissected and circulated. But
both episodes are the same insofar as they were calculated
to rouse scattered people into concerted action.) The response
saved the day.

Saul's gaining of prestige through his rescue of Jabesh-
gilead touched off a feeling of rivalry between him and
Samuel, so that the interests of state and church clashed. A
series of crises progressively deteriorated the relations between Saul and Samuel until there was finally a rupture.
Samuel, who represented the more firmly established theocracy, won out against Saul, who represented the newer and
still delicate institution of the crown. Samuel was able to
reject Saul and anoint another king in his stead.

Samuel went to the house of Jesse in Bethlehem to find the
new anointed of the Lord to rule Israel after Saul. This time
the family was of a large tribe, Judah. But characteristically,
it is David the youngest of the sons who is chosen. Moreover,
it is the eighth son who prevails over the other seven, which,
as noted above, is paralleled as worthy of saga in Ugarit
(compare I Samuel 16:1-14 with Ugaritic text 128:II:24-
28 [16]; cf. III:16).

David becomes not only Saul's armor bearer but also his
harper to drive away the fits of melancholia that come over

---

[16] In these lines it is predicted to Keret of his bride that
   "She will bear thee seven sons
       Yea 'octuple' an eighth for thee
    She will bear the lad Yasib (= the eighth son)
       Who will suck the milk of Asherah
          Even suckle the breasts of the Virgin [Anath]
             The wetnurses [of the gods]."

Saul from time to time. Saul was an impetuous, religious man capable of falling into states of prophetic ecstacy for which he became notorious. The proverb "Is Saul also among the prophets?" [17] was applied to men of high station found behaving disreputably in bad company.

With the anointing of David, inspiration had departed from Saul and gone to David. Or, as the Hebrew text expresses it "the spirit of Yahwe lit upon David" (1 Samuel 16:13) "and the spirit of Yahwe departed from Saul" (verse 14).—The modern reader of the Bible should try to cope with such factors (where the concept, not the event, is the important thing) as within the realm of the history of ideas.

David was gifted, charming and handsome; a man with the kind of loyalty toward his friends that won in return loyalty toward him. His versatile talents as poet and musician as well as warrior contributed to his becoming the national hero.

The Goliath episode, which is part of David's history in the mind of posterity, may well have been attached to him wrongly. The Bible gives us contradictory evidence concerning it. According to the main narrative David killed Goliath. However, this account occasions quite a bit of difficulty in that after the reputed episode is over, Saul and Abner forget completely who David is, whereas he is supposed to have been on the court staff for quite some time. Aside from this and other contradictions, the Bible itself contains a more plausible variant tradition: In 2 Samuel 21:19 it is the hero Elhanan who slays Goliath at the town of Gob. Furthermore, the name of Elhanan's father is obviously connected with the weapon used (the weaver's beam), whereas the latter is inappropriate in the case of the account whereby David is credited with the slaying of Goliath. The author of the Books of Chronicles had before him the Books of Samuel with both variants,

[17] Ecstatic prophets did not have the stature of the great literary prophets.

which he tried to harmonize. Thus 1 Chronicles 20:5 makes Elhanan the killer of Goliath's brother. Since it is much more natural for a heroic event to be transferred from a minor personage to a great hero, than vice versa, the situation may be summed up as follows: Elhanan slew Goliath but the victory was popularly transferred to David. Both the true and the transformed versions appear in Samuel. The Chronicler, seeing the discrepancy, tried to harmonize them.

An interesting factor in the relationship between David and the House of Saul is that there was a friendship between the crown prince Jonathan and David, although nowhere does Jonathan doubt for a moment that David is going to succeed to the throne. The reason is in part this: The idea of hereditary kingship was not yet firmly entrenched in Israel. Rather the concept of inspirational leadership, not passing from father to son, was still in the minds of the Israelite tribesmen. Therefore it took no great adjustment for Jonathan to realize that he was outclassed by David and that in the natural course of events, David would succeed to the throne. This feeling was shared by many of the people, including the girls who sang after a battle that while Saul had slain thousands, David had slain tens of thousands. Being less popular than David made a frightful impression on Saul and increased his suspicion of, and enmity toward, David.

David was finally obliged to flee from the court; for while playing for Saul, Saul had heaved a javelin at him with intent to kill. Later, to eliminate David from the scene, Saul had made him a captain of a thousand on a dangerous mission which he hoped would be fatal. When this did not succeed, he said David could marry his daughter at the brideprice of a hundred Philistine foreskins.[18] David got two hundred in

[18] Ordinarily, proof that enemies were slain consisted of heads or hands cut off from the victims. In the case of the Philistines the foreskins were produced, because the Philistines were "the uncircumcized." The circumcized Egyptians counted their slain foes by heads or hands, except in the

less than the time specified, much to Saul's disappointment and embarrassment. Thus David married a princess, which strengthened his claim on the throne (1 Samuel 18:17-27).

His royal wife, to protect David from emissaries sent by Saul to kill him, let David escape but told the emissaries her husband was sick in bed. She had put teraphim in the bed to fool the searching party into thinking David was sick and in no condition to be moved. This shows that even in the household of David and of Saul's daughter, idols (and, at that, approximating human size) were still on hand.

David, in need of supplies, went to a shrine at Nob, where Ahimelech was the priest. After getting the supplies, he went to a Philistine ruler named Achish, King of Gath. To avoid being hurt, David played insane, and later fled to Adullam, which had close connections with his tribe since the days of Judah himself, according to Genesis 38:1-2. There David gathered together four hundred fellow tribesmen, all desperadoes who had not gotten along with organized society. Upon becoming their chief, David began his career of leadership among men, on his own; a leadership that was to culminate in the establishment of a long dynasty.

Saul, after hearing about Ahimelech's role in supplying David, had him killed along with eighty-five priests of Yahwe. Only Ahimelech's son Ebiathar escaped; and fled to David. Ebiathar came with the ephod. David retained him and from him sought the oracles of Yahwe which he consulted at every turn, in peace and war. The military use of oracles applied, as we have indicated, to tactics as well as strategy. David began by scoring military successes in keeping with Ebiathar's oracles. When on a subsequent occasion the oracle advised him to retreat, David wisely obeyed.[19]

---

case of the uncircumcized Libyans, whose phalli were often amputated for counting.

[19] Obviously, a priest giving military oracles would have to understand warfare if he hoped to be of any use. For this reason, priests were some-

David was now an outlawed gangster.[20] During his exploits he had a couple of chances to kill Saul but he refrained from doing so because he would not lay a hand on the anointed of Yahwe. This is in keeping with David's character; rarely did he fail to do what would command the respect of the public. David usually treated people as he himself would want to be treated. His refraining from laying a hand on Saul probably had much to do with the fact that no one successfully laid a hand on David, when he attained the throne. (In a society where blood is avenged, bloody usurpation is repaid with bloody usurpation; as proved to be the case repeatedly in the northern Kingdom of Israel.) David, as distinct from many orientals of the biblical world, and even of later times,[21] was not bent on extirpating the line of his predecessor. To the contrary, he vowed he would not destroy Saul's seed; a vow of which he was later mindful.

The incident of Nabal is interesting because it reflects conditions in the days of David's brigandage. Nabal, a well-to-do citizen rich in flocks, was giving a party. David sent ten of his men to convey good wishes and collect tribute. The argument was that since David was keeping the peace and had never attacked Nabal's interests, David was entitled to Nabal's tribute. In other words, a band of outlaws could be a force to be reckoned with in a given district in Israel and impose the payment of "protection money" on private citizens. Nabal refused to pay and would thereby have brought on himself destruction from David's gang, had not Nabal's wife Abigail gone to David with gifts to appease him. David accepted the lady's offer and was so impressed with her that

times assigned on regular duty with the army in the ancient Near East. For Ugaritic and Mari examples, see *Ugaritic Literature*, p. 125.

[20] The reader must not conclude that the role was as disreputable as it would be in modern society.

[21] The butchery of princes in Turkish and Iranian history is almost unbelievable.

they married after Nabal's death. David also married another
girl from the north: Ahinoam, the Jezreelite. His wife Michal,
the daughter of Saul, was taken from him and given to another; an insult that he later rectified.

David complained that Saul's driving him to the Philistines
meant David's being cut off from the inheritance of Yahwe
and being forced to worship strange gods (reflecting the idea
then held, that each god could be worshiped only on his own
soil). See 1 Samuel 26:19.

David returns to Achish, King of Gath, who accepts him
as a subject and assigns to him the town of Ziklag. David was
careful to make raids only upon the foes of Israel; he spared
his brethren. The Philistines about this time were arrayed for
battle against Saul, whose desperate plight is described as
follows: "And Saul beheld the camp of the Philistines, and
he feared and his heart trembled much. And Saul sought
oracles of Yahwe. But Yahwe would not answer him, neither
in dreams, nor through *urim* [ = cult objects] nor through
prophets" (1 Samuel 28:5-6). To the Israelites, national
poverty did not consist so much of economic, fiscal or political deficiencies, but rather of being forsaken by God, Who
refused to give His precious words to His people. The word
of God was being denied to Saul; Saul was without inspiration. Samuel was now dead. David, the other anointed of the
Lord, was in a foreign land. Saul in his desperation resorted
to the one means he knew, though it was illegal,[22] of appealing to the man who had given him oracles in the past, to give
him God's word on this occasion. That means was witchcraft.

---

[22] The three legal means, as stated in the Bible, were dreams, cultic
instruments and prophets. The fact that priests and prophets refused to
give oracles might be interpreted as meaning that the branches of the
clergy had united against Saul. That we must beware of so simple an
explanation is indicated by the including of dreams, which the clergy could
not prevent Saul from having. The psychology of ancient religions, or for
that matter of ancient life in general, will always confront us with elusive
phenomena.

Saul went to Endor, where a woman, who surreptitiously engaged in spiritualism, lived. Saul, by disguising, persuaded her to call up the spirit of Samuel from below. The document describing the meeting of Samuel's ghost with Saul (1 Samuel 28 :7-25) clearly mirrors many ideas of the period. Samuel is indignant that the man who had not listened to him sufficiently during his lifetime, was now disturbing his rest in the underworld. The prophet tells him that God has departed from him (Saul) and that defeat is a foregone conclusion. Samuel announces that Saul will soon be entering the underworld, Sheol, where (as we know) the good and evil alike were then believed to go after death. The righteous Samuel and the erring Saul were to be side by side in the roomy underworld of Sheol.

The Philistines preparing for battle against Israel, noticed that David with his contingent was to join them. They suspected his loyalty and therefore Achish found it wise to excuse him and send him back home. When he and his men returned to their base at Ziklag, they found it burned, and all their children and womenfolk and property carried off. He consults Ebiathar to find out whether he can overtake the band that inflicted the disaster. After consulting the ephod, Ebiathar tells him to proceed, for he will be successful. On the way, some of the troops had to be left behind because of exhaustion. On returning, the troops that were with David and had gotten back the captives and property, plus spoils, did not want to share the spoils with those that had stayed behind. But David ruled that in the army, all must share alike; regardless of whether a man participated in combat or whether he was assigned to guard property in the rear (1 Samuel 30:24). The Davidic precedent may have been coined to lend weight to an army policy of some later generation of Israel.[23]

The wisdom, diplomacy and generosity of David are again

[23] We have already noted the Homeric parallel.

shown in that he sent a share of the booty to the elders of
Judah, his own tribe, for it was these elders that some day
were to make him king, before the other tribes of Israel would
accept his sovereignty.

Saul and Jonathan met their doom in the fateful battle of
Gilboa, in which the Philistines crushed the Israelite army.
The heads of Saul and Jonathan were cut off and their corpses
hung on the walls of Beth-shan. The grateful men of Jabesh-
gilead, mindful of how Saul had once rescued them, went by
night to the walls of Beth-shan, recovered the corpses of Saul
and Jonathan, and buried them with condign rites and mourning. An Amalekite bore David what he thought would be
welcome news; namely, that he himself had killed Saul, the
anointed of Yahwe, so that David could now rule.[24] David did
what was in keeping with his character: he killed the bearer
of the tidings. He had no time for those who specialized in
treachery. David composed a dirge (2 Samuel 1:17-27) on
the death of Saul and Jonathan. Part of it runs:

> "O mountains in Gilboa
> Let there be no dew
> Nor rain upon you !" (verse 21).

It was believed that when heroes were slain, the land on which
they perished would be cursed by drought and sterility. When
the Ugaritic Daniel curses the site of Aqhat's murder, he uses
quite similar words. This unmistakable parallel is of special
importance because it provides the key to the origin of Hebrew historiography. Other nations of the ancient Near East
had annals but not real history in which personal character
and motivation were delineated. Such delineation had been
limited to the epics that dealt with gods and legendary men.
We have observed that historic events (such as Deborah's
victory) were celebrated in poetry as well as prose. David's

[24] This, however, does not agree with 1 Samuel 31:4.

dirge, as the Ugaritic parallel proves, is in the epic tradition. Thus the Hebrews achieved true historical composition by transferring human values from the epic to current events. In reading the account of the Battle of Gilboa, we see that while the political and military developments are mentioned, the real interest is in the fate of Saul and Jonathan, and in how their fate affected the hero David. With the rise of the monarchy, Hebrew historiography comes into its own, for the sense of national greatness evoked a pride in the story of the nation. The composition of real history is the greatest achievement of that period. It antedates Greek historiography by over five hundred years. Prior to the Ugaritic discoveries, the origin of Hebrew historiography was a mystery. But now that we know it was created through the application of epic values to current events, it still remains a miracle that not the large nations (such as Babylonia, Assyria or Egypt) but tiny Israel made that momentous contribution to civilization. National, like individual, genius, cannot be explained by analysis in a test-tube. Every nation in the Bible World had epic traditions and experienced current events. It took the genius of Israel to create historiography by combining them.

# Chapter XI

# ISRAEL UNITED UNDER THE HOUSE OF DAVID

SAUL's fall made it possible for David to return to his own tribal land of Judah, where he settled in Hebron and was chosen as king over the tribe. Israel [1] (as the northern tribes are called in contradistinction to Judah) still remained faithful to the House of Saul and accepted as king his son Eshbaal, [2] whose capital was Mahanaim in Transjordan; because all of Palestine west of the Jordan was at the mercy of the Philistines. David was doubtless a puppet of the Philistines at this point and it is quite possible that the division of the kingdom was favored by the Philistines, who were applying the well-known principle of "divide and rule." However, David was not the man to remain in such a servile state.

Wars between David and the House of Saul were inevitable and at Gibeon the armies of the two factions met. The army of the House of Saul was led by Abner, while David's army was led by Joab. By mutual consent, twelve champions of each army were selected to fight each other. All twenty-four

[1] Since the northern Israelites have disappeared, while the southern Judeans have survived, it would have been historically more correct if the Zionist State had chosen as its name "Judah" instead of "Israel." However, the desirability of differentiating Israeli citizens from Jews (= Judeans) of other citizenship was a factor in deciding on "Israel."

The context alone can tell the reader whether "Israel" (in the time of the Hebrew monarchies) refers to all the tribes or only to the northern ones.

[2] Meaning "Man of Baal"; usually altered in Scripture to Ish-bosheth ("Man of Shame") out of religious prejudice. Actually, Saul's naming a child Eshbaal no more brands Saul a pagan than our calling a daughter "Minerva" would brand us pagans today.

met their death in the fray, thus leaving things as unsettled as ever. Then followed another combat between the two armies. A brother of Joab whose name was Asahel chose to pursue Abner, who advised him to desist and instead go after one of the other lads whose belt he could try to take as a trophy. Abner, who was a seasoned warrior, was able to cope with Asahel but he knew that if he slew the youth, it would start a blood feud of the most dangerous kind with Joab. Asahel, however, would not desist and Abner was forced to kill him, which sealed Abner's fate.

Abner was soon to fall out with the House of Saul because he sought in marriage Rizpah, a concubine of Saul. Eshbaal upbraids Abner for the presumptuous request,[3] and Abner thereupon decides to transfer his allegiance to David. David accepts his allegiance on condition that Michal, Saul's daughter, be restored to David as his wife. So Michal is torn away from her second husband, who is grief-stricken as she leaves him to go to David. Abner then proceeded to win the northern tribes over to David; and Abner would have been put in command of David's army, had David had his way. But Joab, although loyal to David, was jealous for his own position. Through treachery Joab got Abner aside and murdered him, thus getting revenge for his brother Asahal and at the same time eliminating his rival. David turned all these delicate situations to his own advantage, through diplomacy and generosity. David fasted and recited a dirge for Abner. Everyone saw David mourning, which made an excellent impression on the northerners.

Soon after, Eshbaal was murdered and his head was brought by the assassins to David (2 Samuel 4). David, instead of rewarding them, had them put to death as murderers, which again enhanced David's reputation.

The northern Israelites then transferred their allegiance

[3] Marrying a king's widow could easily suggest designs on the throne.

to David and came to Hebron to establish a covenant with David and to anoint him. They quote Yahwe as saying: "You shall pasture my people Israel." This is the terminology of the old theocratic ideal. The king is thus like a Sumerian *ensi,* claiming only to be the shepherd who pastures God's human flock. God is the official ruler; the human head of the state is only His agent. It is worth noting too that a covenant was made between the king and the people. The people were not ready to submit to an ancient Near Eastern dictatorship. The Israelites always maintained a sense of tribal and individual dignity and privilege, and so the king had to abide by a covenant which was a sort of constitution he had to grant if they were to accept him. In order to be nearer the center of the country, David moved the capital from his own tribe to the strategically situated and walled city of Jerusalem, which he captured by stealth from the Jebusites. That city remains the only conceivable capital of those devoted to the Davidic Line; it makes no difference whether the devotees are Israelis confronted with practical politics, or Christians contemplating the Messianic Age.

David not only conquered his enemies but established wise alliances. Thus with Hiram, King of Tyre, he made an alliance that was to last long after David's death.

The ark was transferred to Jerusalem and thus the trend toward centralizing the cult there, had made its modest start. David, bearing the ephod, danced before the ark. The spirit of the Lord had come upon him and he leaped ecstatically in public. (His well-born wife Michal disapproved of his behavior [4]; so David indignantly decided to neglect her from that time on.) During the celebration, David further won the hearts of the people by passing out gifts to them. He was a man who by nature won many friends, who appeased most

[4] Ecstatic religion, as we have noted, was not approved of in the best Israelite circles.

of his enemies and who knew how to eliminate what few people were irreconcilable.

David felt that now that he had a house to live in, he should build a temple for his God. He consulted Nathan the Prophet, who later had a dream and reported its message to the King. Nathan represented the conservative element and could not adjust himself to the idea of transforming the shrine from a tabernacle to a temple. Nathan's oracle informed David that a king whose hands were bloody from war, was not the king to build God's temple; and that the temple would better wait for the peaceful reign of David's son. The transition was thus postponed for a generation.

David's conquests extended in all directions. In some cases brutality was resorted to. Moab was conquered and two-thirds of the population were put to death. According to 2 Samuel 8:6, the land of the Arameans around Damascus was conquered and governors were sent by David to rule there. The nascent empire was equipped with more administration than Israel had ever known before. Joab was commander-in-chief of the army. There were also the official recorder, scribe and priests. Sons of David also acted as priests, for there was still some leeway in priestly appointments and also some nepotism in the government whereby sons of the king could be put into responsible positions contrary to the ideals of society.[5] At the head of the foreign troops was Benaiah, who led the Cherethites and Pelethites: troops of Caphtorian origin. It is worth pondering the desirability of such mercenaries. Natives tend to have family or local loyalties. Foreign mercenaries have no such ties and tend to be well disciplined, loyal to their commander, and interested in his personal welfare, for on him depends their professional welfare. Thus these mercenaries were eventually

[5] E.g., the ideal that priests should come only from the tribe of Levi.

instrumental in preserving David's life and throne when his own flesh and blood betrayed him.

David, who had vowed not to destroy Saul's family, sought out Mephibosheth,[6] the son of Jonathan, restored Saul's estate to him and gave him support at the king's table; that is to say, rations at government expense.

Although David is the darling par excellence of the Hebrew people and the model for all kings to come, and the ancestor of the Messianic Line, there is no attempt in Scripture to whitewash him. He committed a great crime in the case of Bathsheba; not only the crime of adultery but the murder of an innocent man (his loyal mercenary, Uriah the Hittite). The Bible makes no attempt to cover David's sin, for which he was soon punished:[7] The child born of the adultery died (though Solomon, who was also the child of David and Bathsheba, succeeded to the throne).

The personality and loyalty of Joab are borne out clearly in the capture of Rabbath-Ammon (now Amman), where Joab was in a position to conquer the city but called for David to come so that David might deal the final blow and get the glory.

Although David was an effective ruler and natural diplomat, he was a poor master of his own household. The disobedience and misbehavior of his own children shows that his forte was not the role of father.

His firstborn son was Amnon. It is interesting to note that at this period there was a fratriarchal organization of brothers

---

[6] This is a puritanic distortion of his name; for "bosheth" has replaced "Baal" as the variant Merib-baal (1 Chronicles 8:34; 9:40) shows.

[7] The history of the early monarchy is not primarily religious. The widespread idea that good and evil deeds are fittingly requited is simply the concept of a Nemesis which can be found in Greek epics and other secular literature. Throughout the history of the early monarchy, the agency of God and the influence of His priests or prophets are in the normal proportion that we would expect in a secular history of those times.

whereby there was not only a chief of the brothers but also a second in command. David's son Chileab was the prince known as "his second"; i.e., Amnon's second-in-command. Only after the firstborn and his second-in-command do the Hebrews number the brothers, "third, fourth, fifth, sixth, etc." This fratriarchal organization was widespread throughout the East, including Israel.[8]

Amnon conceived a passion for his half-sister Tamar and instead of asking for her hand in marriage, which would have been permissible as the biblical text informs us, he seduced her. Her full brother, Absalom, who was the third of the royal sons, slew Amnon to avenge the dishonor. Absalom took refuge, typically enough, in the house of his mother's father, Talmai, the King of Geshur. In polygamous society, where a man has children born by different wives; when strife breaks out among half-brothers-and-sisters, those in trouble will seek refuge with the mother's family.

Joab, who was a powerful figure behind the throne no less than on the battlefield, resorted to a stratagem to effect a reconciliation between father and son. Joab enlisted the services of a clever woman, called the Wise Woman of Tekoa, who told David that one of her sons had killed the other and now the family was going to kill the slayer with the result that she would lose both her children. (This reflects, incidentally, that the king was the highest court of appeals and could even reverse basic laws of society.) David saw the humanity of her argument and said that the slayer should not be touched. The woman now hints that David should apply the same verdict to his own household and spare his guilty son. David then realized who had put her up to it and she confessed that every word she had uttered had been put into her

---

[8] See "Fratriarchy in the Old Testament," *Journal of Biblical Literature* 54, 1935, pp. 223-231. Note also the fratriarchal etiquette, whereby brothers at a banquet are seated in order of seniority (Genesis 43:33).

mouth by Joab. Yet the king was won over to forgiving his son, as his verdict for the woman had indicated. Absalom thereupon came home and although for some time he was not allowed to see David personally, the king eventually relented and permitted him full freedom and the intimacy of the court.

Absalom was a handsome fellow. We are told that the hair on his head was so luxurious that when he had his yearly shave, the hair weighed two hundred shekels, according to the king's weight. (The existence of a royal standard is of some interest. Each country in the ancient Near East had standard weights and measures; but they were not designed to establish honest weights and measures in the bazaars to protect the public from dishonest merchants. Standards were set up for the benefit of the crown, so that when the king got his taxes he should not be given short weight or short measure. Of course, once the government standard was fixed, private citizens could also resort to it for their own protection.) Absalom's long hair was to be instrumental in his downfall.

The handsome prince played up to the public. His father, who had the responsibility of giving decisions, naturally could not favor all the litigants. Absalom, however, was in an ideal situation to do a lot of talking without any responsibility; and he gave the impression to the dissatisfied that if he were king, he would give satisfaction to them. He thus built up a following to support him in a revolt. In order to carry out his plans, he went to Hebron ostensibly to pay some religious vows, for the old family shrine was still there. Once he was in Hebron, he mustered enough forces to launch a full-fledged rebellion. His advisor, the wise Ahitophel, came along with him. David could not assemble enough troops quickly enough to combat those of his son Absalom. Instead he fled with those that were loyal to him. Thus Ittai of Gath, the Philistine in charge of six hundred of David's foreign mercenaries, insisted on going along with David, even though David offered to release him from sharing so precarious a future (2 Samuel 15:18-22). When David's own son betrayed him, and when his own nation rebelled, his best friends included foreign mercenaries, who gladly followed him "whether for death or for life" (verse 21). The fact that these mercenaries were Philistines is in part accounted for by David's Philistine friendships in the days when Saul had driven him into exile.

David left some of his harem, notably the concubines, behind as part of a fifth column in Jerusalem: a fifth column that also included other elements. David insisted that priests should remain with the ark in the capital. He also left behind a counselor by the name of Hushai with instructions to nullify the wise advice that Ahitophel would doubtless give the rebellious Absalom, and to arrange for liaison between the fifth column and the priests so that messages could be relayed to David in his Transjordanian place of refuge.

On his way, while fleeing from Jerusalem to Transjordan, David had some disagreeable experiences. Ziba, a servant of Mephibosheth, the son of Jonathan, offered gifts to David and informed him that Mephibosheth was disloyal to David and favored Absalom's revolt. Another Benjaminite named Shimei came out and reviled David for David's treachery against the House of Saul. It is important for us to remember that from the standpoint of the Israelites, particularly of the tribe of Benjamin, David was a usurper who had sinned against the House of Saul. This fact was detrimental to the unity of the Hebrew tribes because the feeling that the Davidic Line was a line of usurpers contributed to the division (never to be mended) after Solomon's death. Abishai, the brother of Joab, wanted to kill Shimei but again David with his usual magnanimity toward enemies, insisted that Shimei be spared.

Ahitophel advised Absalom to take over his father's harem that had been left behind, and thus show that he was his father's successor. He further told him to gather 12,000 troops that were then available and immediately pursue his father. This practical advice would have granted David no time to assemble adequate forces and Absalom's rebellion would have succeeded. However, Hushai slily advised Absalom to wait until he could gather an overwhelming force so that David's able generals and veteran troops would have no chance militarily. The deceptive picture painted by Hushai was so attractive that Ahitophel's sound advice was rejected. Ahitophel felt he had lost face so badly that he went home, set his house in order, and committed suicide: one of the few suicides in biblical history.

Through the priests, David's intelligence service kept him informed of developments at home. Absalom at last felt ready to move his army under the generalship of Amasa to Transjordan.

David had been well received in the Transjordanian town of Mahanaim. He organized his troops into thousands and then subdivided them into hundreds. The whole army was divided into three; one third under Joab, one third under Abishai, the other third under Ittai. The King, already well advanced in years, was obliged to remain behind because his safety was of great importance to his partisans, and at his age he would have been more of a liability than an asset in the field. His last wish was that his men should deal gently with Absalom, if Absalom should fall into their hands.

Absalom's luxuriant hair caught in a low tree while he was riding on a donkey. Suspended in midair he fell into the hands of David's troops. Joab, who later came up, slew Absalom against David's orders. This is typical of Joab because he realized what was best for David, even when David's desires went against his own best interests. David, who was already senile, let alone soft-hearted especially where family and friendship were concerned, instead of being overjoyed at the

victory, went into the most abysmal grief over his son. Again
it was Joab's forcefulness that saved the day. The troops felt
that far from having pleased their king and having won the
victory, they were guilty of a heinous crime in killing Absalom. Joab therefore reproached the King and forced him to
refrain from all expression of grief. David, thus brought to
his senses, again sat in the gate as ruler of his people and the
morale of his victorious troops was raised to the height they
so well deserved.

Through the mediation of the priests, David made up with
the elders of Judah and amazingly agreed to appoint Amasa
as general to replace Joab. Like so many despots, David resented the presence of so able and forceful a man as Joab,
despite the latter's flawless loyalty.

The tribe of Judah came to the Jordan to welcome the King
across. David showed magnanimity to all; to Mephiboshet
(who denied any disloyalty), and even to Shimei, who had
reviled David in his darkest hour. One of the most touching
incidents is that of Barzillai, who had supported David in
Transjordan. David now wanted him to come to the royal
court where he would live in ease for the rest of his life. But
Barzillai replied: "How old am I that I should go up with the
King to Jerusalem? I am now eighty years old! Can I distinguish the good from the bad? Or can I taste what I eat or
drink? Or can I listen any more to the voice of male and
female singers? Why should I be a burden to my lord, the
King?" (2 Samuel 19:36). So Barzillai returned home, accepting David's offer to lavish his gratitude on a member of
the younger generation, who could make better use of a career
at court than could an octogenarian.

The old rivalry between Israel and Judah that was to prove
disastrous after the division of the monarchy, could be felt
even during the united kingdom of David and Solomon. On
this occasion the Judeans claimed that they after all were the

flesh and blood of the King, while the Israelites claimed that they constituted ten tribes as against the one tribe of Judah. (As we shall soon see, the Hebrews reckoned their tribes as twelve, even though they recognized that there were actually only eleven at this period.)

The kingdom was far from firmly established because the appetite of Israel for independence had been whetted by the disruption of David's House in the time of Absalom's revolt. Accordingly, a Benjaminite named Sheba started another revolt that gained support throughout Israel. David designated as commander-in-chief Amasa, who got off to a bad start by being late. This obliged David to send Abishai, the brother of Joab, to hasten things along. Joab and his men, including the Cherethite and Pelethite mercenaries, proceeded on the march. Joab met Amasa and, with his usual treachery where his honor was at stake, he approached Amasa as if to kiss him, got hold of his beard, drew his sword and slew him (somewhat as he had gotten Abner out of the way).

Joab lost no time. He pursued Sheba till he cornered him in a small fortress. Joab then threw up earthworks against the wall and would have captured the place, except that a wise woman there, pointed out that there was no sense in destroying a whole group of people when the head of one man could settle the issue. Joab agreed with her analysis of the situation, whereupon the head of Sheba was cut from his body and tossed over the wall. Joab ordered a blast on the trumpet, and each man went to his tent: the biblical expression for signifying that the war was over and the army demobilized then and there. The formula "each man went to his tent" is a holdover from nomadic times. By this time Israel did not live in tents but were an agricultural people; yet the old cliché, whereby home was a tent, still lingered on in the language.

Joab went back to Jerusalem and things returned to normal. In 2 Samuel 20:23 we get an idea of some of the internal developments in David's time. David's reign saw an increase in the organization of the realm. David had carved out the largest empire then in existence. Joab was in charge of the army. Benaiah was over the Cherethite and Pelethite mercenaries. Adoram (otherwise called Adoniram) was director of forced labor; for the empire required taxation in labor as well as in kind. There were furthermore the offices of recorder and scribe. The chief priests of the realm were two in number: Zadok and Ebiathar (together with their families) but it is also interesting to note that David had also a private priest by the name of Ira, so that in addition to the so-called legitimate priestly households in the service of the national cult, there were also private priests including one for the King himself.

2 Samuel 21 narrates that the land was afflicted with a three-year famine and the people felt that the nation had incurred guilt through the breaking of faith with the Gibeonites by the House of Saul. The Gibeonites required that the crime be expiated by the killing of seven sons of the House of Saul. Mephibosheth, the son of Jonathan, was spared by David in order to keep his promise not to exterminate the House of Saul. But David did take seven other descendants of the House of Saul and slaughtered them so as to give satisfaction to the offended Gibeonites. Two of these children were born of Rizpah and five of a daughter of Saul. David, however, was able to salvage part of his popularity by retrieving the remains of Saul and Jonathan and burying them in honor in the tomb of Saul's father, Kish. He also got back for decent burial the seven sons who were slaughtered to appease the Gibeonites. According to the scriptural narrative, God was satisfied and the famine ended.

David was now able to entrust the wars against the Philistines to his heroes whose names we know in considerable detail (2 Samuel 21:15, 17).

The King was impelled to take a census of the realm. This alone was a great tribute to the national organization, for a census requires a great deal of administration.[9] But the census was exceedingly unpopular because the people resented interference in their private affairs. In general, people unused to the compilation of statistics regard census-taking as a prelude to conscription and taxation; a viewpoint that was not without justification in the ancient Near East. The census was assigned to Joab, who strongly advised David against it, but then gave in out of loyalty to his sovereign. He started with Transjordan, went up to the borders of Sidon, and then down into the Negeb of the south. The totals of the census are given in round numbers: 800,000 men of fighting age for Israel and 500,000 men of fighting age for Judah. Thus the purpose of the count was to estimate military potential. The figures show that Israel was the greater part of the united kingdom.

To atone for the sin of the census, David was offered a divine alternative through a prophet.[10] The first choice was a regular phenomenon in the thought processes of the ancient Near Easterners: a seven-year famine. The next was three months of defeat; the third alternative, three days of pestilence. David chose the third alternative. He did not so much as consider the first, for it was the most terrible thing that could befall a country. He chose pestilence rather than defeat, in that pestilence is dealt out by God; whereas defeat at the hands of one's enemies puts one at the mercy of man; and human foes show far less mercy than God. God was appeased by the erection of an altar and by sacrifices so that the pestilence and other calamities of the realm were brought to an end.

[9] This is the first serious attempt at a census in Israel. Earlier statistics in the Bible do not rest on actual census figures. The fact that this first attempt met with an unpopular reception confirms that it was an innovation.

[10] Such narratives are of value primarily for reflecting beliefs and institutions.

David was already well advanced in years, and we are told the curious story that in his dotage a Shunammite girl named Abishag was brought to him to nurse him and keep him warm. The latter service means only the physical therapy of keeping the old man warm through the application of young body heat to his body. Sexual implications should not be read into the text.

Like so many despots, David lost his will in his old age. He was played out, for he had exerted his will so powerfully and so long in making weighty decisions and in building and ruling an empire, that he was spent by the time of old age. So now, another one of his sons, Adonijah, a brother of Absalom, began to plot another revolt. Interestingly enough, the two rebellious princes, Absalom and Adonijah, were sons of the same woman. She may well have been an ambitious woman with a hand in her sons' maneuvres for power; even as Bathsheba was to have a hand in Solomon's succession. The element of harem intrigue runs right through Israelite history even as it does through the history of the entire Bible World.

Adonijah enlisted the help of Joab and Ebiathar, which would seem to be a powerful combination. But he snubbed a still more powerful combination. In giving a party, he failed to invite his half-brother Solomon, who was the son of the favorite Queen; he failed to invite Zadok, the priest who was the equal of Ebiathar; he failed to invite Benaiah, who was in charge of the mercenaries; he failed to invite Nathan, the leading prophet. Adonijah snubbed also a few other prominent men in military circles. Accordingly, Nathan and Bathsheba decided that this was the time to take matters in hand; and he instructed her to go to the King and remind him of his promise to put Solomon on the throne and to tell him that at that very moment Adonijah was engaging in subversive activities aimed at seizing the throne that was destined for another.

Nathan informed her that as soon as she should leave the hall, he would make preparations to have a royal audience and in his own way (independently as far as the King was concerned) confirm the fact. This was done cleverly and the favorite Queen and the favorite prophet convinced the old man that this was the time to crown his son Solomon king, while he, David, was still alive.

Once Solomon sat on the throne, he began to eliminate his enemies one by one. Adonijah foolishly requested as a wife Abishag, the girl who nursed David during his last illness. The request was indiscreet in that taking over a handmaid of the former king might be an opening wedge to laying claim on the throne. Adonijah eventually paid with his life for his temerity. Ebiathar, who had cast his lot with Adonijah, was defrocked and sent home. Joab, who had taken refuge at the altar of the Lord where he was entitled to sanctuary, was ordered to leave. Upon stating he preferred to die at the altar, he was killed there in cold blood by Solomon's agents.

Shimei, who was also on the list of *personae non gratae,* was ordered to live in Jerusalem, where he could be watched, and where he discreetly stayed for three years. At the end of that time, he lost a couple of slaves whom he pursued into Philistine territory to retrieve them in the city of Gath. (Apparently, relations between the Houses of the Judean David and the Philistine Achish were so good that citizens of one realm could cross the frontier into the other realm, and be accorded sufficient cooperation from the authorities to retrieve fugitive slaves.) On coming back to Jerusalem, Shimei was put to death for disobeying the order to remain in the city (1 Kings 2:36-46).

Hebrew historiography had reached its height under David. With Solomon, there is already deterioration in the records, which are excerpted with special reference to his building operations and his material accomplishments. Thus we have correct dates (such as that the building of the Temple began in his fourth year and ended in his eleventh) but Solomon's personality on the one hand, or the general activities of the realm on the other, are not portrayed with the fulness of David's history. The exact specifications of Solomon's buildings are small compensation for the lack of the human richness of David's account.

David had shaped a realm; he had been too active to make time for excessive luxury. But Solomon could enjoy the fruits of his father's labor. Egypt had declined and Israel grown. Accordingly, at this time we find that a daughter of Pharaoh (perhaps the daughter of Psusennes II, the last Pharaoh of the Twenty-first Dynasty) is a member of Solomon's harem. Her need to live up to the style of her father's court gave added impetus to Solomon's building program. Solomon built several high-places. But the existence of high-places around Jerusalem was a necessity in the capital of a king, who married princesses from foreign lands. To extend to his brides the common courtesy of religious freedom, he had to grant them chapels where they could worship their native gods. Also the foreign traders that frequented Jerusalem appreciated the courtesy [11] of access to shrines where they could worship their own gods.

Among the topics included in the history of Solomon are two dreams in which God promised him wisdom and admonished him to adhere to the good way of life. As we have shown, there is no basis for the view that such items must be late accretions. There is no reason to doubt the antiquity of the account of Solomon's dreams any more than the antiquity of Gudea's, which are known to have been recorded, in the form that we have them, in Gudea's reign.

---

[11] It is strange that we who pride ourselves on extending religious freedom to men of other faiths, are often shocked when biblical characters show the same liberality.

Solomon's regime marked a further growth in administration and accordingly a further weakening of the tribes. I Kings 4 is a list of Solomon's twelve administrative districts. These districts for the most part do not correspond to the tribes but are new administrative areas set up for the smooth implementing of national policies. The reason for the twelve is explicitly stated: each district was to maintain the royal household and the cost of government for one month of the year. Thus twelveness was still essential in the concept of national administration, although Solomon's districts had replaced the traditional division into tribes. Two of the district governors happen to be sons-in-law of Solomon's: signs of nepotism. It is interesting to note that Azariah, son of Nathan (= David's son rather than Nathan the Prophet), was in charge of the King's commissioners. Although we were told that Ebiathar had been defrocked and sent home, we now read that both Zadok and Ebiathar are official priests: a discrepancy showing that the material available to the compiler of Kings has not been edited systematically.[12] Instead of one official scribe there are now two, reflecting how the administration, while following the lines set by David, was increasing. Zabud, another son of Nathan, is a private priest of the King; so through two important appointments (the private priest of the King and the chief of the royal commissioners) the sons of Nathan enjoyed considerable power with the crown. Another official was over the Royal House which required lavish supplies. Adoniram was still over the *corvée* (or forced labor).

The figure for the Israelites at forced labor is given at 30,000; 10,000 of them worked each month. Mines had to be operated and trees cut for the building program. A man

---

[12] Perhaps at the beginning of Solomon's reign both of the priests were in office; while at the end of his reign, Ebiathar was eliminated. The apparent contradiction in the Bible would then be due to a false arrangement of individually correct facts.

obliged to render such service for the King, would spend two months at home and one away at forced labor. The Canaanite elements of the population were no longer sufficient for doing all the rough work and Israelites were now being reduced to servitude, which was quite unpopular among the people who cherished traditions of freedom. The King's horses required extensive stables both for cavalry and chariotry. Some of his stables have been excavated by the Oriental Institute, of the University of Chicago, at the northern city of Megiddo. The chariots and horses had to be bought at great cost, cutting into the living standard of the peasant population. The King's officials were furthermore encroaching upon the prerogatives of local government. Each city had its elders who sat in the gate and gave decisions, but now they had the competition of the King's servants (as officials of the central government were called), who had more power than they. Thus the people's king (as Saul had been) had changed into an oriental despot, which was against the natural inclination of the citizenry. With the growth of wealth in royal and official circles, came the growth of poverty among the masses of the people.

Solomon was able to facilitate his construction program by maintaining alliances, notably with Hiram of Tyre. In his message to Hiram, Solomon states: "There is none among us who knows how to cut trees like the Sidonians" (1 Kings 5:20). To the inexperienced reader it might look like a faux pas for Solomon to praise the Sidonians in an appeal to the King of Tyre. But since "Sidonians" is a general term for all the southern Phoenicians, even the men of Tyre are "Sidonians." The famed cedars and other Lebanese evergreens were cut down, brought to the coast, tied into rafts, and floated down to Joppa, where the rafts were broken up and the trees hauled to Jerusalem. All this had to be paid for and almost the only thing the Hebrews had to spend was the produce of the soil; so their wheat and olive oil were shipped in large quantities to Hiram of Tyre.

The building program of Solomon, contrary to the general impression, was not focused on the Temple. He built a royal complex of which the Temple was only a part. Scripture tells us that the Temple required seven years to build but that the King's palace took thirteen. His house for Pharaoh's daughter was quite elaborate too.

The skilled metal work was executed by another Hiram, whose father was a master craftsman [13] of Tyre and whose mother was a widow from the tribe of Naphtali (pointing to the intermingling of south Phoenicians with north Israelites).

Base metal (but not, as far as we know, precious metal), notably copper, was obtained from the famed "Mines of Solomon." The mines, together with their adjacent smelting plants, have been found by Nelson Glueck at a number of points along the Wadi Arabah (which runs between the Dead Sea and the Gulf of Aqaba). The pottery found alongside the smelting furnaces is from the same period as the pottery from the Megiddo level containing Solomon's stables. The archeological evidence ties in with the statement in 1 Kings 7:46 that Solomon had casting done in the "Plain of the Jordan."

The dedication of the Temple and the moving of the ark from the City of David to Zion, where the Temple was erected, were solemnly celebrated. The elders of Israel and the heads of the clans were assembled. God is said to have showed His acceptance of the Temple by permeating it as a cloud called "The Glory of Yahwe" that filled the interior. (In the Bible, "The Glory of Yahwe" must often be envisaged as a mist that enveloped the Divine Presence.) There then follows Solomon's dedication prayer, in which divine sanc-

---

[13] It must have been quite common for sons to follow the trades and professions of their fathers, not only because of environment and natural emulation, but because tradesmen and artisans in Canaan were organized into closely knit guilds as attested in the Ugaritic tablets.

tion is regarded as an integral part of justice. It is God's will that justice should be done and in exchange for service to God and the carrying out of His commandments, defeat can be averted, drought can be avoided or terminated, people can be saved from famine, from pestilence, from locusts and other catastrophes of nature which so often make life difficult in Palestine. God's rewarding His People's devotion will show foreigners all over the world that God's name is really associated with His Temple; for how else could the service in it be effective? The sinning captives from among His People ("for there is no man who does not sin," 1 Kings 8:46), by turning to God will be rescued by Him and brought home again to the only land where they can possibly worship Him [14] and live their national life.

In the second theophany of Solomon (1 Kings 9), it is characteristically noted that the covenant made is conditional: God's protection will continue only as long as the royal line obeys God's will.

Whatever the value of Solomon's constructions, the price was great. King Hiram had to be paid with more than just wheat and oil. Twenty Galilean cities were turned over to him in partial payment for his services.

The Pharaoh made an incursion into Palestine and took the city of Gezer away from the Canaanites, who were still occupying and ruling it. (This shows that the Israelite Conquest of the Promised Land was still incomplete.) Pharaoh's army killed the Canaanites of Gezer and he gave the destroyed city as a wedding gift to his son-in-law Solomon.[15] We are fur-

---

[14] The idea that God could be effectively worshiped by His People anywhere, had not yet developed. It was only the destruction of the Temple and the Exile that liberated Yahwistic worship from localism.

[15] The incorporation of Gezer into the realm brings up the question of the calendars, for a list of local agricultural month names has been found at Gezer. In the Bible there is another such ancient calendar whose spring season opens with *hodesh ha-abib* (Exodus 13:4 etc.) "month of (freshly ripened) barley" (cf. Exodus 9:31; Leviticus 2:14). Moreover the Phoeni-

ther told that the remnants of the Amorites, Hittites, Jebusites, etc., who were not of the Children of Israel, were reduced to the status of laborers (1 Kings 9:20), whereas the
officials and warriors were Israelites (verse 22). However,
this can only have been a partly fulfilled ideal. The forced
labor actually exacted from among the Israelites made a
stronger impression on the people than the pretension that
they were exclusively a ruling class.

Solomon included in his ventures a fleet sailing from the
port of Ezion-geber (at the head of the Gulf of Aqaba).
Expert sailors were supplied by Hiram of Tyre. The ships
fetched gold, precious stones and wood (particularly good for
the manufacture of musical instruments) from the land of
Ophir. Solomon thus had a fleet of Tarshish (which means
simply any sea-going fleet) that made a trip every third year
bringing back gold, silver, ivory, monkeys and peacocks.
These commodities show that it could not be a Mediterranean
fleet although Tarshish is probably in Spain. The source of
the cargo has to be India or some place attainable from the
Red Sea.[16] (The statements in 1 Kings 9:26-28; 10:11-12,
22 may well refer to one and the same fleet.)

---

cian calendar (wherein "month" is normally *yerah* instead of *hodesh*) was
also used in official records (1 Kings 6:1, 38; 8:2). Probably many
towns under the early Hebrew kings had local cultic agricultural calendars. Centralization under the crown necessitated a uniform calendar for
federal administration. Thus was invented the practical though colorless
calendar "First Month," "Second Month" - - - "Twelfth Month" (e.g.,
throughout Jeremiah starting with 1:3). The inspiration for this development may have come from Egypt where the year was divided into three
seasons, each consisting of four numbered months. But even so the Hebrews
deserve credit for eliminating seasonal names and streamlining the calendar
with simple numbers from one to twelve. After the Exile in 586 B.C. the
Jews learned the Babylonian month names, starting with the spring new-
year month of Nisan; cf. Esther (3:7 etc.) where dates are given both in
terms of the numbered Judean and the Babylonian systems.

[16] Modern Israel has exerted every effort to hold on to a bit of shore
on the Gulf of Aqaba, near Ezion-geber, with a view to developing sea-
borne trade with the East.

A Queen of Sheba, who visited Solomon, came with a caravan of camels bringing spice, gold and precious stones from her realm in South Arabia (1 Kings 10:1-3). The historic evaluation of this incident implies that caravan trade bringing minerals and spices was already established with South Arabia. The biblical tradition also reflects the fact that queens frequently ruled among the ancient Arabs: a phenomenon corroborated, as we shall see, in cuneiform records concerning relations between Mesopotamia and Arabia.

All of this trade by caravan routes and by sea, plus all the new edifices, brought splendor hitherto unknown to the simple Hebrews of the past. The capital and the bigger provincial cities saw more luxury than ever before. But the price paid depleted the resources of the country. The new glamor was for the most part unprofitable. The imported chariots cost six hundred shekels of silver apiece. The imported steeds cost one hundred and fifty shekels of silver each. The royal harem was an expensive establishment with wives from Egypt, Moab, Ammon, Edom, Sidon and the Hittites. Solomon's wives led him, especially in his old age, to acts of apostacy including the worship of Astarte, the goddess of Sidon, and Milcom, the god of the Ammonites (1 Kings 11:1-6). Solomon's high-places to the god Chemosh of Moab and Molech of Ammon lasted for three and a half centuries in Jerusalem until the reign of Josiah (2 Kings 23:13).

What the Israelites (particularly the northerners, who felt abused by the Judean King) had to pay in labor and wealth for Solomon's prosperity, was regarded as plain oppression. The situation was aggravated by the fact that the subjugated provinces of the empire grew rebellious as the warlike qualities of Israel gradually petered out. An Edomite prince named Hadad, who had taken refuge in Egypt and married into the Pharaoh's family, now returned to Edom to regain his country to the chagrin of Solomon, who still wished to keep it in his realm. Also an Aramean prince named Rezon, who had also taken refuge in Egypt, returned to Damascus to rule over Aram. Thus, while Solomon's Kingdom still held together, the provinces of the Empire were being lost, so that his territory toward the close of his reign was considerably smaller than what he had inherited from David.

We might ask why the Pharaonic family, into which Solomon had married, was allowing his neighbors to dismember his empire. It is well to remember that Hadad the Edomite was also a member of the Pharaonic family through marriage. Egypt was at the old game of "divide and rule." Pharaoh was playing politics in Canaan to keep the area as weak as possible. Thus he would play one group against the other, for the weaker Canaan was, the better for Egypt.

An able man named Jeroboam was fatefully chosen by Solomon to be chief of the *corvée* in the House of Joseph, as the north was called. A prophet named Ahijah of Shiloh, met Jeroboam and symbolically tore Jeroboam's garment into twelve pieces giving ten to Jeroboam and reserving one for the House of David (1 King 11:29-32). The contradiction of ten plus one equaling twelve is obvious, but since it has been explained we need not comment on it further here. To take the incident out of the prophetic sphere and put it into the sphere of politics: Jeroboam used his opportunity to work with the enslaved masses of Israel to win their support and make things ready for the right moment when a crisis should confront the realm. When his activities and designs became known, he fled to Egypt, where the Pharaoh Shishak protected him.

Our Book of Kings cites earlier sources. The compiler here refers us to the Book of the Deeds of Solomon (1 Kings 11:41)—unfortunately now lost—constituting, or at least based upon, the court chronicles of Solomon.

On the death of Solomon, it is noteworthy that his son

Rehoboam had to go north to Shechem [17] for acceptance by the Israelites, who had at best mixed feelings toward the Judean Dynasty and its capital. There was still the feeling that there had to be a covenant between the ruler and the ruled, so that a new king had to lay down a platform acceptable to the people before they would receive him as their sovereign. The Israelites naturally wanted to know whether Rehoboam's rule would be oppressive like Solomon's or whether it would be mild. He consulted the elders, who urged him to reply mildly to the people. As the elders put it : "If you will be a slave today to this people, and serve them and answer them and speak good words to them, they will be your slaves for all the days" (1 Kings 12 :7). Instead of following this sound advice, Rehoboam turned to his young cronies, who ill-advisedly got him to lay down a get-tough policy and say that he would be even stricter than his father. The dissatisfied northern tribes thereupon deserted him, never to rejoin Judah or the House of David. Whatever chance there might have been for the Hebrews to regain political strength, and be masters of their own national destiny, was shattered for millennia.

[17] The location suggests that the nation as a whole still regarded Shechem, with its shrine at Gerizim, as the true center versus the newer Davidic capital at Jerusalem with its still more recent shrine.

# Chapter XII

# THE DIVIDED KINGDOMS TO JEHU'S PURGE

REHOBOAM failed to grasp fully the seriousness of the situation. He sent Adoram, who was still in charge of the *corvée,* to exact forced labor from the Israelites. The indignant Israelites assassinated Adoram. Rehoboam fled by chariot to Jerusalem, behind whose walls he found refuge from the hostility of his former subjects in the north.

1 Kings 12:19 expresses the verdict of the biblical author: "And Israel has sinned against the House of David down to this day." We must bear in mind that the sympathies of the Bible are squarely Judean and therefore against the Israelite North. As long as Israel was detached from the House of David, there could be no virtue in Israel. Moreover, all cults (even for the worship of Yahwe) in Israel will be condemned from this time on, in the Bible, whose authors recognize only the legitimacy of the Temple in Jerusalem. The Bible judges the Kings of Judah as good or bad depending on their devotion to the Jerusalem Cult; but the Kings of Israel were of necessity all bad, because they could not adhere to the Jerusalem Cult which lay outside their borders.

The Israelites, after rejecting Rehoboam, summoned Jeroboam to a council in order to interrogate him and oblige him to make a covenant with the representatives of the people. Israel crowned Jeroboam as King and the rupture with Judah was complete.

Economically the resources of the Hebrews were too limited to secure any continuous or solid prosperity. They had virtually no coast land and so could not profit from Mediterranean trade. The coast was in the hands of the Phoenicians and to some extent of the Philistines. The caravan routes were in the hands of the desert nomads and Arabian kingdoms, so that the Hebrews could derive nothing from that source other than limited toll charges. The arable land on which the people depended was quite circumscribed in quantity. There was some good land in the "Valley" [1] of Jezreel and a few other narrow plains; and, though less productive, something could be done with the hill country; but it all added up to very little agricultural land to support the population. Furthermore, the seasonal rainfall was precarious, and droughts brought famine as well as thirst. And even in years when the rain was sufficient, locust plagues and blights might ruin the crops. Sometimes the poor land underwent the worst of all calamities : a succession of famine years. All such disasters were regarded as punishments from God for the sins of the people and their rulers [2]; so instead of undermining the faith of His devotees, misfortune simply intensified religion.

Rehoboam was wisely dissuaded by a "man of God" named Shemaiah from launching an attack on Israel. Judah, throughout all her history, never had the means or will to attempt to reconquer Israel.

Jeroboam had problems on his hands. How was he to prevent his subjects from renewing their contacts with Judah? Israel and Judah accepted one and the same God. Furthermore, by this time, the shrine at Jerusalem was considerably more impressive than any other shrine in the land. From political necessity, Jeroboam strengthened the Yahwistic shrines at Bethel and Dan. The Judeans, however, regarded

---

[1] The Hebrew word *'emeq* is often translated "valley" even when it really designates a plain between two mountainous areas or between mountains and a sea (or lake).

[2] This was also true of the neighboring people with reference to their national gods.

them as spurious, and viewed the religion practiced there as the worst kind of apostasy.

The priests were to a great extent non-Levitical. They were professional and perhaps formed guilds such as we encounter in the Ugaritic texts, where the priests are organized into guilds just as craftsmen are. It was only later that the hereditary and Levitical character of the priesthood became more firmly established. The functions of the priests were to provide oracles, perform rituals (particularly with reference to sacrifice) and to teach the Law of God. It was proficiency in these three functions that qualified a man for the priesthood. The Levitical priests had a great deal of trouble in obtaining, as they later did, exclusive recognition. The situation is reflected in the blessing for Levi (Deuteronomy 33:8-11), where the Levite is described as a man who forsakes his father and mother and devotes himself to the oracles and Law of God. Hostility from non-Levitical guilds may be reflected in the curse heaped on those who are giving the Levites trouble (verse 11). The fact that there were non-Levitical priests in the North is stressed by Scripture (2 Chronicles 11:14-15) as one of the sins of Jeroboam's Kingdom. Also the calves associated with Yahwistic worship at Bethel and Dan are repeatedly mentioned as abominations.

Despite the frequent biblical condemnation of Jeroboam, he was in fact not one to flout either the religion of Yahwe or the legitimacy of Yahwe's prophets. When his son Abijah takes sick, he sends his wife in disguise to Ahijah, a prophet of Yahwe, in order to receive an oracle to tell what would happen to the child. The oracle is unfavorable and the boy dies (1 Kings 14). The story is interesting in that it represents Jeroboam as going out of his way to consult a true prophet of Yahwe. While condemning all the Israelite Kings, the Bible often lets slip data that show that not all of the condemnation should be left unqualified.

It is to the lasting credit of the Judean authors that they do not whitewash their rulers of the House of David. Judah is repeatedly guilty of worshiping on high-places,[3] of setting up monuments (*maṣṣebôth*) of paganizing character, and of worshiping on high hills and under green trees (favorite sites for popular worship). Also priests known as Kedeshim (and priestesses called Kedeshoth), reputedly given to immoral practices, could still be found in the land, at times even in the Jerusalem Temple.

We have an exact date taken from authentic chronicles of the Kings of Judah for the reign of Rehoboam, in whose fifth year, Shishak, the first Pharaoh of the Twenty-Second Dynasty invaded Palestine somewhere around the year 930 B.C. According to Shishak's records, he invaded both Israel and Judah, and carried off rich plunder from a considerable number of towns. The Bible tells nothing of these extensive operations other than that Shishak came against Jerusalem so that Rehoboam had to strip the Temple and royal treasury to appease the Pharaoh and get him to move on. Why does the Bible tell us nothing about Shishak's wide operations throughout Israel and Judah? The reason is that the biblical author's chief interest is the Jerusalem cult. He cared little about the secular history of Israel; nor was he very deeply concerned about the provincial cities of Judah. His attention was focused on Jerusalem, with special reference to Yahwe's cult in the Temple there.

Alongside the partisan selection of data and the propagandistic attitude of the compiler, the Books of Kings contain many reliable dates and facts from authentic court chronicles; e.g., as we have already mentioned, the dates of the beginning and completion of Solomon's Temple and of Shishak's invasion. Dates are given in terms of the king's reign. Each reign

---

[3] "High-place" comes to mean any shrine other than the one legitimate Temple in Jerusalem.

was a unit unto itself. We do not usually know precisely when a given reign began or ended in terms of absolute B.C. dates; though within a reign, dates such as those just cited are correct. The names and order of all the kings of Israel and Judah are also accurate. Furthermore, the ages at which the Kings of Judah ascended the throne, and their mothers' names, are reliable. In the daily life of the people (as distinct from the court chronicles), dating by events was the usual type of chronology.[4] Thus the Book of Amos is dated "two years before the earthquake." The numerical errors in the Books of Kings have defied every attempt to ungarble them. Those errors are largely the creation of the editors who set out to write a synchronistic history of Judah and Israel, using as sources two sets of unrelated court chronicles. Combining two elaborate sets of figures was not an easy task. But even with due regard for the difficulties involved, the editors did not execute the synchronisms skilfully.

1 Kings 15:2, 10 show that Abijam and Asa of Judah are brothers born of the same mother. Accordingly, Asa is not Abijam's son as he is erroneously stated to be in verse 8. Another problem is raised by the fact that 1 Kings calls the king "Abijam," whereas 2 Chronicles 12:16 ff. changes the name to "Abijah." The older Kings tradition is correct. His name does not contain the divine name "Yah" (for "Yahwe") but the pagan "Yam" (the Canaanite sea-god). Puritanically this was revised to "Yah" by the Chronicler[5] who did not like to see any trace of paganism in the name of a Davidic king. Asa is singled out as one of the good kings of Judah for putting aside pagan images and removing the illegitimate priests of the Kedeshim class. He went to the extent of demoting his mother, who had gotten involved with the Asherah cult, from

---

[4] This is essentially the type of dating used in Mesopotamian tablets of the Third Dynasty of Ur and of the First Dynasty of Babylon. The uneducated people of the Near East still use that method.

[5] As the author of the biblical books of Chronicles is called.

the queenship. But, at the same time we are told that Asa did not wipe out the high-places so that while his virtue was great, it fell short of perfection.

Jeroboam was succeeded by Nadab who warred with the Philistines and, while besieging a city, was assassinated by one of his army officers named Baasha who usurped the throne. There is a sharp contrast between the histories of Israel and Judah with respect to the continuity of the royal lines. Judah ran its long course under the one Davidic House, whereas Israel experienced a succession of bloody usurpations, whereby one line followed another. Baasha proceeded to fortify the city of Ramah, just north of the border, as a defense against Judah and perhaps as a base for making incursions into that country. Asa reacted by bribing the Arameans of Damascus to attack Israel, thus touching off the Israelite-Aramean wars which were to continue for a long time to come. Asa then mobilized all of Judah, so that none was exempt, and proceeded to Ramah, now abandoned by the Israelites who had their hands full in the north. Asa tore down the fortress and reused the building materials to construct Gibeah of Benjamin and Mizpah as strongholds for defense against Israel.

The situation in Israel rapidly deteriorated. Baasha was succeeded by his son Elah, who while with the army got drunk and was killed by Zimri, a captain of the chariotry, who usurped the throne. However, an able army officer named Omri had himself crowned by his own troops and proceeded against Zimri, who, realizing that his cause was lost, set his palace afire and died in the flames. But another Israelite, named Tibni, set himself up as ruler, so that Israel was divided between two kings, Omri and Tibni. Upon Tibni's death, Omri became sole ruler and proved to be one of the ablest kings throughout Israelite history. Fortunately for him and his dynasty, he was known as the avenger of his master

(Elah) and not as a usurper. Zimri was the usurper as is shown by the taunt of Jezebel in 2 Kings 9:31.

Omri purchased, in a fair and honest way, the site of Samaria and made it the greatest of all the Israelite capitals. It is a good site with an excellent view of the mountains all around, well-protected and not dominated by any near height. It is conveniently located near a road down to Dor (a seaport south of Haifa) as well as near the main north-and-south highway of the country. Omri encouraged Aramean trade by inviting his Damascene neighbors in the north to set up bazaars in Samaria (note 1 Kings 20:34). He was wise in his foreign policy, for it was he who also ended the Judean wars so that for a long time to come, there was no political or military friction between the two Hebrew kingdoms. Omri's greatest accomplishment (completely omitted in Scripture!) is the conquest of Moab, as we learn from the inscription of the Moabite King Mesha, who relates that Omri conquered Moab so that Moab was suppressed by Israel all the days of Omri and half the days of his son ( = Ahab). This is a good illustration of how the Judean author leaves out data that do not suit his purpose. The chief triumph of a great King of Israel is thus known to us only through a pagan source outside the Bible. Another sign of Omri's greatness is that even long after his death, Israel was known politically to the Assyrians as the "House of Omri."

Possibly Omri was responsible for the wedding of his heir Ahab, who was married to a Phoenician princess of dynamic personality and force of character. Unfortunately those qualities were in the wrong direction. Her name was Jezebel.

The marriage of Jezebel to Ahab meant that the courtesy due to a queen required the building of a Baal shrine with an adjacent Asherah, plus the introduction of the pagan priesthood necessary for the cult. Viewed objectively, it was no worse than what Solomon had done for his wives, although the Bible is far more critical of the Israelite Ahab than of the Judean Solomon.

Ahab was capable. He recovered from Damascus cities lost by his predecessors Baasha and Omri. He established favorable trade relations not only with the kingdom of his father-in-law, who ruled Tyre, but also with Damascus. When he defeated Damascus, he gave generous terms to the fallen foe. At the same time that he retrieved the lost territory of his own people, he established mutual concessions in the bazaars, so that Aram had bazaar stalls in Samaria, and he, in return, had stalls for his merchants in the bazaars of Damascus. Irresponsible fanatics of Israel (whose opinions are given with approbation in Scripture) condemned his restraint and statesmanship as disobedience to God. Actually, his mildness was politically sound because Damascus and Israel were neighbors of comparable size and strength. It was an age when they had to stick together. For Israel to try to reduce Damascus to vassaldom would have exhausted Israel and ended in disaster. To the contrary, circumstances were soon to require Israel and Aram to hang together or hang separately.

It is in Ahab's reign that we have the first absolute date, that can be controlled historically, in the entire history of the Hebrew people. Shalmaneser III ended an era when the small nations of Palestine and Syria had only each other to contend with. Assyria had been developing and growing from strength to strength and in 853 B.C. Shalmaneser III was ready to attempt to extend his empire into Canaan. In that year he waged a battle at Karkar on the Orontes River in Syria. It was this threat that effected a union of the Canaanite nations including Israel, but with Damascus as head of the coalition.

Damascus was able to throw into the field 1200 chariots, 1200 cavalry and 20,000 infantry. Ahab had the second largest force, but in a technical sense the strongest of all, for he supplied 2000 chariots (the most prized of the military arms) and 10,000 infantry. The coalition also included kings from Phoenicia, Cilicia (in southeast Asia Minor), Ammon, camel-riding Arabs and a contingent from Muṣur.[6] Thus the nations of the West forgot their local animosities and united against their common Assyrian foe. Shalmaneser claims a stupendous victory. In one account he tells us he slaughtered 14,000 of his enemies. Later in his reign, when he rewrote the "history," the number had grown to 25,000. This illustrates how little we can trust statistics meant to glorify monarchs rather than to state sober facts.

Such attacks by Assyria did not incorporate the enemy countries into the empire, as was to happen later, notably under the Sargonid kings of Assyria. Shalmaneser's expeditions cost many lives and enriched Assyria with plunder of gold, silver, slaves, animals and so forth. But the large walled cities remained intact; and as soon as the invader departed, the local kings reasserted themselves, and politically things were much as they had been before the nightmare. In spite of the great victory claimed by Shalmaneser, he had to return to Hamath and Damascus six years later.

The marriage of Jezebel into the royal house of Israel meant that Baal had a cult in competition with Yahwe's. The Baal worshiped throughout Israel at this time, was not a foreign Baal. He was the Baal of the Earth: a universal god who could just as well be associated with the land of Israel as he could with the land of Tyre, Sidon, Byblos or (in for-

---

[6] Not Egypt, which has the same name ("Mizraim") in Hebrew. This Muṣur was in the north, as its combination with Que (in Cilicia) shows in 1 Kings 10:28-29 (concerning the sources of Solomon's horses and chariots).

The absence of Judah shows that the coalition went only as far south as Israel. The fact that Judah (together with Edom, which often was dominated by Judah) was the convenient buffer between the Mesopotamian Empires and Egypt, explains why Judah bore so much less of the brunt of the Assyrian invasions and why it was spared to the extent that it was.

mer times) Ugarit. The discrepancy between the "universal" and "local" nature of Baal, or any other god, did not disturb ancient devotees nearly so much as it does philosophically minded modern scholars.

In Ahab's reign there was a drought attested not only in the Bible but also in Phoenician history which has come down through Greek channels. In the minds of the Yahwists, particularly of the prophets, there could be only one cause for this prolonged drought and that was that Yahwe, Who alone could send rain or withhold it, had been offended; and it was only through the annihilation of the Baal cult and the reestablishment of Yahwe's cult, that rain would come and the nation be saved. The leader in defending the cause of Yahwe is Elijah, whose narratives are among the finest in the Bible. His showdown in 1 Kings 18 with the priesthood of Baal is one of the most vivid and moving passages in the Old Testament.

The great event which was to be remembered for a long time to come was not so much the wars of Ahab [7] but the affair of Naboth. The latter, a private citizen, who in accordance with Hebrew tradition could stand up for his rights even against the King, had a vineyard adjacent to Ahab's estate. Ahab made every reasonable offer to pay Naboth for the land so that Ahab might enlarge the royal estate. Naboth stubbornly refused to sell, because it was his own inheritance handed down from his father and typically enough from the Israelite viewpoint, Ahab went home disturbed and frustrated, because there was nothing he could do against the rights of his subject. Jezebel, however, had a different approach. It may have been her Phoenician background, where

---

[7] To the Judean compiler of Kings, so unimportant were the wars, that the Battle of Karkar (in which Ahab figures conspicuously according to the annals of the greatest empire of the time) is not even mentioned in the Bible.

kings had more rights; and citizens, fewer.[8] By trumping up
a false charge against Naboth and by procuring a few good-
for-nothings as witnesses and using the King's seal to authenticate her nefarious case, she had Naboth convicted of
blasphemy and of reviling the King, so that Naboth was
stoned to death by the multitude ostensibly in accordance with
the law, whereby Naboth's property was also forfeited to the
crown. The affair made a terrible impression on the people
and determined the downfall of Ahab's line because innocent
blood had been shed. Israel's institutions of desert origins
required that innocent blood be expiated by blood; and even
if Ahab should die a natural death, his descendant(s) would
have to pay for the crime, as actually came to pass. A single
miscarriage of justice was enough to destroy the most powerful and effective dynasty that northern Israel ever had.

Elijah held himself more or less aloof from practical politics. He stuck to religion and morals, in his defense of
Yahwism. It was his successor Elisha who gave Elijah's program political implementation.[9] If we strip the narratives
about Elisha of their anecdotes, he appears as an important
historic personage: a maker of kings and a man who inter-
vened boldly, at the psychological moments, in international
affairs.

Some of the details in the anecdotes about Elisha are often
misunderstood. When he counted on the possession of Elijah's
cloak for magical powers to show he had inherited his master's inspiration, he says in 2 Kings 2:9 that he wants, not
twice the power of his master but two-thirds thereof. The
Hebrew fraction is often misunderstood. No disciple of a

[8] See the interesting light in which the affair is put by H. L. Ginsberg,
"Ugaritic Studies and the Bible," *Biblical Archeologist* 7, 1945, p. 52.
[9] The reason the Judean editor is so interested in the northern prophets,
Elijah and Elisha, is that they championed the cause of Yahwism against
the cult of Baal. The same holds for the lengthy account of Jehu, King of
Israel, who later abolished Baalism and vindicated Yahwe.

great prophet would hope to have twice his master's power. The only other possible interpretation is "a double share" such as the chief heir gets in contradistinction to his brothers who get a single share. But then the Hebrew idiom could not mean Elisha got twice Elijah's power, any more than an heir could get twice the whole estate.

Another detail in the cycle of Elisha is easily misunderstood to the point of being ridiculous. It is the story of Elisha in Bethel, where he was called "baldy" by local children, upon whom the Prophet heaped a hearty malediction so that a couple of bears came out of the forest and ripped open forty-two of the disrespectful youngsters. In traveling through Arab Palestine I observed that in certain villages the hospitality toward all strangers (in spite of political tension) was admirable; like Abraham's hospitality to the angels. But at other villages (which had bad, but deserved, reputations) children would without provocation throw stones at strangers. Bethel was a town where there was no respect for strangers or for age. Accordingly the point of the story is not that just children were punished, but that specifically the children of a rotten community were given a punishment they so fully deserved, as everyone in Israel knew.

Among the accomplishments of Ahab is the fortification of Jericho and a number of other cities. He also embellished Samaria and built an ivory palace there (1 Kings 22:39). That type of palace soon spread to the upper classes (Amos 3:15). Such palaces were not built of ivory, but as we know from actual ivories found in excavations, were houses adorned with inlays, panels, jewel boxes and other small objects of artistically carved ivory. Thus the ivory was used for ornamentation and not for construction (which would require more ivory than the supply could meet). Carved ivories and other luxuries were often imported from Phoenicia. Trade with Phoenicia was favored by a pact between Israel and Tyre (Amos 1:9).

Ahab's worst defeat was his loss of the province of Moab. Mesha's inscription dates Moab's successful war for independence in the middle of Ahab's reign. Mesha relates that some of the Israelite tribes, such as Gad, were still in Transjordan. Mesha took those Hebrews captive and forced them to work on his public projects as slave laborers. He visualized his success as a victory of his native god Chemosh over the foreign God Yahwe. Chemosh had been angry with his people but had finally forgiven them and so rescued them out of the hand of Yahwe and Yahwe's subjects. We note that the rivalry of gods was imagined to be the source of warfare. Putting war on a religious plane justified the ever-growing brutality in warfare such as we read on Mesha's stela and other documents of the ancient Near East.

Good relations between Israel and Judah were enhanced by the marriage of Jehoshaphat of Judah to Athaliah, daughter of Ahab. This union gave Judah so much additional strength that it was able to reconquer Edom, which was thereafter administered for a time not by its own king but by a governor stationed there. It should be noted that just as the sign of Israelite strength is its domination over Moab, the criterion for inferring the strength of Judah is its domination over Edom. When Judah has military striking power, it dominates Edom; when Judah is weak, Edom regains independence.

Ahab and Jehoshaphat got together fraternally [10] to try to win back Israelite territory in Transjordan by fighting for the key city of Ramoth-gilead. Before embarking on the campaign, Ahab consulted four hundred prophets available in his court for what passed for the agreeable [11] word of God. One

[10] Though with Judah subordinate to Israel's interests.

[11] If agreeableness is demanded of oracles, the oracles soon prove false and become discredited. Furthermore, inspired men never occur in droves. Such prophets as these were simply a variety of court flatterer.

of the prophets named Zedekiah, presented a pair of iron horns, which symbolically were to be worn by Ahab to gore Aram and score a victory. This optimistic prophecy did not impress Jehoshaphat who wanted to know whether they might consult some more genuine prophet of Yahwe. Reluctantly Ahab admitted there was one, Micaiah son of Imlah, who in the past had consistently prophesied evil for Ahab. Micaiah was fetched and he at first sarcastically confirmed the agreeable prognosis of the court prophets. But on being prodded to speak the truth, Micaiah declared that God wanted to ruin the House of Ahab and for that very reason He had sent a lying spirit into these prophets. (The point had not yet been reached in Hebraic theology, where a lying spirit sent by Yahwe would be unthinkable. As we have already observed, Yahwe is here represented as acting much like Zeus who intentionally misled Agamemnon by a false dream.) Micaiah finally gives a true prophecy and predicts disaster for the kings in their venture at Ramoth-gilead. He is sent to jail pending the outcome, but in 1 Kings 22:28 enunciates the test of prophecy, in saying to Ahab: "If you return in peace, then God has not spoken through me." The kings go off to the battle, meet with their defeat and Micaiah is vindicated. Ahab was mortally wounded at Ramoth-gilead. The judgment of Scripture concerning Jehoshaphat is typical of several good kings of Judah: He was good except for one thing; the people were still worshiping on the high-places. However, he did wipe out the remnant of the unsavory Kedeshim priests.

Jehoshaphat felt sufficiently strong, what with his conquest of Edom, to launch a fleet for the purpose of trade on the Red Sea. His ships were wrecked before they could sail from their home port of Ezion-geber (1 Kings 22:49) in keeping with Judean ineptitude at navigation. King Ahaziah, son of Ahab, offered to cooperate with Jehoshaphat in further naval exploits but Jehoshaphat had had enough and declined (1 Kings 22:50).

Ahaziah consulted the pagan god Baal-zebub. Conversely, Naaman of Damascus turned to Elisha, a prophet of Yahwe, for healing. Often people have the notion that foreign talent is superior to domestic skill. In any case, Naaman came to Elisha seeking to be cured (2 Kings 5:1-19) through powers derived from Yahwe. Naaman was so convinced of the efficacy of the cure and of Yahwe's supremacy that he embraced Yahwism and carried back two mule loads of soil from Israel so that in Damascus he might worship Yahwe on His own earth. (This reflects the belief that a god could only be effectively worshiped on his own soil.) Inasmuch as his official duties included accompanying his sovereign into a pagan temple where he had to bow down, he received in advance an indulgence from Elisha permitting him to do this.

In this period of history, the interrelations between Israel and Judah are quite close and the names of kings reigning simultaneously in the two monarchies may be identical to the confusion of the reader. We now enter a period where both the north and the south are ruled by J(eh)orams; one Jehoram is the son of Ahab, the other is the son of Jehoshaphat. Though the son of Ahab destroyed his father's Baal monument, he is nonetheless condemned as wicked for the simple reason that as a northern king he could not adhere to the Jerusalem cult. But we discern by his attack on Baalism that the reform of Elijah and Elisha was meeting with a positive response in Israel with the result that Baalism was giving way to the return of Yahwism.

The two Jehorams and the ruler of Edom pooled their resources to march against Mesha and win back Moab for Israel. To understand their relationship it is necessary to bear in mind that the greatest of the three rulers was the King of Israel. Indeed the expedition was for Israel's benefit. Judah was subordinate to Israel; and Edom was Judah's vassal. The three unequal allies proceeded against Mesha of Moab.

Elisha accompanied the armies to give oracles. When an oracle is finally sought of him, he gets into the prophetic mood by listening to music (2 Kings 3:15). (The use of music either to induce the spirit of the Lord, or to drive out an evil spirit are both attested in Scripture. Psychiatrists know both the good and bad effects that can be produced on patients by different types of music.) A water shortage threatened the three armies and Elisha predicted that without observing wind or rain, the dry wadi before them would be filled with water (2 Kings 3:17). The hosts and their beasts were saved by a torrent in the wadi, although they saw no rain to account for it. The phenomenon is not a miracle: It sometimes happens that a sudden heavy rain at a distance in the hills sends a raging torrent through the wadis leaving the natural holes in the wadi bed filled with water for hours, or even days, to come. The only remarkable feature of the story is the timing. The Arabs call such a wadi torrent a *sayl*.

The expedition against Moab was typically destructive and inconclusive. The invaders filled up wells and cisterns with stones, cut down trees and devastated the countryside. Finally they surrounded the fortified town in which the Moabite King had taken refuge. From the military standpoint, the impregnability of the town wall doomed the expedition to failure, as so frequently happened in ancient warfare. The invaders had plundered and ruined the country but could not win the war. Since Israel did not succeed in its attempt to reconquer Moab, Mesha's earlier war for independence, related on his stela, had not been in vain. Mesha sacrificed to the national god Chemosh his crown prince on the town wall, where everyone could see it. The Israelites and their allies chose this moment to withdraw to their homeland lest the rage of Chemosh should destroy them in his own territory. His pity, aroused by the extreme sacrifice of King Mesha, had brought his "great rage against Israel" (2 Kings 3:27). The incident shows that Israel still shared with her neighbors the national concept of divinity. Just as Yahwe had His land and people; Chemosh had his land and people.

While Mesha's victory over Israel preceded the two Jehorams' invasion, it is probable that the building operations mentioned in his stela were required to repair the damage inflicted during that invasion. The fact that Mesha's program included waterworks as well as buildings and fortifications jibes with 2 Kings 3:25. The question arises why Mesha does not discuss this invasion. The answer is probably that he had very little to boast about in a war where the enemy effected an unopposed withdrawal after devastating Moab. To sum up Moabite relations with Israel: Omri conquered Moab; quite a few years afterward (described as "forty" years by Mesha in accordance with a well known idiom not meant to be taken literally) Mesha regained independence from Ahab; Jehoram of Israel tried to win back Moab but succeeded only in devastating that land; and Mesha repaired the damage by a building program outlined in his stela.

King Ahaziah of Judah (the son of Jehoram of Judah and of Ahab's daughter Athaliah) joined forces with Jehoram of Israel against the usurper Hazael, who had seized the throne of Damascus. Hazael is called in Assyrian annals "the son of a nobody" which means a usurper. 2 Kings 8:7-15 states that Elisha was instrumental in Hazael's usurpation, for Hazael was viewed as God's tool against the iniquitous line of Israel that had been contaminated with Jezebel and Baalism, and that had polluted the Davidic Line via Ahab's daughter Athaliah.

The Kings of Israel and Judah were wounded in the battle, and went to Jezreel to recuperate. Elisha, with his usual effectiveness and timing, chose that moment to send a prophet to

Ramoth-gilead to anoint in secret the army officer Jehu, as
King of Israel. (The prophet is referred to as a madman by
other officers at Ramoth-gilead because prophetic inspiration
and insanity were overlapping concepts; see 2 Kings 9:11).
Jehu, now anointed by a prophet of Yahwe, is hailed as king
by his own officers. Having thus secured the support of the
army, he proceeds by chariot to Jezreel. Jehoram's scout
identifies the impetuous charioteer, for "the driving is as the
driving of Jehu the son of Nimshi; for he drives furiously"
(2 Kings 9:20).

Jehu himself slew the King of Israel and soon after had the
King of Judah slain too. Eventually he got around to Jezebel,
who with painted eyes looks down from a window and de-
fiantly calls the usurper a "Zimri who has slain his lord"
(2 Kings 9:31). Jehu dispatches two or three of his hench-
men who throw her out of the window to her death. The
mauled remains of the hated Queen were buried by Jehu's
orders, because, as he admits, "she is the daughter of a king"
(2 Kings 9:34). Few personalities are more colorful or positive than Jezebel. She stopped at nothing—not even murder
—to achieve her goals. Her royal husband was like putty in
her hands. Born to the purple, she perished without flinching.

2 Kings 10 is one of the most magnificent and terrible and
strictly historical narratives in all of the Bible. Jehu proceeded
to wipe out the entire House of Ahab. He also got hold of a
party of Ahaziah's kin and slew them in cold blood. Naboth
was at long last avenged. There could be no peace in the country until that wrong had been righted and only now could the
affair of Naboth be considered closed.

In a still more treacherous fashion, stopping at nothing
and without any scruples, Jehu now turns to slaughtering the
Baalists in fulfilment of his obligation incurred by the circumstances of his coronation. He had been anointed by a
prophet of Yahwe to secure the victory of Yahwism and to

annihilate Baalism from Israel. He enlisted the help of a puritanical idealist named Jonadab son of Rechab. (Jonadab is the founder of the Rechabites: a group we are to hear more about later in the time of Jeremiah. Their ideal is the God-fearing austerity of the desert. Thus they shunned alcoholic drinks. This prohibition had long been practiced in Israel by individual "Nazirites," who were men destined for particularly holy lives in token whereof they did not shave or drink intoxicating liquor. But the Rechabites extended the prohibition to the whole community. They furthermore lived in tents instead of houses and refrained from agriculture in the true nomadic spirit. They were strict devotees of Yahwe.) Jehu with the help of Jonadab lured all of the Baalists into the Baal temple for a religious celebration; then by stationing eighty well armed men at the exits, all the congregation was killed in cold blood. The House of Baal was destroyed and left as a dung heap. Israel was purged of Baalism, and Yahwism had triumphed.

Jehu's purge was fatal not only for the history of Israel but for all of western civilization down to the present. It was a precedent of exclusivism, of fanaticism, where no toleration for any other cult was permissible. This frightful precedent had its reflexes not only on the rare occasions where Jews were in a position to implement such a policy, but more particularly in the history of Christianity and the history of Islam. Thus the bloody religious wars of Christian Europe in the sixteenth and seventeenth centuries A.D., hark back, though indirectly, to Jehu's precedent in ancient Israel.

In spite of Jehu's unswerving zeal for Yahwe (and no one can deny that he left no stone unturned in reestablishing Yahwism), Jehu is condemned by the biblical writer (2 Kings 10:31). No amount of Yahwistic devotion could atone for Israel's separation from Jerusalem.

# Chapter XIII

## DISCOVERIES AT KARATEPE

WE interrupt our account of the Hebrew Kingdoms for an interlude on one of the most important discoveries from the ancient Near East, since the unearthing of the Ugaritic tablets in 1929. In a palace at Karatepe in Cilicia, a royal bilingual inscription was found after the Second World War. The two languages of the text are Phoenician, which can be translated with but few difficulties; and Hieroglyphic Hittite, which could not be interpreted except for a number of details. The importance of the discovery lies in the fact that at last there is a key for accelerating the decipherment of the corpus of Hieroglyphic Hittite texts.[1]

The Phoenician version comes in three recensions; the Hittite version, in two recensions. The two versions are idiomatic rather than slavish translations of an original. Transpositions, plusses and minuses, and other changes are introduced freely to fit in with the spirit and idiom of the Phoenician and Hittite media, respectively. Moreover the recensions within either version, are not in absolute verbal agreement. There too, there are plusses, minuses, minor alterations and even transpositions. The requirement of ancient copyists and translators was to reproduce the same sense but not to be slavish in detail.[2]

[1] While Cuneiform Hittite (except for problematic texts) has for some years been quite intelligible, Hieroglyphic Hittite has been virtually untranslatable in spite of the painstaking work of Bossert, Gelb, Hrozný and Meriggi. Although both kinds of Hittite are Indo-European, they differ considerably from each other linguistically.

[2] Professor G. D. Young has pointed out, on the evidence of Karatepe, that scribal and translational laxity in the ancient Near East is not due to differences in time or place or faction.

Aside from the fact that Karatepe provides a major clue to Hieroglyphic Hittite, the texts happen also to be the longest known inscriptions in either Phoenician or in Hieroglyphic Hittite.

The date of the text has been put by various scholars in different periods ranging from the middle of the ninth to late in the eighth centuries B.C. The consensus of opinion tends to favor the lower date. But regardless of which precise date proves to be correct, the text [3] belongs to the general period of small statehood discussed in the chapter that precedes and in the one that follows. It is therefore of value for giving us some insight into a non-Hebrew state resembling Israel in some respects and differing from it in others.

The ruler for whom the text was written is Azitawadd, King of the Danunite city state of Adana, who boasts of enlarging his borders, of establishing prosperity and public security and of building the royal residence where the inscription was discovered.

The reason that the text was not written in the Danunite language is that the latter was not a literary medium. The two international languages used then for writing in that part of the Near East were Semitic Phoenician and Indo-European Hieroglyphic Hittite. That Phoenician enjoyed such a status in Asia Minor had been unsuspected. Early in the eighth century B.C. Aramaic began to displace Phoenician as the *lingua franca* of Canaan—a process that swept all of Western Asia and lasted until the Islamic Conquest (in the seventh century A.D.) substituted Arabic for Aramaic.

Azitawadd's Phoenician text, in the best preserved of the recensions, runs as follows:

"I am Azitawadd, the blessed of Baal, the servant of Baal, whom Awrikk, King of the Danunites, exalted. Baal made

[3] *Journal of Near Eastern Studies* 7, 1949, pp. 108-115.

me as a father and a mother to the Danunites.[4] I quickened the Danunites, enlarged the Land of the Plain of Adana, from the rising of the sun to its setting, and in my days the Danunites had every good and plenty and goodness. And I filled the *arsenals*[5] of Paar[6] and I multiplied horse upon horse and shield upon shield and camp upon camp by the grace of Baal and the gods and the *assemblage of lares*.[7] And I wiped out all the evil that was in the land. And I erected the house of my lordship in goodness and I did good for the root of my lordship. And I sat on the throne of my father and made peace with every king. And even (as) in fatherhood every king treated me because of my righteousness, wisdom and goodness of heart. And I built mighty walls in all the outposts on the borders, in places where there had been bad men with gangs, none of whom had been subservient to the House of Mopsh[8]; but I, Azitawadd, put them under my feet and I built settlements in those places for the Danunites to inhabit in the ease of their hearts. And I subjugated mighty lands in the west,[9] which all the kings before me had not subjugated, but I, Azitawadd, subjugated them, bringing (them) down and settling (them) in the extremity of my borders in the east, and Danunites I settled there.[10] And there were in my days, in all the borders of the Plain of Adana, from the rising of the sun to its setting—and in places which had formerly been feared, where a person would fear to walk the road, but in my days a woman could *stroll* with hand on spindles by the

---

[4] Note that Baal is the head of the pantheon and that he confers kingship so that the ruler should look after the people kindly.

[5] Italics indicate uncertainty of translation.

[6] The name of a city?

[7] For *meliṣim* "ancestral spirits," see Isaiah 43:27.

[8] The name of Azitawadd's dynasty.

[9] The "might" of those lands is not as great as the word conveys to an unwary modern reader. Azitawadd is referring to small states like his own.

[10] Note the technique of transplanting populations to break the spirit of the conquered. Not only were the victims exiled but their land was resettled by Danunites who precluded the hope of the exiles' returning.

grace of Baal and the gods—yea, there were in all my days plenty and goodness and good living and ease of heart for the Danunites and all the Plain of Adana. And I built this city and made the name Azitawaddiyy because Baal and Reshef-of-the-*Bucks* [11] sent me to build and I built it by the grace of Baal and Reshef-of-the-*Bucks,* in plenty and in goodness and in good living and in ease of heart so that it would be a stronghold for the Plain of Adana and the House of Mopsh. For in my days there were unto the land of the Plain of Adana, plenty and goodness; and in my days it was never night for the Danunites. [12] And I built this city and made the name Azitawaddiyy. I installed Baal K-r-n-t-r-y-sh [13] in (it) and a sacrifice went for every idol; a head of large cattle (as) an annual sacrifice, and in the plowing season a head of small cattle, and in the harvest season a head of small cattle. [14] And Baal K-r-n-t-r-y-sh blessed Azitawadd with life and peace and great strength above any other king [15] so that Baal K-r-n-t-r-y-sh and all the deities of the city might give to Azitawadd length of days and multitude of years and good authority and great strength above any other king. And this city was one of plenty (of food) and wine, and this people which dwells in it constituted owners of large and small cattle and owners of plenty (of food) and wine, and (who) *abundantly* [16] *pay taxes,* and *abundantly* render adulation and *abundantly* render service to Azitawadd and to the House of Mopsh by the grace of Baal and the gods. And if any king

[11] Another possibility for this god's name is Reshef-of-the-*Birds.* Since the Phoenician text lacks vowels, it is not uncommon for different words to fall together in the consonantal script.

[12] H. L. Ginsberg was the first to detect the right reading here.

[13] This is the epithet of the local Baal in the role of national god. The vowels are uncertain.

[14] Phoenician (like Hebrew) includes sheep and goats under "small cattle" as distinct from cows which are "large cattle."

[15] The exaggeration is typical of royal inscriptions.

[16] Or "publicly," if *brbm* has the meaning of Late Hebrew *barabbim.*

among kings, or prince among princes, or person of renown, who obliterates the name of Azitawadd from this gate and puts (on his own) name, or even covets this city and removes this gate which Azitawadd made, and reuses (it) for a strange gate and puts (his) name on it; whether he removes from covetousness, or from hate and evil he removes this gate; then may Baal of the Heavens and El Creator of Earth,[17] and the Eternal Sun [18] and all the Generation of the Gods [19] obliterate that prince and that king and that man of renown but may the name of Azitawadd endure forever like the name of the Sun and Moon!"

Professor H. Th. Bossert is now in the course of using the Phoenician to decipher the Hittite version. He has published the first third of the Hittite text deciphered (by correlation phrase for phrase with the Phoenician) under the title "Die phönizisch-hethitischen Bilinguen vom Karatepe," *Archiv Orientální* 18, No. 3-4, 1950, pp. 1-33. The scholarly world awaits the rest impatiently. Meanwhile there is a growing literature on the part of the text that is available; e.g., P. Meriggi, "La Bilingue di Karatepe in Cananeo e Geroglifici Etei," *Athanaeum* new series 29, 1951, pp. 25-99.

There is every indication that Anatolia may be the most productive area in ancient Near East archeology for some time to come. Surface exploration (without digging) has not been exploited there as it has in most of the Semitic areas. While Karatepe (discovered by a school teacher hiking during vacation) is not likely to be matched for a long time— if ever—among surface finds, Anatolia will probably produce

---

[17] Note how the younger Baal is mentioned before the old head of the pantheon, El who created the earth. Note too that Baal is already elevated to "Baal (= Lord) of the Heavens," who was widely worshiped centuries later.

[18] The Sun is frequently invoked in oaths and imprecations because as the god of light he witnesses everything everywhere.

[19] This expression for "The Pantheon" occurs also in Ugaritic.

richer epigraphic remains without excavation than the Semitic Fertile Crescent to the south. Excavation (in all those areas) will, of course, yield rich discoveries, whose magnitude cannot be predicted. That Hieroglyphic Hittite (along with other discoveries in Asia Minor) will illuminate both Near Eastern and Greek civilization is a foregone geographical conclusion. Needless to say, this is bound to result in a better understanding of our own biblical and classical heritages.

# Chapter XIV

## FROM ISRAEL'S LARGEST EMPIRE
## TO THE FALL OF SAMARIA

THE House of Jehu, founded in usurpation and established in bloodshed, could not be fundamentally strong. All of the territory that Israel had in Transjordan was seized by Hazael (2 Kings 10:32-33) and Israel became a vassal state of Damascus. Shalmaneser once more invaded the area in 841 B.C. : another fixed date in Israelite history. The Assyrian proceeded against Hazael but again failed to capture the well fortified Damascus. He received tribute from quite a number of vassal kings, including Jehu of Israel, who is mentioned on the Black Obelisk of Shalmaneser III. Whether the portrait in relief given with Jehu's name is supposed to be Jehu or a representative of his, is an open question. The value of the portrait resides more in its worth as a record of authentic costume than of personal physiognomy. This expedition which Shalmaneser claims to be a great triumph was another one of those ephemeral raids. He did not return to the area until 838, when Jehu did not have to pay him tribute, which implies that Shalmaneser did not menace Israelite territory although he invaded surrounding countries.

Jehu begins to reign in Israel, and Athaliah seizes control in Judah, simultaneously in the year 841. The synchronism is established because the upheaval of Jehu's usurpation led to the assassinations of the kings of both Israel and Judah. If we go back to the Division of the Kingdom, upon the death of Solomon, the synchronistic history of the Books of Kings gives us fairly consistent figures for the duration of the two

Kingdoms. 98 years are attributed to Israel and 95 to Judah; the discrepancy is not excessive. If, however, we go from 841 to 722 (when Israel was destroyed), both of which are controlled dates, the reigns add up to 143 years and 7 months for Israel but to 172 years for Judah (instead of about 120 years for each kingdom!).[1] The arithmetical errors in the Bible are serious here; they cannot be corrected by scholarly ingenuity alone. If the true chronology of Israel and Judah is ever established, it will require the use of extrabiblical sources some of which are yet to come to light.—H. S. Gehman (in J. A. Montgomery's *The Books of Kings,* New York, 1951, pp. 58-64), wisely avoids forcing a solution upon the problem in his valuable chronological tables.

At this juncture we may well turn to some of the ideas and institutions of the age. In the realm of theology we note (2 Kings 5:1) that Naaman is regarded as an instrument of Yahwe's plan to grant salvation to Aram. This marks an advance over the older view which made of Yahwe a more narrowly national god; and constitutes a step in the trend whereby God is to become the God of world history. For the first time a Hebrew prophet (Elisha) is connected with the crowning of another nation's king (Hazael of Damascus). The prophets have not yet become literary prophets. They wander about in bands and have a kind of organization. They make a living from fees offered for services rendered; for example, the rich gift which Naaman offered to Elisha, and which was accepted in part by Elisha's servant. 2 Kings 4:42 shows that people also gave "the bread of first-fruits" to the prophets, who were therefore partially supported by offerings resembling the gifts given by laymen to priests or Levites.

The most familiar holidays are those of the New Moon and

[1] The figures may be checked by consulting the numbers with their sources conveniently listed by E. R. Thiele in *The Mysterious Numbers of the Hebrew Kings: A Reconstruction of the Chronology of the Kingdoms of Israel and Judah,* Chicago, 1951, pp. 281-2.

Sabbath. On those occasions people might make a trip to a prophet (2 Kings 4:23). The incident of Naaman is also noteworthy because of his being cured in the Jordan River: the earliest recorded example of baptism in that river for the sake of healing.

The nations of Canaan would be welded into coalitions in the face of Assyrian invasions, but between those invasions Canaan would relapse into small states fighting each other. Intrigue was rife and little nations did not hesitate to bribe a foreign king to attack their neighbors. In 2 Kings 7:6-8 the Arameans abandon their camp, with all their supplies, because of a rumor that the King of Israel bribed the kings of the Hittites and Musur. ("Hittites" mean the people in some of the Aramean kingdoms [2] of North Syria, which were in some cases relatively powerful in this age.) The same kind of bribery appears in inscriptions of the Aramean kings. Thus around the year 800 B.C. King Kilamuwa of the far north Syrian state of Samal relates that he paid the Assyrians to attack his neighbors the Danunites of Cilicia.

With the growth of commerce and wealth, there was a corresponding increase in poverty. The common people frequently fell into debt and were often unable to repay on time. Debtors and their families were often seized as security and thus enslaved. Poverty could oblige people to sell their own children. In a particularly bad state were widows, who had to look after themselves and their children without a man's protection and support; 2 Kings 4:1 tells of a widow whose creditor is about to take away her children as slaves. The old ideal still persisted that every Israelite sat under his own vine and fig tree; but that ideal was little more than a literary cliché, a distant memory and a vain hope because the population consisted of a large poor class and a small rich class.

---

[2] They sometimes (like Carchemish) used Hieroglyphic Hittite for royal inscriptions. Thus they maintained some Hittite tradition.

2 Kings 7 shows that lepers were not allowed in the city but were obliged to remain outside. For the history of medicine this is of interest as an early example of quarantine. But the motivation was not identical with that of modern quarantine; the Hebrews abhorred corpses and diseased bodies because of ritual purity. Their instincts were good and were conducive to healthy living but we must refrain from reading into Hebrew civilization, modern notions of contagion and of preventive medicine. For the Hebrews, the etiology of disease was the displeasure of the Lord; thus when King Azariah of Judah falls sick it is simply because the Lord afflicted him (2 Kings 15:5).

Jehu, who reigned from about 841 to 814, had weakened the country by his bloody purge. After 838, when Shalmaneser attacked the area and withdrew, there were no more Assyrian invasions for over thirty years. Yet Jehu lacked the resources to emerge as one of the greater powers in Canaan. Instead Hazael reduced Israel and rendered it so impotent that he was able to turn on both the Philistines and Judeans. Hazael destroyed Gath and would have proceeded against Jerusalem had he not been bought off (2 Kings 12:18-19). Accordingly it was Damascus, not Israel, that became dominant among the local kingdoms.

Athaliah, who controlled Judah from about 841 to 836 B.C., was intolerable to the Yahwists. If the House of Ahab was not acceptable to Israel, it was even less so to Judah. In the tradition of the brutality of the day, she proceeded to wipe out the House of David, but a royal baby named Joash was rescued and seven years later, the priest Jehoiada, in concert with the army, staged a revolt which resulted in the coronation of the boy king around 836 B.C. and the assassination of Athaliah (2 Kings 11). Joash began his reign under the regency of Jehoiada who was professionally interested in the Jerusalem cult. The boy king, indoctrinated under the priest's tutelage,

devoted himself to religious reform. The Temple had fallen
into disrepair and the most memorable activity of his reign
(2 Kings 12) was his restoration and repair of the Temple.
However, his virtue is regarded (verse 4) as not quite up to
the idealized standard of his great ancestor David for the
people were still worshiping on the high-places. Nor was his
reign altogether blessed from a political or military standpoint. His buying off Hazael with the sacred vessels of the
Temple and with the treasures of the Temple and palace
(verses 18-19) could not escape criticism. Dissatisfaction with
Joash led to his assassination about 802 B.C.

Jehoahaz, who ruled Israel from about 814 to 798 B.C., was
a vassal of the King of Damascus. The report that the King
of Damascus left to Jehoahaz only 50 cavalry, 10 chariots and
10,000 infantry (2 Kings 13:7) is probably an authentic
statement taken out of the peace treaty. Damascus was making
a bid for the domination of all Canaan. Its King, Ben-Hadad,
with his allies, marched against the northern Kingdom of
Hamath but failed to conquer it. The resulting weakness of
Damascus meant a full-fledged revival of small statehood from
which Israel could profit. Israel regained its independence
under Jehoash (or Joash—not to be confused with the Judean
king of the same name), who ruled from about 798 to
783 B.C., and scored victories over Aram and regained cities
that his predecessors had lost.

The period was not one for bringing out the best in the
Canaanite peoples, including Israel and Judah. They all took
shameful advantage of each other's misfortunes. The state of
affairs is vividly reflected in the initial prophecies of Amos,
where he lists the countries, enumerates their sins and justi-
fies their misfortunes.

We learn from 2 Kings 13:20 and Amos 1:13 that there
were Moabite and Ammonite raids. This meant the capture
of people as slaves, and the Philistines and Phoenicians in the

coastal cities gladly profited from the resulting slave trade. This was particularly perfidious in the case of Tyre, which had a pact of friendship with Israel (Amos 1:9). Then too, Moab turned against Edom, making incursions and desecrating the royal grave there (Amos 2:1). The age was one of unethical and treacherous international relations.

King Amaziah of Judah avenged his father Joash on the actual murderers but not on their children; which is singled out as a good deed in keeping with the law of Moses.[3] Amaziah conquered Edom and took the city of Sela ( = Petra). Emboldened by his victories, he committed the indiscretion of challenging the more powerful King Jehoahaz of Israel, who accordingly invaded Judah, breached the wall of Jerusalem and plundered the Temple and royal treasury. Amaziah's costly folly may well have had something to do with the fact that he too was assassinated. He was succeeded by his son Azariah, who enjoyed a measure of prosperity. He rebuilt the Edomite port of Elath ( = Ezion-geber) on the Gulf of Aqaba. He contracted leprosy which unfitted him for ruling so that his son Jotham acted as regent.

In 805 B.C. Adadnirari III resumed the Assyrian invasions of the area, overrunning all the surrounding nations but not Judah. Israel, Philistia, Moab, Edom, Phoenicia and Aram bore the brunt. When the Assyrians withdrew with their plunder and captives, things became much as they had been before, so that Israel was again in circumstances from which it could profit materially and politically.

Jeroboam II (who ruled from about 783 to 743 B.C.) was the most vigorous member of the House of Jehu and forged by far the greatest empire ever won by the northern Kingdom of Israel. The biblical statement that he ruled from Hamath

---

[3] Whether the reference to the Law of Moses is Amaziah's reason, or the exilic compiler's observation is hard to say. In any case, all knowledge of the Law was forgotten by 621 B.C., when the Law was rediscovered.

to the Sea of the Arabah shows that his empire had a huge
spread from north to south. In spite of this phenomenal conquest, his reign is slurred over in the few verses of 2 Kings
14:23-29. Being wicked, as every king of Israel had to be
from the Judean viewpoint, Jeroboam did not merit a fuller
account. Yet we are thankful for the few revealing facts given
in the Bible about the extent of his realm. The *crux inter-
pretum* in verse 28 I am inclined to render "he restored
Damascus and Hamath from Yehuda into Israel." Yehuda is
not the southern Judah but the kingdom of the same name in
far northern Syria (also known as Samal). The prepositions
are in accordance with uses now fully familiar from the
Ugaritic tablets. The reason there are three apparent anoma-
lies in the two crucial words ("from [4] + Samal" [5] and "into [6]
+ Israel") is due to the fact that, as the verse itself tells,
the information is derived from the court "Chronicles of the
Kings of Israel." The dialect and history of Israel were full
of pitfalls for the Judean author, who may well have excerpted
his Israelite source without understanding it.

The splendor of the reign of Jeroboam II was ephemeral,
both for external and internal reasons. Externally, because
any time the Assyrians would put in another appearance, no
country in Canaan, no matter how strong, could defend itself
effectively. Internally, because society was unsound due to the
cleavage between the rich upper class and the large and ever-
growing poor class. The institutions of Israel were such that

[4] *Ugaritic Handbook*, p. 86, §10.11.

[5] In the Samal inscriptions, the native city state is called the "Yaudi"
(= Judean) kingdom. The Hebrew form is *Yehudi* "Judean." Aramaic
substitution of *aleph* (not represented in our English transliteration) for
*h* is common. Hence the omission of the *h* is linguistically explicable. At
a time when northern Judah (= Samal) was the great Syrian power defeated by Jeroboam II, the court chroniclers at Samaria knew that southern Judah was not meant in this context. Bible readers, however, have
not had the background necessary to know about the north Judah.

[6] *Ugaritic Handbook*, pp. 82-83, §10.4.

the royal line (because of the bloodshed in which Jehu had founded it in Jezreel) would have to suffer the same fate as Omri's line (Hosea 1:4 [7]).

God's wrath was evident to every Yahwist because of the natural ills that befell the land. The locusts, droughts, famines and other catastrophes could only be the hand of God (Amos 4:6-13). The fact that the people suffered, far from making them turn to another god or abandoning their own God, merely intensified their religion as manifested in cultic fanaticism; but this was not satisfying to the great prophets of Israel. Hosea has very little to say in favor of cultic practices; for example, he points out in 4:14 the abhorrent impurities of sexual rites connected with the Kedeshoth.

The woes that beset the land evoked a new concept in the prophecy of this time: the Day of Yahwe (e.g., Amos 5:18), the terrible day of reckoning when God would deal out punishment to the wicked and inaugurate a godly era. Alongside such severe prophets, there were to be sure also the cheerful prophets of victory such as Jonah son of Amittai (2 Kings 14:25) to bolster the morale of the established regime.

There was a balance of power in the life of the Hebrews that contributed to their strength in the future course of mankind, if not to a spectacular glory in antiquity. Just as the Books of Kings contain elements from court chronicles, from true human histories and from tales of the prophets, there were the officialdom, the literary men with keen powers of observation, and also the prophets. The prophets were not of one mold; some were optimistic, others gloomy, but none devoid of ultimate hope. The wonderworking or ecstatic prophets continued to exist but they were eclipsed by the new literary prophets such as Hosea and Amos, whose messages

---

[7] The symbolic naming of a child (here called "Jezreel") is a feature of Hosea that served as a precedent for future prophets; notably Isaiah, whose messianic prophecy about Immanuel is in line with this tradition.

were aimed at social reform within the matrix of Yahwism.
Religion was represented at radically different levels ranging
from priests interested in sacrifices at shrines, to a prophet
like Amos who attached no value whatever to cultic practices
but held that morality and social justice could alone please
God. The common people, with traditional rights, retained a
measure of their democratic heritage in spite of encroachments thereon. The elders of the people exerted influence in
local, and sometimes in national, affairs. Social institutions,
such as blood revenge, exacted their penalties of any violator
from the king down. Hebrew society had thus many checks
and balances and was not a dictatorship by some vested
interest.

The Aramean wars of Ahab are not the jejune listing of
names, numbers, idle boasts and trivia that one finds in court
annals. The account of Ahab's reign is enriched by that magnificent school of historiography that ripened with the United
Monarchy. No mere court chronicler would dare record the
incident of Naboth's vineyard as we have it in Scripture, on
pain of losing his job, if not his life. The fateful affair of
Naboth was described by a historian, who knew the court
well but was not subservient to it. Also Jehu's purge and the
triumph of Yahwism is historical writing of a high order and
not the formulaic scribbling of a hack annalist. (In Judah,
the incident of Athaliah and her removal may be in the same
historiographic tradition.) In these accounts there is none of
the narrow sectarianism such as we find in the compiler's
stereotyped condemnations of all the Israelite kings.

In addition to the historiography concerning royal personages, there is another charming literature about the lives of
the prophets, in no way inferior as writing, but different in
motivation, atmosphere and content from the work of the
royal historiographers. The lives of the prophets have religious as well as human interest; perhaps the best example is

the Elijah Cycle (1 Kings 17-19) including the superb account of his showdown with the Baalists on Mount Carmel (chapter 18). Here again it is the battle for Yahwism but without any sectarianism (such as propaganda for the Judean or any other cult) or political axe to grind (such as the legitimacy of one particular kingdom or dynasty). Unlike the royal historiography, the lives of the prophets contain legend as well as history. The reader of the Bible must not let the miracles and anecdotes obscure the historic missions of Elijah, who led the Yahwistic reaction against Baalism; or of Elisha, who gave that reaction political implementation.

With the prophet Amos during the reign of Jeroboam II there emerges into history a creative individuality in spiritual life, the like of which is not attested earlier anywhere in the world. Amos was a herdsman from Tekoa in Judah. All we know of his ministry is limited to his fearless preaching in Bethel on an occasion "two years before the earthquake." He left his land of Judah because of an inner urge that he was unable to resist. Crossing the Israelite border, he went to the royal shrine at Bethel, enumerated the recent historic sins of all the nations round about, culminating with a terrible indictment of Israel: the chief target of his message. He predicted the fall of Jeroboam by the sword and the exile of the Israelites for their iniquity. This was hardly popular with the authorities. The priest of Bethel, Amaziah, could not have Amos killed because Amos enjoyed prophetic immunity. Prophets could be unpopular but normally their lives were spared, whether their divine message was agreeable or not. Amaziah reported the affair to Jeroboam and came back to tell Amos to go home to Judah, where he could eat bread and prophesy all he liked, but not to bother Bethel: a royal shrine where his ranting was not welcome. Amos denied the implication that he was professional; he was not preaching to earn his bread. "I am neither a prophet nor the son of a prophet" means he did not belong to any prophetic guild. He was a shepherd[8] who had left his flocks in Tekoa because God had sent him to Bethel. As is typical of the great prophets, Amos remained fearless and proclaimed that Amaziah, whose family would suffer the worst disgraces and bloodshed, would himself be taken captive to an unclean land. Amos was not concerned with the establishment of a cult in Jerusalem or anywhere else, nor does he stress idolatry as one of his grievances against the Bethel community or the Israelites in general. He is against all cultic practices, which, insofar as they do not go with good living, are meaningless and offer no pleasure to God. He speaks of the unethical practices of the day: how the merchants sit around waiting for the end of the Sabbath or the New Moon when they could again cheat the public "making small the *ephah* (measure) and making large the shekel (weight)"; that is to say, selling short quantities but overcharging the customer, who pays with weighed silver. Amos hated hypocrites who frequented the shrine and altar but accumulated ill-gotten gains and abused the poor. He had no time for the rich who were living in "houses of ivory" with both summer and winter homes, in luxury all year, while the poor who were ground down under them had to pay for that luxury and groaned under the oppression. For Amos, God has no concern with the cult but only with ethics. The following passage (5:21-24) will suffice to sum up Amos's attitude toward what God wants of men:

"I hate, I loathe your pilgrimages,
　Nor will I inhale the odors of your convocations.
　Though you make sacrifices to Me
　I shall not accept your offerings
　Nor shall I regard the peace offering of your fatlings.

[8] It might seem strange for a shepherd to be so well informed of international events. However, the watering holes frequented by shepherds are often the best places to gather foreign news from caravan personnel.

Take away from Me the noise of your songs
For I will not listen to the music of your harps.
But let justice roll on like the waters
Even righteousness like a mighty stream."

Amos pronounces the doctrine that things have gone so far that Israel must be destroyed except for a remnant. Certainly the rotten upper class, whose members reclined on couches in Samaria and Damascus (Amos 3:12),[9] were doomed to destruction. As for the shrines, Amos (7:9) declares:

"The high places of Isaac shall be destroyed
Yea the sanctuaries of Israel laid waste."

For what pleasure could a righteous God have in shrines frequented by hypocrites?

In 8:11 Amos predicts that the physical hunger and thirst experienced by the people are nothing compared with the impending hunger and thirst, not for bread and water, but for Yahwe's word. Thus persists the old[10] idea that national bankruptcy has come only when God stops talking to men. Such would be the culmination of the period of disaster that must precede the Day of Yahwe when things will be righted.

Amos had risen above the narrow idea that God could only be interested in His own Chosen People. For Amos, God's concern for all mankind was equal; and in 9:7 He asks:

"Are ye not to Me as Ethiopians
O children of Israel?---
Have I not brought up
Israel from the land of Egypt
And the Philistines from Caphtor
And Aram from Kir?"

[9] This confirms the statement in Kings that Jeroboam's empire included Aram.

[10] It will be recalled that national bankruptcy in Saul's reign came when the oracles of God could not be obtained through any of the legitimate channels.

Thus Israel's Exodus from Egypt is not unique in history. God, Who has also arranged an exodus for the uncircumcized Philistines, cares not a whit less for the black Ethiopians than for Israel.

But the destruction that is to come will not strike the remnant, small though it be, because those devoted to Yahwe must not disappear from the earth. Yahwe's religion must continue; but it is to be an ethical, not a cultic, religion. Amos (9:14-15) ends his book with an undying message of hope:

" 'And I shall return the captivity of My people Israel
    And they shall rebuild desolated cities and dwell therein
And plant vineyards and drink their wine
    And make their gardens and eat their fruit.
And I shall plant them on their land
    And they shall not be separated any more from the land
        which I gave to them'
Saith Yahwe
    Your God."

These are great words that make history. Centuries later, in the time of Ezra and Nehemiah, people thought that these words were being fulfilled. But history has shown that the Second Commonwealth [11] was not the fulfilment of Amos's prophecy. Yet Amos's immortal words will continue to cry out for fulfilment until every promise comes true. His words are inseparable from the vigor of Israel down to the present time; and his message of hope has encouraged Israel to survive millennia of disaster. It was by warning the Hebrews that, before their remnant could be saved, they would undergo devastating vicissitudes, that their morale was prepared for withstanding the blows of destiny, which have wiped out the

[11] This designates the period of the Second Temple, from the late sixth century B.C. to the late first century A.D.

historic continuity of every other people from remote antiquity. Jewish suffering, instead of proving fatal, thus became
an assurance of the truth of the promise that the remnant will
survive. Amos and the other immortal prophets of Israel,
will continue as a vital force in the unfolding of human history, as long as men dwell upon the earth.

During the reign of Azariah (also called Uzziah) of Judah,
many changes took place in the Kingdom of Israel. These
changes were typical of Israel's history as contrasted with
Judah's. Judah enjoyed dynastic continuity, whereas in Israel
dynasty followed dynasty in bloody usurpation. Zechariah,
son of Jeroboam II, succeeded his father, but lasted only six
months. He was assassinated by Shallum, who reigned only
one month, to be assassinated around 742 B.C. by Menahem,
who seized the throne and perhaps enjoyed the reputation of
an avenger of his sovereign (Zechariah) rather than that of
usurper. Menahem was doubtless confronted with a civil war
and his atrocities in quelling it included the ripping open of
pregnant women in the city of Tiphsah (2 Kings 15:16).

In Menahem's reign, an Assyrian king sometimes called
Pul, but more often called Tiglathpileser [12] III, who began to
rule in 745 B.C., made changes throughout the entire Near
East, including Israel. Tiglathpileser was a vigorous monarch
who inaugurated new policies. Hitherto the incursions of the
Assyrian kings into the West meant that they would strike,
make off with as much booty and as many slaves as possible,
exact as much tribute as they could collect, and go home;
whereupon the old dynasts would reassert themselves. Or, if
the old dynasts were too unpopular or too weak to regain
control, a native opposition party or native usurper would
take over. To reconquer the state, Assyria would have to

---

[12] As king of Assyria he was Tiglathpileser; but as king of Babylonia,
he took the name Pul. The Bible confusingly uses both names without
explanation.

begin all over again in a future campaign. Tiglathpileser began the policy of incorporating the conquered territory into
the empire as provinces. The Assyrian kings before him had
done this with territory nearer at hand, so in a sense Tiglathpileser's policy was the extending of an old principle to Syria,
Babylonia and Anatolia. Brutality to any resistance was
justified from the Assyrian viewpoint on religious grounds.
The god Assur had willed that his country and his king
should achieve world domination; and all other gods, kings
and peoples had to be subservient to Assur's will. Any resistance meant rebellion against the great god and was put down
with condign severity.

Tiglathpileser also put into greater effect than had ever
been known before, the efficacious but cruel policy of transplanting conquered populations. This did not mean just exiling people from their homeland; it meant also putting other
exiles from distant areas into the evacuated territory so that
there would be no continuity between the old population and
the new. Moreover, any hope the old population might have
to return would be shattered by the presence of the new
population which would forbid their homecoming.[13]

The transplanting of populations reduced rebellions to a
minimum and explains why the northern Kingdom of Israel
has not had any effective continuity in Jewish history. Men
will fight for their own, but not for a strange, country.
Tiglathpileser and his successors transformed the East permanently. The shifting of populations meant a leveling-out
process that terminated the individuality that had characterized the nations of the Near East. One of the leveling-out
features was linguistic; Aramaic displaced other varieties of
speech with accelerated tempo throughout the area. The

---

[13] This is one important reason why Israel (conquered by Assyria) was
wiped out; while Judah (whose Babylonian conquerors did not repopulate
the land with aliens) survived.

Assyrian regime had to have as its backbone the army which was progressive, and mastered, as it went along, all the new techniques of warfare. It developed siege warfare to a greater extent than had ever been attained before; battering rams and other devices for breaching strong city walls reached an unprecedented degree of development.

It is during this period that there was a usurper in Syria named Azriyau [14] of the Yaudi land. (Yaudi, as noted above, is the same word as the Hebrew for "Judean.") It is not likely that Azriyau (in spite of Eduard Meyer's very attractive theory) was an Israelite adventurer; he was probably a native north Syrian with a Yahwistic name. [15] Azriyau headed up a large coalition that was suppressed in 740 B.C. by Tiglathpileser, who restored the old Yaudi dynasty, under King Panamuwa II.

In 738 Tiglathpileser again struck at the West and collected tribute from Asia Minor, Syria, the Phoenician cities, and from King Rezin of Damascus, King Menahem of Israel and Queen Zabibe of an Arab tribe. According to 2 Kings 5:19-20, the tribute Menahem paid was a thousand talents of silver. The sum was raised by imposing fifty shekels of silver on each tax-paying citizen, [16] implying that there were 60,000 such citizens in the Kingdom of Israel. Upon the payment of this tribute, Pul (= Tiglathpileser III) withdrew from Israel.

[14] Azriyau is the Assyrian transliteration of the same name that appears in the English Bible as Azariah. It is hardly possible to identify the two kings, even though some scholars have tried to do so.

[15] Ya(h)u (= Yahwe) names occur among non-Hebrews. Thus Yaubidi of Hamath and not a few Amorite names compounded with Ya(h)we-. Indeed Hamath had long been fostering some sort of Yahwism to judge from "Joram" of Hamath (2 Samuel 8:9-10), which the puritanic Chronicler modifies to the pagan "Hadoram" (1 Chronicles 18:10).

[16] The Hebrew term is literally "a hero of valor," which had evolved from its original sense of "stalwart warrior" to "upstanding landowner" who could be counted on to meet economic obligations. Boaz, in the Book of Ruth, who bears that title, is just such a man.

Menahem's son and successor Pekahiah was assassinated in 735 B.C. by one of his charioteers, Pekah, who was accompanied by a group of fifty Gileadites. Pekah combined with Rezin to attack Judah around 734 B.C. but none of their specific operations are known from the brief statement in 2 Kings 15:37. Tiglathpileser had conquered and exiled the populations of Transjordan and the northern part of Israel west of the Jordan to Assyria as is related in 2 Kings 15:29.

The inevitable disaster that faced the people of Israel (and doubtless, too, the surrounding countries) was one of the major factors leading to rampant pleasure-seeking and immorality. This immorality evoked the appeal for moral reform, from the earliest literary prophets.

Prophetic reform in Israel (unlike Judah) stopt short of demanding the removal of the golden calves at the northern shrines.

Amos had set a new precedent: his work was put in a book. His example may have caused the writing of Hosea's prophecies as a permanent record. Hosea, unlike Amos, was not a broad mind with worldwide horizons. Amos introduces his prophecy to and against Israel with a survey of the entire surrounding world, mentioning the misdeeds of the individual kingdoms as the reason for the punishment that was to descend upon them. Hosea's is a much smaller spirit. He knew only Israel well; plus Judah incidentally. The world beyond, was outside his interests. He realized of course that Israel and Judah were related people worshiping the same God; but Hosea's country was his beloved "Ephraim." He cried out against the moral evils of the cult in Israel, and against Israel's ignorance of God. He pictured Israel's betrayal of God in terms of marital infidelity because God had, so to speak, accepted Israel and Judah as His brides but they were unfaithful to Him.

It is impossible to understand the literal meaning of Hosea's prophecy without knowing some of the background in terms of daily life and social institutions. In Hosea 2 :4-5 the following words are addressed to children :

> "Take action against your mother
>     Take action!
> Because she is not my wife
> And I am not her husband.
>
> - - - - - - -
>
> Lest I have her stript bare
> And set out as the day she was born."

The first part of this declaration ("she is not my wife and I am not her husband") is a legal divorce formula. The penalty whereby a reprehensible wife is to be prosecuted by her own children and driven out naked is attested in earlier cuneiform tablets and in later Jewish Aramaic texts.[17]

Hosea was a religious spirit and not a practical politician. He envisaged a return to the covenant, when God would reaffirm His relationship to His People through a second Exodus from the land of Egypt.

Hosea, unlike virtually all the other biblical authors was a northerner; not a Judean. Before the fall of Israel (722 B.C.), his book was transplanted and adopted in Judah, where for linguistic and psychological reasons it was misunderstood; with the passing of time that misunderstanding has increased. Its linguistic and psychological obscurities have facilitated scribal errors in transmission. The conjectural methods used to correct those errors have (as usual) led to fallacious results. The Book of Hosea is a parade example of the rule that while an individual correction may conceivably be an im-

---

[17] For the cuneiform and Aramaic parallels see K. Kuhl, *Zeitschrift fuer alttestamentliche Wissenschaft* 11, 1934, pp. 102-109; and C. H. Gordon, *ibid.* 13, 1936, pp. 277-280; 14, 1937, p. 176.

provement, a hundred corrections invariably lead us farther
from the truth than does the present traditional text, no matter how many difficulties be in that text. (This holds even
when the emendations are made by profound Hebrew scholars
gifted with ingenuity. When unqualified Hebraists emend the
text, their corrections are impossible as compositions in the
Hebrew language. Unfortunately new Bible translations often
palm off such impossibilities on the unsuspecting reader.)

Tiglathpileser's departure from Syria in 737 B.C. was the
signal for the small states to reassert themselves. It was then
that Rezin and Pekah attacked their neighbors including
Judah, to strengthen themselves in the area while they were
free from Assyrian pressure. The King of Damascus took
away the port of Elath from Judah and resettled Edomites
there (2 Kings 16:6); though possibly the text instead means
that he supplanted the Judeans there with Arameans.

When Ahaz succeeded to the throne of Judah, Jerusalem
was surrounded by the forces of Rezin and Pekah. Ahaz consulted the prophet Isaiah, who had already received his call
around 740 B.C. (Isaiah 6) via a vision in which he had
beheld the Lord of Hosts enthroned between the cherubim.
(Such visions are related to the art of the times. Just as Gudea
in his visions sees Imdugud, the divine storm-bird, as it is
portrayed in Sumerian art; Isaiah sees God on the throne
between cherubim in the manner of the royal throne as illustrated on the Megiddo ivories and elsewhere in Canaanite
art.) On this occasion, Isaiah's answer to Ahaz is described
in Isaiah 7. The Prophet comes with a child who bears the
symbolic name "A-Remnant-Will-Return." (Isaiah's device
of giving symbolic names to children had already been practiced by Hosea.) Isaiah tells King Ahaz not to fear for all
will end well. Isaiah (7:14) then comforts the King with a
reference to a child Immanuel ("God-is-with-Us") just, or
about to be, conceived; for before that child is old enough to

reject evil and to choose good (by which the Prophet must
have meant at least the age of two), Aram and Israel will
be desolated.

To give further comfort to the harassed Kingdom of Judah,
Isaiah (8:3) went home to the Prophetess (which suggests
that "prophet" was a professional term to the extent that even
his wife was automatically accorded the title of "prophetess"),
who is to bear a child called "Hasten-Plunder-Hurry-Spoil."
Before that child will be able to say "father" or "mother,"
Assyria will plunder Damascus and Samaria. It is probably
the military and political impracticability of Isaiah's message
that drove Ahaz to the desperate step of sacrificing his own
son (2 Kings 16:3) and to the practical expedient of bribing
Tiglathpileser to attack Aram and Israel and thus to save
Judah from them (2 Kings 16:7). In any case, Tiglathpileser
conducted military operations in Syria from 734 to 732 B.C.

Ahaz, a vassal of Tiglathpileser, visited the victorious
Assyrian monarch in the captured city of Damascus. There
Ahaz saw an altar that appealed to him. He had the specifications of the altar recorded and sent to Jerusalem where the
priest Uriah executed the specifications to duplicate the pagan
altar for Yahwe's Temple.

Tiglathpileser's invasions, as we have noted, resulted in the
conquest of the northern and eastern territory of Israel and
in the exile of the captured inhabitants to Assyria (2 Kings
15:29). Pekah could not retain the confidence of his subjects
after his military fiasco. The last king of Israel, Hosea,
usurped the throne by killing Pekah, and became Tiglathpileser's vassal over a truncated state of Israel without
Transjordan or the northern provinces west of the Jordan.
Tiglathpileser's annals, however, give a slightly different
version to the effect that the Israelites ousted Pekah, whereupon Tiglathpileser made Hosea king over them. No contra-

diction is involved but only a difference in emphasis and interpretation.

After the capture of Damascus, Tiglathpileser marched against some Arabs who were ruled by Queen Shamsiyya. The Arab tribes, however, were willing to come to terms with Assyria because they depended on caravan trade for their prosperity. It was only by fitting into the Assyrian Order that they could live in peace and carry on their vital commercial pursuits.

Tiglathpileser assigned the tribe of Idibail (mentioned in Genesis 25:13) to guard the Egyptian frontier against Pharaonic interference in the Assyrian sphere of influence that now included Palestine. Tiglathpileser then went to conquer Babylonia. In addition to his conquests, he is also known for his constructive activity. He built up ruins and converted bad-lands into cultivable tracts. His reign marks a considerable refinement both in art and in the writing of annals. He made one fatal mistake. He took away the privileges of the two sacred cities of Assur and Haran. The people there had been exempt from taxation and military service. By rescinding these privileges he caused the downfall of his dynasty at the end of his son's reign. Tiglathpileser was followed by Shalmaneser V (726-722 B.C.), who warred against Israel and in whose reign Hezekiah, whom the Bible commends as a righteous King of Judah, sat on the throne in Jerusalem (about 726-697 B.C.).

King Hosea, who started out as a vassal, turned out to be unfaithful to his Assyrian overlord and rebelled. He found numerous anti-Assyrian allies ready to join hands with him; notably the Egyptian whose name in the traditional pronunciation of the Bible is "So," though Siwi would be more correct. He is called King of Egypt in 2 Kings 17:4, but he was actually the right-hand man of the Pharaoh at this time, as we learn from contemporary Assyrian records. Siwi and

King Hosea and a number of other small potentates around Palestine, joined forces in the uprising. Hosea was captured and carried off in chains. However, Samaria continued its resistance and it took three years before the city fell in January 722, whereupon the inhabitants were exiled to Assyria and Media. According to the annals of the Assyrian usurper Sargon, who finished up the war, 27,290 inhabitants were carried off from the Kingdom of Israel. The biblical account is related in 2 Kings 17:6 to 18:11.

# Chapter XV

# JUDAH ALONE

SARGON, though a usurper, enjoyed the role of avenger for the god Assur, from whose city Tiglathpileser had taken away time-honored privileges.

Sargon blames the King of Hamath for stirring up the rebellion in Syria and Palestine. That king is called Yaubidi. His name is to be compared with Ilubidi (also of Hamath and perhaps the same person). Ya(h)u (=Yahwe) and Ilu ("god") are variants of the divine element in the name. We may compare 2 Kings 23:34, where Eliakim is renamed Jehoiakim, with the identical substitution of the same elements ("El" = "Ilu"; "Jeho" = "Yahu").

The coalition had many members besides Hamath, Damascus, Israel and Egypt. For example, Hanno, the ruler of Gaza, who had escaped to Egypt, came back to lead his city in the rebellion.

Sargon's reprisals were severe. Israel was put under a governor and had to pay permanent tribute. Samaria was strengthened as an Assyrian stronghold and the land was settled by an alien population.

The trouble that broke loose for Assyria on the death of Shalmaneser V took time to clear up. Merodach-baladan, aspiring to the throne of Babylonia, went to Babylon for the New Year (= the first of the month of Nisan) 721 B.C. and grasped the hands of the Marduk idol there. This was the way to claim kingship over the country for the year to come. He found allies in the Elamites and in tribes that had been suppressed by Assyria.

Hamath was sacked in 720. Babylon was crushed in 709, although Merodach-baladan escaped and lived to stir up future rebellions indefatigably. Exiles from Hamath and Babylon were sent to Israel (2 Kings 17:24). So not only were the deported Israelites being punished for their rebellion, but the new settlers were being punished for theirs. The new population in Israel account for the founding of the Samaritan nation, which was to play a considerable role in Palestinian history and to figure prominently in both Testaments. The new settlers reacted to difficulties in the land by turning for protection to the local authentic religion, which they recognized to be Yahwism. They had the wide-spread idea that only the god of a particular area could be effective in that area. Accordingly they requested a genuine Yahwistic priest to teach them the religion of Yahwe. Such a priest was sent by the Assyrian government and he set up headquarters in Bethel. But the fact that numerous other priests were taken from various strata of society, constituted one of the offenses of the Samaritans according to the Bible. Yet the adherence of the Samaritans to Yahwe has been constant throughout their subsequent history, although at this early time the accusation is made in Scripture that they mixed their Yahwism with the cults they had known before their advent to Israel.

The treatment that Sargon meted out to the whole area, was typically Assyrian in its cruelty. Yaubidi was flayed; Hamath incorporated into the Empire; the people were exiled; the land was resettled. Sargon's victory was complete. Siwi of Egypt was defeated. Hanno of Gaza was sent in chains to Assur. But other sovereigns who were allowed to pay tribute and live in peace, included the rulers of Philistine cities, Judah, Edom and Moab. Both the Cypriotes and Arabs paid tribute and made peace with Sargon; the Cypriotes because of the necessity of maintaining sea trade with the mainland,

and the Arabs on account of caravan trade. Sargon built the new capital of Dur-Sharrukin for himself, not far from Nineveh. It was excavated first by the French and more recently by the Oriental Institute of the University of Chicago, and has yielded rich finds. Dur-Sharrukin, which was never quite completed, was abandoned after Sargon's death.

Sennacherib, son of Sargon, came to the throne in 705 B.C. The change in sovereigns was the sign for Merodach-baladan to return from exile in Elam and stir up a rebellion in his bid for the throne of Babylon. It might have been then that he sent his delegation to Hezekiah (2 Kings 20:12). Merodach-baladan was able and enterprising. Nothing discouraged him. As long as he lived, he was ready for a comeback and it is probable that his mission to Hezekiah was not merely one of banal diplomacy and the extending of kindly wishes, but rather part of a bold attempt to found a great alliance for ridding the world of Assyrian tyranny.

The verdict of the Bible on the character of Hezekiah is exceedingly favorable. 2 Kings 18:3 ff. informs us that he was the best of the Judean kings and was like his ancestor David. He put an end to the high-places, the paganizing monuments and Asherah. He went so far as to destroy a bronze serpent called Nehushtan that had been used as a cult object and was ascribed to Moses himself. His waterworks (2 Kings 20:20) which have been identified, are now called the Siloam Tunnel. In it was found the Hebrew inscription telling how the tunnel was hewn.[1] Through this tunnel water was brought from a source outside the city to within the fortifications. The project contributed to the ability of Jerusalem to withstand siege.

Hezekiah took the lead in organizing a regional rebellion against Sennacherib. He smote the Philistines unto Gaza (2 Kings 18:8) to force them into the anti-Assyrian camp.

[1] Some skeptical authors contest the date of the inscription.

This was done in concert with Egypt, whose dominant figure was now Tirhakah (though he had not yet become Pharaoh), and with the Philistine city of Ascalon, the Phoenician city of Tyre and perhaps also with Babylon under Merodach-baladan. The result was that in 701 Sennacherib invaded Judah and took all the walled cities except Jerusalem (2 Kings 18:13). Sennacherib's annals record that he took forty-six walled cities and carried off 200,150 Judeans as captives. All that was left to Hezekiah was the capital. Sennacherib parceled out the captured Judean territory to his Philistine vassals at Ascalon, Ekron and Gaza.

Egypt had tried to relieve Ekron but was defeated by Sennacherib. By this time Hezekiah felt obliged to send emissaries to sue for peace from Sennacherib, whose headquarters were at Lachish. He had to release Padi, a Philistine vassal of Sennacherib, and pay (according to the Assyrian annals) 800 talents of silver and 30 of gold. According to the Bible, however, he paid 300 of silver and 30 of gold. Outside of the discrepancy between the figures 300 and 800, there are no contradictions between the two versions, although the viewpoints naturally differ and each version supplements the other.[2] Sennacherib declares that he had shut up Hezekiah in Jerusalem like a bird in a cage, which confirms the biblical account to the effect that Jerusalem escaped the fate that Sennacherib had planned for it.

[2] There is no doubt that the biblical and Assyrian accounts refer to the same invasion. What has misled some scholars into assuming two invasions, is the fact that the Bible mentions Hezekiah's tribute at the beginning of the narrative, whereas Sennacherib's annals state that the tribute was paid in Nineveh after Sennacherib had gone home. Hezekiah offered tribute during the invasion but on condition that Sennacherib first withdraw. Since the offering of the tribute occurred early in the episode, the editor of Kings decided to finish the subject before going on to other items; especially since the tribute was recorded in the royal chronicles, while the Rabshakeh speech hails from a different historiographic source. Aside from desiring to keep his word, the reason Hezekiah paid tribute after Sennacherib had withdrawn was so that the Assyrian should not have cause to return to Judah in future campaigns.

One of the purple passages of the Bible is 2 Kings 18:17 ff., in which an Assyrian official, called by his title Rabshakeh, is sent to Jerusalem to get the city to capitulate by breaking down public morale. He addresses the representatives of Hezekiah within the hearing of the people crowded on top of the city wall. He starts out with advice against Judah's laying any reliance on that "broken reed" of Egypt, which was in no condition to render any effective help. He furthermore points out that trust in Yahwe is without justification because Yahwe is angry at Hezekiah for closing Yahwe's shrines all over the country and forcing the people to come to the one shrine at Jerusalem. This ties in with the statement that Hezekiah abolished the high-places of the land, which must have been an unpopular act for those who did not live in Jerusalem. The weakness of Judah is then high-lighted by a sarcastic wager that the King of Assyria would provide 2,000 horses for Hezekiah, if the latter could supply the men to ride them. Rabshakeh then states it was Yahwe who ordered Sennacherib to destroy Judah. This agreed with what certain prophets had been proclaiming for a long time. The Assyrian was probably sincere in believing that Yahwe was the God of the land Who presided over its destiny.

Hezekiah's representatives, worried about the effect Rabshakeh's words would have on the people, requested him to continue in Aramaic, the diplomatic language, which the common people could not understand. But Rabshakeh cleverly insisted on speaking "Judean" (= Hebrew) because he said his message was vital not only to the King and officials, but especially to the common people who have to bear the consequences of official policy. He then proceeds to tell, in the earshot of all the people present, not to let Hezekiah deceive them, that Yahwe will not save them and Yahwe's will is being carried out by Sennacherib, not by Hezekiah. Then he promises that, if they surrender, they could go back home outside the city to their own vineyards and groves and drink water from their own cisterns, until the King of Assyria saw fit to deport them to good territory, just as good as their own, where they could enjoy a successful life with all their needs gratified. He observes that all of the gods had failed to save their lands from the hands of Assyria; and he significantly includes Samaria, which Yahwe Himself had not saved from Assyria. This was psychological warfare of a high order. The Assyrian annals, by their very nature, tell us nothing of such factors. It was the Judean historiographers who had the interest to preserve the account of Rabshakeh, even though what he said was hardly agreeable to Judean sensibilities. That the episode is authentic cannot be doubted.

It is a tribute to the Judeans that their morale was not broken. They kept perfect discipline and clung to their faith in Yahwe and remained loyal to His anointed one, who ruled over them.

2 Kings 19 relates how Hezekiah, on receiving the news of Rabshakeh's ultimatum, expressed his grief and sent for Isaiah, who consoled him with the prediction that Sennacherib would hear a rumor of trouble in his realm and depart. Hezekiah, in his prayer to Yahwe, expressed the conviction that the gods Sennacherib had destroyed were simply the creations of human hands out of stone and wood but that Yahwe is alone the God and that therefore Rabshakeh's claims were vain. Hezekiah's prediction (verses 20-34) was followed by a plague that smote the camp of the Assyrians so that, according to the biblical figures, 185,000 men perished (verse 35). Many an army that had succeeded by the sword, has been doomed by disease! This plague is independently attested via an Egyptian source in Herodotus, and so there is no reason whatever for doubting its authenticity. Although Isaiah had not correctly predicted the cause of Sennacherib's departure (a rumor is not the same as a plague), the sudden

salvation of Jerusalem had vindicated Isaiah's optimism and his reputation was established.

The biblical statement that Sennacherib returned to Nineveh and was murdered by his sons (2 Kings 19:36-37) is true, but we know from Assyrian records that the assassination took place years later.

Isaiah has come down in tradition as the greatest of the writing prophets. He enunciated prophecies concerning foreign nations as well as Judah. Here he is following the precedent of Amos. Far from being a practical, down-to-earth politician, militarist or statesman, Isaiah is concerned solely with morals and religion. For him, God is the cause of everything that happens or exists. It is obvious that Isaiah was not the spirit of resistance. We have every reason to believe that it was Hezekiah's own idea to start the rebellion against Sennacherib; in no case was he aided and abetted by Isaiah. For Isaiah, Assyria is simply God's tool for meting out punishment to the nations of the world and particularly to Judah. But Assyria in turn is to be destroyed, though by God and not by man (Isaiah 10:5 and especially 31:8).

According to Isaiah (3:1-7; 24:2)—and this is in the tradition of Egyptian prophecies of the second millennium B.C.—there is to be an upheaval of society,[3] with chaos and distress, when the respect of the young for the old will go by the board, and when the distinction between master and slave, priest and layman, ruler and ruled, will be reversed or obliterated. Only after that unbearable upheaval, will salvation come. In the spirit of all the Hebrew prophets, Isaiah urgently tells his people to mend their ways so that there may be national salvation. (For the Old Testament prophets, salvation is national, not personal.[4])

[3] Cf. Hesiod, *Works and Days* 180-201.
[4] This is still prevalent in Judaism, where the continuity of the People is important but where very little emphasis is placed on personal salvation.

In the spirit of Amos and Hosea, Isaiah (1:17) proclaims that God does not want ritual and sacrifices but rather justice and morality. In spite of the fact that national salvation is so important, there is no chauvinism in the total picture of Isaiah's message. In 19:24-25 he mentions three nations that are to turn out to be blessings: Egypt, Assyria and Israel. It is thus through all of mankind that God's plan is to unfold. The disaster that confronts the world, and particularly Judah, is to be followed by a glorious and happy future. Thus Isaiah shares with his predecessors the conviction that after all the many woes that are in store, a wonderful and eternal age lies ahead. Isaiah incorporates the concept of the End of Days, which was to grow into the eschatology that figures so prominently in later Judaic development.[5]

In the End of Days there will come into its own a remnant which will include not only Judeans but Israelites. The remnant will have to be assembled from the ends of the earth, when God will show His majesty in leading the remnant back to Zion, even as He showed His divine power and purpose when He led Israel out of Egypt. The whole world will then accept Yahwe Who will reign alone as God over a perfect world (18:7).

Long before Isaiah there had been, as we have noted, a school of Egyptian prophecy, which dealt with a punishment to Egypt for offending the gods. The punishment was to be in terms of foreign domination, widespread destruction and in social upheaval whereby classes would no longer retain their former relationships. These woes would be terminated

[5] Eschatology is the school of thought devoted to the idea that the historic process with all its dislocations, will come to a close at the End of Days toward which all history moves. At that time an eternal era of static perfection will be inaugurated for the righteous. Birth, growth, death, wars, all types of change will then be unknown. The more the Jews suffered, the more they cherished their eschatological dream. It is obvious that this static ideal can have little attraction for modern westerners who cannot conceive of a desirable order without progress.

by a godly king who would be victorious in temporal and
spiritual affairs, so that he would inaugurate the divine order.
These elements plus ethical Yahwism (such as we find in
Amos and Hosea) add up to the Hebrew prophecy such as
we find in Isaiah. The Messiah or king who will inaugurate
the golden age at the end of days, must be of the Davidic
Line. That Messianic Age will be a perfect world, a kingdom
without end, in which justice and peace, but not violence,
will be the determining factor. Isaiah 11:5 states that righteousness or faithfulness will be the girdle on the loins of the
Messiah. That is to say, he will not be a hero of physical
combat whose strength is symbolized by the wrestling-belt,[6]
but who instead will be symbolized by morality and virtue.
He will inaugurate eternal peace and right, replacing all the
world empires.

There are still other elements in Isaiah; for example his
innovation that the animal kingdom will change its nature
in order to fit in with the ideal age. According to 11:6-9 the
lion will have to give up eating meat and turn to eating straw
because in that perfect world all the beasts shall live together
in peace with a little child leading.

Isaiah had complete conviction that Zion was inviolable.
Samaria could fall but not Zion; for how could Yahwe
abandon His holy city and His holy Temple? Sennacherib's
invasion had strengthened the doctrine of Zion's inviolability,
for every surrounding nation had fallen, every city in Judah
had been captured, but not Jerusalem and its holy shrine.
History enabled the Judeans to adhere to this doctrine for
some time to come. Prophets like Micah (3:12) and later
Jeremiah were to oppose it but the majority of the people

---

[6] The terminology harks back to the heroic age of the Near East (illus-
trated on seal cylinders) when combat took the form of belt-wrestling.
Cf. C. H. Gordon, "Belt-wrestling in the Bible World," *Hebrew Union
College Annual* 23, 1950-1, pp. 131-6.

in and around [7] Jerusalem cherished the illusion until Jerusalem fell in 586 B.C. [8]

Micah, in chapter 4, enunciates the doctrine of the End of
Days, when all nations will flock to Zion and enjoy an eternity
of peace. Micah thus follows the lead of Isaiah in the idea
that all nations will participate along with the remnant of
Israel in the golden age. Micah, like nearly all of the prophets,
holds that God is not interested in ritual and sacrifices. His
outcry against sacrifices of the fruit of the womb (6:7) may
have been evoked by the atrocity of Ahaz, who sacrificed a
son in his misguided concept of Yahwism. Micah (6:8) points
out that Yahwe wants only justice, uprightness and humility
with God; all the rest is unessential. In chapter 7, Micah
(like all the other prophets) preaches faith in ultimate salvation from Yahwe. There will always be a remnant (7:18),
which God will spare and to this remnant God will carry
out the promises He made to the patriarchal fathers of the
Hebrew people (7:20).

Hezekiah's brave struggle for independence had resulted
in loss of land, people and livestock. The Judeans had suffered materially in consequence of his policies. Isaiah's optimism might have made a favorable impression on the Jerusalemites, who heard his message and witnessed the salvation
of the capital; but there was little consolation for the inhabitants of the rest of the country. It is only natural, then, that
there should have been a reaction to the era of Hezekiah
and Isaiah.

Around 697 B.C. Hezekiah's twelve-year-old son Manasseh
became King of Judah. He reacted away from the prophets

---

[7] The people in the nearby villages and fields took refuge in Jerusalem
from invading armies.

[8] Micah (from Moresheth-gath) and Jeremiah (from Anathoth), not
being Jerusalemites, were for that reason not devoted to the doctrine of
Zion's inviolability. Isaiah, a court aristocrat of Jerusalem, was preconditioned to adhere to that doctrine.

toward cultism, hand in hand with the priesthood throughout the country. This does not mean that he abandoned
Yahwe as the national God but only that Yahwe was now
the chief of a group of popular deities (largely astral) that
had a great appeal at local shrines and among the common people. He revived institutions that the biblical authors
always regard with abhorrence. Thus there reappeared male
and female sacred prostitution in the shrines, a usage which
was widely practiced in the surrounding countries. Manasseh's
reactionary brand of religion was also expressed by his sacrificing his firstborn, which, to the biblical authors who judge
him, is not piety but the shedding of innocent blood. We
have very few facts from the long reign of Manasseh (about
697 to 641 B.C.). Probably the facts are so few because very
little happened and his reign was peaceful. He represented
a reaction against the spirit of resistance as well as the spirit
of prophecy. He was discreet enough to stage no revolts, to
pay his tribute promptly,[9] and to keep out of mischief as a
vassal within the world empire of Assyria. His were days of
economic prosperity and political tranquility, for after the
suppression of Hezekiah's revolt of 701, Canaan enjoyed
peace and trade under the *Pax Assyriaca*.

In rebuilding the high-places destroyed by Hezekiah (2
Kings 21:3), he gained the support of most of the people
outside of Jerusalem, especially the priesthood and other
leaders at the various centers, who had strong feelings in

[9] He is listed as Minashi among the vassals who paid tribute to Assyria.
Assurbanipal's campaigns encompass Judah but do not touch it, showing
that Manasseh behaved himself to Assyrian satisfaction. 2 Chronicles
33:11-16 mentions an Assyrian invasion (unsupported by Assyrian annals
or the Kings account), the deportation of Manasseh to Babylon, followed
by his reform and return to sound Yahwism. Perhaps we should regard his
deportation and reform as unhistorical midrash (to teach the moral that
wickedness is punished but a sinner can always repent). On the other hand,
his otherwise unattested defense works in verse 14 have a true ring and
may well go back to authentic annals.

favor of their own shrines as against that at Jerusalem. In bowing down to all the host of heaven, he was following the trend of the times, because in the Assyrian empire, the importance of astral worship would be great in that the Mesopotamians were the most star-conscious people of history.

The altars he set up in the spirit of paganism were even erected within the Temple itself in Jerusalem. The sacrifice of his son may have set a fashion that gave rise to the charge that his reign saw Jerusalem gorged from end to end with innocent blood. He also revived the popular religious institutions of divination and spiritualism which had been suppressed in the preceding reign. Accordingly the Bible condemns him as exceedingly wicked and as having misled the people into being worse than the nations God had expelled to make room for the Hebrews. Therefore the fate of Samaria would have to befall Jerusalem. However, it is likely that the trades-people who enjoyed better business than usual were in favor of Manasseh. It is likely too that he had the support of the provincial priests in a way that Hezekiah could not have obtained. But the Jerusalem faction and the prophetic movement, which could not tolerate his policies, reacted against them and crushed them shortly afterwards.

Amon followed his father Manasseh not only on the throne but in his policies. After a short reign of two years, Amon was assassinated and the reaction had asserted itself. Amon was succeeded by his eight-year-old son Josiah, who reigned from 638 to 608 B.C. and effected a tremendous impact on all subsequent history. The Bible approves of him and compares him with David. There is also the statement (2 Kings 23:25) that no king before or after him was as good.

It was during the reign of Josiah that the Assyrian empire tottered. In 626 B.C. Babylon broke away and the collapse of Assyria was just a matter of time. This gave the signal for independence movements and national restorations all through the Assyrian empire.

In his eighteenth year, Josiah sent the scribe Shaphan to the Temple to investigate the progress made in repairs. The situation is reminiscent of that in the time of Joash, who also was a boy king under priestly tutelage, in whose reign the Temple was repaired.[10] The terminology is largely the same; e.g., in the repetition of one fact that appears important to the biblical writer, namely that there was no bookkeeping in financial matters because everyone could be counted on to work in good faith.

The Highpriest Hilkiah had found in the Temple a book, which he turns over to Shaphan, who, on reporting to the King, reads the book to the King. On hearing the text, Josiah rends his clothes in grief because he and his predecessors had not been following this Book of the Law which had just been found. To know what to do, he sought an oracle from the Lord so as to avert the wrath of God which would befall him in accordance with the message of that Book, since the Law had not been followed. For the oracle he turned to the prophetess Huldah, who announced a favorable prognosis for his reign, although the ultimate wrath of God for previous disobedience was to bring on destruction thereafter. The religious reform was instituted without delay.

It is worth noting who backed the reform. It was supported by the priesthood of Jerusalem, notably Hilkiah; by the officialdom of Jerusalem such as Shaphan; by the crown; and by the prophetic movement; if we are to infer that the individuals who took part in the initial stages of the reform represented, as men often do, the interests of the groups from which they came (2 Kings 22).

Josiah then convokes all the elders of Judah and Jerusalem

---

[10] The similarity is due not only to the fact that history was repeating itself but also that the historiographic style is the same.

(2 Kings 23). The division is no longer that of Israel and Judah; now the factions of the Hebrew people are the Jerusalemites and the provincial Judeans. Already in the time of Hezekiah, Rabshakeh, in his oration, speaks of the people of Jerusalem and those of Judah. That is the cleavage that lasted down to the end of Judean independence. Josiah convokes not only the elders but also the common people of Judah and Jerusalem. Furthermore, two other categories of leaders are specified: the priests and prophets. It was before this impressive aggregation of leaders and citizens that Josiah had the Book of the Law read in public.

The traditional view is that the Law, discovered by Hilkiah and now read before the nation, was the entire Pentateuch. Since it would take at least fifteen hours to read through the Pentateuch, and since an ancient scroll is generally much smaller than the Pentateuch, it is conceivable that the scroll covered only a part of the Pentateuch. However, the view that the scroll was forged shortly before its alleged discovery in 621 B.C. is based on false premises. Throughout the ancient Near East, law codes (even when claiming divine origin like Hammurabi's Code) were disregarded in actual life. At the very time when codes were promulgated, the actual business contracts disregard the codes and so, from the standpoint of the codes, the market is black. The judges regularly omit any reference to codes in their court decisions in Mesopotamia. They are instead guided by tradition, public opinion and common sense. This is also true of Israel, where Solomon's suggestion to divide the harlots' baby was certainly not suggested by any code. Disregard of the written law is also illustrated by David's imposition of the death penalty (which is not prescribed by the law against stealing animals) in addition to fourfold restitution (2 Samuel 12:5-6). This does not prove that the Law did not exist. In Israel, as in Mesopotamia, judges and

rulers did not refer to codes or keep law books on hand for
consultation. There were two distinct currents: (1) practice
and (2) written law. Attempts to codify law naturally reckoned with custom and past experience but once such codes
were written, they were at best studied by a few scholars and
had little or no direct influence on legal and social practice.
Accordingly, the fact that neither Josiah nor his immediate
predecessors had known anything of the Law does not prove
it was a forgery by Hilkiah or Shaphan. The rediscovery of
Hammurabi's Code would have come as a complete surprise
to most kings of Babylon after Hammurabi. It is the consensus of conventional scholarly opinion that Josiah's scroll
was a composition of his reign and resembled Deuteronomy,
though it was not coextensive with Deuteronomy. Scholars
call that hypothetical document D (= Deuteronomic Code)
and while no two scholars agree on exactly what it includes
and excludes, virtually all scholars agree on its actuality.
The circumstances of the Josianic discovery fit in with what
we know of the ancient Near East so well that we may take
it at its face value. A forgotten book was rediscovered. Since
only a few scholars studied such books in a world where
illiteracy was the rule, law codes (whose practical value was
quite limited) were generally forgotten in the Bible World.
The significance of 621 is not that a great forgery was
foisted on a gullible world. The significance of that date is
that for the first time in human history, a written document
was *actually* adopted *for all time* and *without interruption*
as the permanent guide of a nation. The fact that it was
regarded as divinely inspired lent it the necessary authority;
but other codes that claimed divine origin had been promulgated long before and failed in the test of survival. Hitherto
in Israel and Judah divine guidance was sought by oracle.
Josiah himself resorted to an oracle when he was jolted by
the discovery of the scroll. But since 621, oracles have been

on the way out, and written scripture holds the field for most of mankind.[11]

The covenant reaffirmed in 621 bound God, king and people for all time. Josiah then proceeded to destroy cult objects that were not within the orthodox repertoire. He burned a number of them and transported their ashes to Bethel (2 Kings 23:4). This implies that he went outside the borders of Judah to bury these abominable remains in evil Bethel; for the boundaries of Judah are stated in verse 8 as extending from Geba unto Beersheba. Whether this expedition to Bethel was done with the permission of an Assyrian governor, or whether it was done without authorization (for the Assyrian empire was already weakening), we do not know. Josiah then put an end to the priests of the high-places who worshiped Baal and the various solar deities. He also destroyed the houses of the Kedeshim priests in the Temple itself, where women too used to weave cult objects called "houses for Asherah." (It is generally assumed that the Kedeshim and Kedeshoth were priests and priestesses given to sacred prostitution, but inasmuch as priests of the same title occur commonly in Canaan as far north as Ugarit, they seem to be too large a category to be limited to so specialized a function.[12])

Josiah also defiled the high-places; his usual method of defiling was to scatter bones upon them. The priests from outlying districts were allowed to come to Jerusalem and eat unleavened broad along with their brothers, but they

[11] The pattern of development follows three stages: (1) oracles, (2) canonical scripture, and (when the changing needs of life are no longer met by the antiquated scripture) (3) interpretation of scripture. We are of necessity in the third stage.

[12] The fact that qedesha (literally, "a holy woman") as a common noun means "a prostitute" (as its equivalent qadishtu does in Accadian) does not necessarily mean that the priests and priestesses designated by the same root must be sodomites and prostitutes respectively. After all, the basic meaning is "holy"; the sexual connotation is secondary.

were not allowed to sacrifice in the Temple. This means that while they were stript of important sacerdotal functions and graded down to subservient positions, they were not liquidated economically. Josiah also defiled the Tophet: the place where the sons and daughters of Judeans had been burned as molech offerings. Solar worship had become established under Manasseh and Amon so that Josiah had to put an end to the solar horses and chariots, which were doubtless regarded as chariots of the solar god identified with Yahwe in the reigns of Manasseh and Amon. Not only Manasseh's but also Solomon's constructions had to be destroyed in the Jerusalem vicinity for in verse 13 we read that Josiah devastated the shrines of Solomon's Sidonian Astarte and Moabite Chemosh and Ammonite Milcom. Josiah put down the witchcraft and spiritualism that had flourished in Manasseh's reign.

The Passover had either fallen into disuse or lost its importance. So, in accordance with the Law, a great Passover such as had not been celebrated since the days of the Judges was now celebrated under Josiah's orders. (The Exilic compiler of the Books of Kings adds (verse 26) that inasmuch as God could not forget the unspeakable evil of Manasseh, the city and Temple eventually had to face destruction although not in the days of the good Josiah.) The reform of Josiah amounted to the inauguration of a divine order whose neglect had occasioned the wrath of God which had brought the nation to such low estate.

The reform brought into world history the effective concept of a canon: writings of a divine origin binding for all time. Subsequently Judaism and its daughter religions added books to their respective canons but the effective idea that unalterable books of divine origin shall be eternally binding, first appears in 621.

The question as to what part of the Law was discovered

in 621 is open to difference of opinion. One of the most applicable parts of Scripture is Deuteronomy 17 and 18, which map out the proper duty and conduct of a king of the Hebrew people. The fact that hitherto the kings had not been living up to this standard because of their ignorance of this Law intensified the reaction of Josiah. Deuteronomy 18:3 ff. specifies the rights and privileges of the priests and Levites, who were to occupy such an exalted position that they are compared with judges in the dignity they were to enjoy (Deuteronomy 17:9; 19:17). Deuteronomy 18:6 outlines the rights of the countryside Levites; but this is significantly contradicted in 2 Kings 23:9, and even more so in the later writing of Ezekiel (44:15), in which only the Zadokite priests are to enjoy the full rights and privileges of priesthood. Such difficulties show the futility of facile, schematic solutions.

Also applicable to Josiah's reform might be Deuteronomy 18:15-22, where it is stated that the prophets are to be obeyed if their messages prove to conform with objective truth. 18:10 might be applicable because of the prohibition against human sacrifice and magic, both of which Josiah abolished. However, the legislation calling for the freeing of Hebrew slaves in the Sabbatical Year was not even attempted by Josiah. The first recorded attempt to enforce it was in the reign of Zedekiah (Jeremiah 34:12-16).

The reform whereby the cult and residence of God was limited to one city was appropriate to and feasible in a small city state. Aside from cultic matters, the actual enforcement of the Law came as a result of the Exile, and we find it in effect only after the Exile when it becomes an integral part of Judaism down to modern times.

The growing emphasis on the Law meant in the long run a curbing of the prophetic spirit; and ultimately the establishment of the Law did away with the acceptance of prophecy as a living institution. However, it is a mistake to shut our eyes to the prophetic spirit in many parts of the Law such as the Ten Commandments, the section beginning "Hear, O Israel" and in admonitions such as those to treat neighbors and foreigners as we would be treated.

One of the most sweeping effects of Josiah's reform was the change of the nation into a church. The community, instead of being a normal body politic, with well rounded national life, became a religious entity. Only since 1948 A.D., when the modern state of Israel came into existence, was the process reversed by the change back from church to nationhood.

A number of prophets flourished during the reign of Josiah. One of them was Zephaniah who predicted God would wipe Baalism and astral worship out of the land of Judah. Thus the prophetic movement helped lead up to the reform. Zephaniah also stresses the Day of Yahwe and prophesies against all the nations round about, including Assyria, which was the most hated one of all, because it was the most powerful and oppressive. Zephaniah 3:9 states the ideal whereby in the End of Days all nations would have one language and one God. Since that God is Yahwe, the Judean ideal would be extended to all mankind. Universality was triumphing over narrow nationalism, at least in the highest strata of Judah's prophets.

Zephaniah 3:12 predicts that the sole survivors who were to have a happy future in Zion, are the poor and humble who trust in Yahwe. The emphasis on "in Zion" had grown since the year 701 and there was a strong feeling among the people and among most of the prophets that Zion would be spared and be the scene of the happy future. It was on this point that the prophets and Jerusalem priesthood could agree, however much they might differ on other matters. This agreement between two groups of religious leaders con-

tributed to the success of Josiah's reform. Few were bothered
by philosophical problems such as the conflict between Yahwe
as the local God of Zion, and Yahwe the World God. And if
we examine the question, we shall see that the conflict does
not really exist; for the ruler of a great empire can reside in
a localized capital. Just as the Assyrian King resided in
Nineveh or a Babylonian king resided in Babylon, while
claiming world dominion; why can not Yahwe, Who rules
the Universe, choose as His capital the Davidic city of Zion?

Since 701 B.C. things had been generally quiet throughout
the Assyrian Empire. The most notable exception was
Babylon, where there was the feeling that Babylon should be
the center of world dominion and hence it was unfitting in
the eyes of gods and men, that Babylon should be subservient
to Assyria. When Sennacherib was slain, his son Esarhaddon
came to the throne and decided to rebuild Babylon and appease the population. His policy went hand in hand, as was
usually the case, with a theology. He held that the gods had
been angry with Merodach-baladan for transporting the
treasures of the Babylonian temples to Elam; but now that
they could be recovered and the city reestablished, the gods
might be conciliated and Babylon might enjoy prosperity
again. It is interesting to note that he resettled the remnant
of Babylon in their old city and restored all their old privileges. Thus we witness a forerunner of the restoration to
Zion.

During Esarhaddon's reign, the Phoenicians, the Edomites,
the Arabs and the Egyptians staged a revolt, from which
Judah remained aloof and therefore suffered no Assyrian
retribution.

Esarhaddon did what none of his predecessors had done;
he conquered Egypt and took the title of King of Lower
Egypt, King of Upper Egypt and King of Ethiopia. His

victories made him head of a world empire including Egypt, Syria and islands such as Cyprus.

The Phoenician cities of Sidon and Tyre revolted in concert with the mulatto Tirhakah of Ethiopia, who again came to the fore and struck for the independence of the Nile Valley. This obliged Esarhaddon to return to Egypt in 671 B.C. His Arab allies helped him with water and supplies en route, especially in the dry Negeb south of Judah. He reached Memphis where the local princes willingly yielded to him, partly because they disliked the rule of the Ethiopian, who, according to Egyptian prejudices, was a barbarian.

There was still more trouble in Egypt in 669, when Esarhaddon headed for that land but died on the way. His successor Assurbanipal is one of the most interesting kings in world history. He was too civilized to concentrate his efforts on war. His father Esarhaddon had already shown signs of reluctance to take part in battles and stayed home much of the time. Assurbanipal sent his Turtan (second-in-command) to Egypt with heavy forces to be further reinforced by Syrian contingents. The Egyptians by this time had learned that the Ethiopians, even though they were negroid, belonged to the same general culture as the Egyptians and were preferable to the brutal and completely alien Assyrians. Upon the invasion of Assurbanipal's army, Tirhakah fled south. Assurbanipal pursued a policy of appeasement toward Egypt. After summoning the Egyptian prince Necho as a captive to Assyria, he sent him back to the city of Sais where Necho assumed the throne (Twenty-sixth Dynasty).

Tirhakah died in 664 B.C. to be succeeded by his elderly nephew Tenuatamon, who managed to reach Memphis, but upon the approach of the Assyrian armies retreated southward to Thebes. The Assyrians pursued him and destroyed Thebes in 660 B.C., which made a deep impression on the ancient Near East. Thus when the prophet Nahum (3:8), who predicted the downfall of Assyria, wants to point out that Assyria deserves the fate that was in store for her, he asks rhetorically: "Are you better than No-Amon (= Thebes)?"

The defeats that the Egyptians suffered under their Ethiopian leaders had meant the end of the Amon World Empire, which had been a fiction for a long time but was now reduced to such limited territory on the Upper Nile that it had to relinquish its pretensions. Vestigially, however, it held on for some centuries as a local religious state in its remote southern refuge.

Assyria was mistress of a famed world empire and was universally hated for that reason. Nahum is the best example of a writer in this period who expresses that hatred and predicted the fall that everyone wished Assyria.

At heart, Assurbanipal, who was anything but a warrior, loved peaceful pursuits. He was from early youth a scholar. He was trained as a scribe and his fondest project may well have been the establishment of his great Nineveh library, which was unearthed by the British in the nineteenth century, and whose tablets provide us with much of what we know of Babylonian and Assyrian civilization. He sent scribes around to copy ancient texts of all kinds so that their transcripts have been preserved for us.

Assurbanipal considered himself divinely appointed by Assur, the god of Assyria, to rule over the world. Therefore anyone who rebelled against him was guilty of heresy as well as treason and so was treated in the cruelest fashion.

His building operations were extensive and of fine quality. The art of this period was enriched by contacts from the West and from Egypt. Greater compositions, especially in relief, were now attempted than ever before. These reliefs have several levels set on different horizontal lines, so that the figures convey a feeling of depth unequaled in earlier

Assyrian reliefs. The animals of this period are particularly
fine when they do not hark back to a stereotyped tradition.
Thus the wounded animals expressing pain in the hunting
scenes are among the finest representations in world art,
comparing favorably with animal representations at their
best in Egypt.

With Assurbanipal Assyrian civilization reached its apex.
There was Egyptian influence, but within the canons of
Assyrian drawing and manner. Moreover, Assyrian concep-
tions of composition were bolder than the more traditional
Egyptians would attempt. But it is also interesting that this
high point of refinement in Assyrian civilization came just
before the downfall of Assyria: a development not rare in
world history.

Assurbanipal was no longer King of Babylonia by 626
B.C., which means either that he died by that time or that the
Babylonians had shaken off Assyrian domination. The new
dynasty in Babylon is called the Chaldean or Neo-Babylonian;
its first great figure is Nabopolassar. In 616 B.C. the Babylonians and Medes, under their respective kings Nabopolassar
and Cyaxares, united to crush Assyria. The union was
solemnized by the marriage of the Babylonian crown prince,
Nebuchadnezzar, and the daughter of the Median king. The
united armies vanquished the city of Assur in 614; and
Nineveh, after bitter resistance, in 612. All four historic
capitals were soon in ruins and have not since been resettled.
The mightiest nation the world had ever known was annihi-
lated. The cruel fate of Carthage at Roman hands was only
the destruction of a single city. But Assyria had been a
whole nation dominating the world and now it was gone
without any survival. Thus Xenophon saw the ruins of Calah
two centuries later without realizing it had been the capital
of a great nation. Never was a dire prediction more literally
fulfilled than Nahum's prophecy against Assyria.

Hatred of Assyria made the rejoicing universal. The spoils were divided. The Medes got the Upper Tigris country; the Babylonians won West Mesopotamia and Syria so that the civilized Semitic areas fell to them.

Media, with its share of Assyrian territory north, east and west of the Tigris became for a time the world's greatest empire. Media happens to be the least known of the large empires of the ancient East. Its contribution to the later Achaemenian Empire of the Medes and Persians was enormous. Media had already absorbed a considerable degree of Accadian civilization which it integrated with its native Iranian heritage. The combination was incorporated when Cyrus of Persia conquered Media to form the Achaemenian Empire. The capital of Media was Ecbatana, the site of the modern city of Hamadan in Iran. The ancient citadel is fortunately an unoccupied mound overlooking the city; so it is accessible for excavation.

The Median Empire extended into Asia Minor, where it came to grips with the kingdom of Lydia. The latter had made a contribution of wide practical significance for commerce. Around the middle of the seventh century B.C. coinage was introduced in Lydia. Prior to coinage, business transactions were by barter. While gold and silver bars and rings had long been known, the seller always had to check their weight and purity to avoid being "shortchanged." Accordingly the metal was more akin to a commodity than to currency.

Early coinage was not the prerogative of only the emperor. The kings and governors of the component parts of the empire could also issue coinage.

The advantages of coinage to trade were considerable. Coinage placed the responsibility for the value of the metal on the ruler, thus relieving the merchant. Moreover, since the ruler established his coinage as a compulsory medium of exchange in his territory, business practices were simplified. Coined currency did not however oust the older system of barter in the East. Both systems continued to exist side by side.

In addition to the monarchs of Babylonia and Media, another king made a bid for power upon the collapse of Assyria. That was Pharaoh Necho II (609-595 B.C.), who wanted Palestine and Syria as his share. The Judeans, however, had other ideas on the subject and wished at long last to have their independence and not to be part of another empire. Necho marched through Palestine on his way to the Euphrates, to join forces with Assuruballit, the Assyrian who was trying to reconstitute the shattered empire from a temporary capital in Haran. The situation is reflected, though with insufficient detail, in 2 Kings 23:29.[13]

The Syrian provinces yielded to Necho but the Judeans under Josiah would not submit. In trying to block Necho at the city of Megiddo, which was well outside Judean territory,[14] Josiah lost his life. His successor Jehoahaz was anointed king by "the people of the land" (2 Kings 23:30), attesting the tradition of democracy whereby the common people had a say in the highest policies including the coronation of kings. Jehoahaz lasted only three months; for Necho arrested and dispatched him to Egypt, crowning another prince in his stead as Egyptian vassal over Judah. That prince was Eliakim, whose name the Pharaoh changed to Jehoiakim on the occasion. A moderate tribute was imposed on the country: a hundred talents of silver and one of gold,

---

[13] The Hebrew text means Necho was going to help the Assyrian King against the Babylonian menace. It is commonly misunderstood to mean that Necho was opposing the Assyrian.

[14] Between the collapse of Assyria and the Babylonian conquest of Canaan, Israelite territory may have fallen within the Judean sphere of influence.

which Jehoiakim raised by taxing citizens, each according to his ability to pay (verse 33).

Jeremiah (46:2) records that Necho opposed Nebuchadnezzar at Carchemish in the year 605/4 B.C. Nebuchadnezzar scored a victory and proceeded to the Egyptian border so that Judah was now within the confines of the Neo-Babylonian Empire (2 Kings 24:7).

Jeremiah's (25:9) prediction that the kingdoms of Syria would be destroyed did not have to be fulfilled. They yielded to Nebuchadnezzar without a struggle. (It may not be out of place to note here that it is not the fulfilment but the nonfulfilment of a prophecy that establishes its historic authenticity; though fulfilment does not prove the reverse.)

Fortunately for the exact chronology of the later kings of Judah, Jeremiah gives double datings as in 25:1 where he informs us that the first year of Nebuchadnezzar is the fourth year of Jehoiakim. Jeremiah's ministry began in Josiah's reign and ended after the destruction of Jerusalem, which took place in 586 B.C. His synchronisms put the period from Josiah to the end of Judean independence on an exact chronological basis.

Jehoiakim remained a vassal of Nebuchadnezzar for three years and then rebelled (2 Kings 24:1) in the spirit of independence and defiance wherewith the Judeans wanted to be masters of their own destiny.

Jeremiah began to preach in 626 upon feeling his call in Josiah's reign. The prophet tells us he would gladly have evaded his unpleasant mission if he possibly could, but the urge was irresistible. As we can see in Jeremiah, chapters 7 and following, the prophet took a view opposed to that of the majority. He felt that only ethical Yahwism, and not the Temple or the cult, could save the country. It was for that reason that he saw dismal destruction in store not only for Judah but for Jerusalem and the Temple. Corruption pervaded the nation. Trust in the outer forms of the cult could not mend this for the simple reason that God wanted what Amos had told the people and not what the priests of the Temple, or any other sanctuary, desired.

Jeremiah was not alone in predicting the downfall of the capital. There was another prophet, Uriah,[15] who had fled to Egypt, fearing the consequences of his doctrine; but the Egyptians turned him back to Judah[16] where he was put to death (see Jeremiah 26:20-23). Jeremiah saw that Nebuchadnezzar would prevail and was politically realistic enough to state that vassaldom was the only practical course and that the idea of independence was an illusion.

Jeremiah (11:13) proclaimed that the number of Judean cities was the number of the Judean gods; that is to say, the Yahwe worshiped at the high-places was not Yahwe at all; for such Yahwism was no different from the Baalism of the Canaanites whereby each town had its Baal.[17] Cult objects meant nothing to Jeremiah; in 3:16 he claims that even the holy ark was no source of protection. For him, true religion was ethical and moral. He finds that Judah was worse than Israel (3:11) and therefore a just God would see to it that Judah shared the fate of Israel. But for the common people, the greater their distress, the greater their hope. When Assyria was at its height, Nahum confidently predicted that Assyria would perish but that Judah would be saved. Subsequently, Habakkuk, when Babylon ruled, predicted that God would destroy Babylon and save Judah.

Jeremiah's contemporary, the prophet Hananiah, prophesied in 593 the imminent fall of Babylon. Jeremiah took the

---

[15] Like most Hebrew prophets, Uriah has not left writings behind him.

[16] The extradition of political refugees (which is included in the treaty between Ramses II and Hattusil) may have been according to a pact between Judah and Egypt, which were now allies.

[17] Jeremiah thus realized the distinction between strict monotheism and local pluralism.

unpopular viewpoint and contradicted him. But with all the prophets, we meet with the common theme of ultimate hope; an unshakable belief in a remnant that would be saved for the Messianic Age; a conviction that Judeans would survive their temporal masters. It has been this conviction that has enabled the Jews to withstand all the trials of history, whereas all their oppressors have one by one disappeared from the creative continuity of civilization.

To return to the march of political and military events: Egypt was in no condition to aid Jehoiakim in his move for independence for all Canaan was in Nebuchadnezzar's hands down to the Egyptian border (2 Kings 24:7). Jehoiakim died, leaving his eighteen-year-old son Jehoiachin (also called Coniah and Jechonias) on the throne to face Nebuchadnezzar's besieging army. After a reign of only three months, the young king capitulated and was carried off into exile to Babylon in 597 B.C. Although Nebuchadnezzar set another member of the Davidic House (Mattaniah, whose name Nebuchadnezzar changed to Zedekiah) on the throne of Judah, Judeo-Christian tradition considers Jehoiachin the legitimate king through whom the Messiah must come (see Matthew 1:11-12). In 597 the Temple treasures were taken to Babylon as booty. The cream of the population was skimmed off and exiled to Babylon. Seven thousand warriors and one thousand artisans were among the ten thousand Judean exiles (2 Kings 24:8-16).

Tablets from Babylon have come to light containing memoranda of rations issued to Jehoiachin and other Judean princes. These documents are of particular interest because they also record rations for artisans of other Canaanite nations. Thus the Judean Exile fits into Nebuchadnezzar's policy of transporting talent from conquered areas to aid in the building program he energetically pursued in Babylonia. His father, Nabopolassar, had begun to repair the damage that

Sennacherib had wrought in Babylonia—damage that Esar-haddon had only repaired in part—and that Assurbanipal had aggravated in suppressing the Babylonian insurrection under his own brother Shamash-shum-ukin.

Nebuchadnezzar boasts very little of his conquests and em-pire. In his own inscriptions, he stresses his constructive work in his homeland. By irrigation and building, he enriched and embellished his country. Prominent among his pious works were the restoration of Esagila, Marduk's temple in Babylon, and Ezida, Nebo's temple in Borsippa. His energy was amaz-ing for any age, including our own. The fact that he erected a palace in fifteen days is not only claimed in his own texts but corroborated in the Greek writings of Berossus. The Hanging Gardens of Babylon (one of the Seven Wonders of antiquity) were his work (rather than Queen Semiramis's, as Herodotus reports). He fortified Babylon with two walls. A stream ran through the city dividing it into two parts con-nected by a bridge whose beams could be removed by night so that if one half of the city fell into hostile hands, the other half could be defended. The stream was walled for some dis-tance from the city to enhance the defenses. The farthest canal to the north, joining the Tigris and Euphrates Rivers, was also walled against Median invasion.

Nebuchadnezzar experienced comparatively little opposi-tion from his empire, whose people had long been accustomed to subservience and for whom the new regime meant only a change of masters. Trade was the better because of the empire. When any of the nomadic Arabs grew restive, Nebuchad-nezzar knew how to quell them (Jeremiah 49:28-33) so that they were brought back into line. Armenian merchants came down the rivers to trade in Babylonia. Ships on the Persian Gulf carried goods between Babylonia and East Arabia. Nebu-chadnezzar so established Babylon that it (or its local successor) remained more or less the commercial capital of the world until the Mongol Invasions.

In foreign affairs, Egypt came after Media as a source of concern for Nebuchadnezzar. The Pharaoh could not view with complacence the loss of Canaanite trade, with which Egypt's prosperity is linked. Therefore Egypt was inciting the states of Canaan to revolt against Babylonia. Nebuchadnezzar wisely extended his empire to the Egyptian border but did not exhaust his resources by attempting to absorb Egypt as Sargonid Assyria had done.[18]

The removal of the aristocracy and talented elements of Judah had produced a social revolution. The poor who had been left behind were able to buy the abandoned land and other possessions of the exiles cheaply. Nebuchadnezzar might have speciously reasoned that the *nouveaux riches* of Judah would be satisfied with the economic and social advantages they had come by so easily because of his policies. But one factor nullified such a view: The Judeans still trusted in Yahwe, Who unlike the other gods of the conquered nations could not be bodily carried off because He alone of the gods had no image. Optimists like Hananiah predicted the early return of the exiles including Jehoiachin. Many of the exiles shared this optimism; but not Jeremiah (chapter 29), who wrote to Babylon assuring the exiles that their stay would be long and that they should settle down to a sound communal life as loyal Babylonian subjects.

Pharaoh Psammetichus II (593-588 B.C.) directed most of his foreign activities to Ethiopia, not Canaan. But when Pharaoh Hophra, who was crowned in 588, resumed a policy of interfering in Canaanite affairs, Nebuchadnezzar returned to Canaan in 587. Syria yielded to him to avoid a hopeless war. Jeremiah advocated surrender to Nebuchadnezzar,

[18] Not realizing Nebuchadnezzar's moderation in foreign policy, Jeremiah and Ezekiel incorrectly prophesied the ruin of Egypt.

whom he regarded as the instrument of Yahwe's wrath. The
Jerusalemites looked upon Jeremiah as a defeatist and would
have killed him had not Zedekiah rescued him from their
hands. It is possible that the King's kindly feelings toward the
Prophet were in part prompted in gratitude for Jeremiah's
discouragement of those who looked to Jehoiachin's return,
which would have meant Zedekiah's dethronement.

There is a new source for the last days of Judah. Eighteen
ostraca, mostly military letters, were found in 1935, and three
more in 1938, at Lachish. The texts were written for units of
the Judean army around Lachish and Azekah, the last provincial cities to hold out against the Babylonian invaders.
The documents show that Yahwism was firmly entrenched.
Not only are the personal names Yahwistic but the officers
swear "by the life of Yahwe" as is prescribed by orthodox
biblical religion. The Lachish letters mention the activity of
prophets; for oracles were still sought for guidance in military
tactics. The texts deal tersely with signal communications and
intelligence reports. Some of the ostraca reflect the eternal
situation of officers in the field trying to square themselves
with headquarters. That Egypt had a hand in the Judean
revolt is reflected by a reference to a Judean mission to Egypt.

Lachish and Azekah fell leaving Jerusalem alone to resist.
The Babylonians at last breached the walls of the capital and
Zedekiah attempted to escape through the gap. He was over-
taken, captured and blinded and many of his followers were
killed. Between thirty and forty thousand additional exiles
were carried off to Babylon leaving little besides the poorest
in Judah. Jerusalem and the Temple were destroyed. Judea
has still not recovered fully from the blow, for many of the
towns devastated in that war are still barren mounds. It was
Jeremiah (30:18) who predicted that "the city will be rebuilt
on its mound." For many Judean towns, Jeremiah's prophecy
is about to be fulfilled only in our own time by the gathering

in of the exiles after 2500 years. While the needs of the living must take priority over historical studies, it is to be hoped that the main mounds will be excavated before they are covered by new settlements which will render them inaccessible to investigation. That Israel will cooperate with archeologists in every reasonable way, is indicated by the activities of the Department of Antiquities under the directorship of my friend, Samuel Yeivin, supported by an enlightened public conscious of its history.

Jeremiah, whose record was regarded with favor by the conquerors, was allowed to remain in Judah. The Judean Gedaliah was made governor of the province of Babylonia. Between the lines of the Bible, it is clear that Judean patriots regarded him as a collaborationist.[19] Ishmael, a member of the Davidic House, who had been harbored and helped by the King of Ammon, treacherously slew Gedaliah and his followers. Fearing reprisals for his violence and rebellion, Ishmael and his men fled to Egypt, carrying Jeremiah off with them. No more is known of the great prophet.

Few of the other Canaanite states resisted Babylonia. King Ithobaal II of Tyre withstood a long siege lasting from 585 to 573 B.C. and while the city island was not actually captured or occupied by the Babylonians, the Tyrians came to terms with Nebuchadnezzar, surrendered its royal princes as hostages, and became part of the Babylonian System.

[19] It was H. L. Ginsberg, who first called this to my attention.

# Chapter XVI

# EXILE AND RESTORATION

AMASIS who became Pharaoh in 569 B.C., again stirred up the Canaanite states to revolt against Nebuchadnezzar, who was thus obliged to return to the West, where he restored order and reestablished his boundary at the Egyptian frontier.

Babylonia had long depended on the personality of Nebuchadnezzar rather than on well balanced national strength. Therefore, when he died, collapse set in relentlessly. He was succeeded by his son Evil-Merodach, who reigned only from 561 to 559. The latter's brother-in-law Nergalsharezer then came to the throne but lasted only until 556. Labashi-Marduk (son of Nergalsharezer) was crowned but was soon deposed by the courtiers who placed on the throne Nabonidus, who was not of royal extraction. For the most part Nabonidus's reign was peaceful. He spent most of his career rebuilding cities other than Babylon; including the northern Haran, where he restored the temple of the moon-god Sin. The propaganda of Cyrus, who vanquished Babylon in 539 B.C., is of interest for the view it expresses about Nabonidus. Cyrus accuses Nabonidus of having neglected Marduk, the great universal god. Furthermore, Nabonidus, in the course of Cyrus's invasion, had offended the pantheon by exiling the various gods to Babylon. (From Nabonidus's viewpoint, the step had been taken to save the gods from falling into the hands of the enemy and to keep the gods on Nabonidus's side.) Marduk therefore summoned Cyrus to restore the gods to their rightful shrines. Aside from the way this explains Cyrus's restoration of Yahwism on Zion, it shows the monotheistic undercurrent of the times : Marduk is identified with the supreme deity that governs world history.

Meanwhile there had been developments in Egypt. Hophra had been solicited by the Libyans west of the Delta to rescue them from the Greeks who had founded Cyrene in 630 B.C. and had ever since been enlarging their coastal holdings. The Egyptian army fared badly, although the Greek mercenaries in Pharaoh's service remained loyal. The disgruntled army chose Amasis as Pharaoh (in 569, as we have already noted). It is to be observed that although he was fighting the Greeks of Cyrene, he was an admirer of Greek culture. The emergence of the Greeks was destined to terminate the history of the ancient Near East within two and a half centuries.

The faith of the Jews in Yahwe had been strengthened by the Exile and concomitant misfortunes because Yahwe's prophets had predicted them. Down to the Exile the rank and file of the Judeans adhered to a localistic religion, for the orthodox view maintained the exclusive legitimacy of the Jerusalem cult. Exile, however, had forced upon the Jews the belief in the universality of Yahwe, Who would follow them wherever they might wander. Thus their loss of land and Temple had forced the Jewish people as a whole to embrace a universal concept of God that had formerly been the concept of only a few select leaders.

The Jews and the other national groups that were now part of the Babylonian Empire, no longer had any political power. They were even losing their national languages and adopting Aramaic. Exile, trade and service in the Babylonian army and government also resulted in some intermarriage. Yet people tended to call themselves by their ancestors' nationality. Thus there were still the Judeans, albeit without political power, without their own soil, without their own spoken language. Such nationalities resolved themselves into religious communities.

The theological universality of the age ran parallel with the theological individuality of each nation. All national groups tended to identify their particular god with the one and only cosmic deity who ruled the universe. The conflicting pretensions of all the national groups led to missionizing for the propagation of one's own national cult or theology. Zoroastrianism, though it started in Iran, was a missionizing religion from the start. But Judaism first became missionizing in the sixth century B.C. under the impact of the Exile milieu.

The age of propagandizing ideas may have given an impetus to wisdom literature, whereby the god-fearing sages of Egypt and Western Asia set forth the principles of the good life in the form of proverbs. Although there is a timelessness and transcendence of national boundaries in wisdom literature that often make it difficult to localize and to date, it is possible that some of the wisdom literature in the Bible was composed or recast in this era.

Exile had replaced the physical bonds between men and god with a personal bond whose incorporeal character made it indestructible. It is the latter quality, fully attained by Judaism in the sixth century, that has imparted lasting vigor to Judaism and its daughter religions: Christianity and Islam.

As all the gods tended to be identified with Re in Egypt since the Old Kingdom, now in the sixth century all national gods throughout the Near East tended to be identified with the divine World Ruler. Thus in Syria, Baal Shamen ("Lord of Heaven"), so identified, was fostered more than ever before. In Mesopotamia, the Jews and their newly won converts so identified Yahwe. Since all great or national gods were thus identified, the cultic practices became more and more important to the masses who lack the sophistication for appreciating lofty ethical concepts and theological refinements. The cults had not only their own distinctive sacrifices but also their own codes of purity.

The oppressed victims of exile and dislocation turned more and more to eschatological ideas whereby they would enjoy personal salvation in paradise. The preëxilic prophets had not been concerned with salvation for the individual but rather for the nation. Weary from the vicissitudes of cruel history people sought comfort in eschatology which offered the welcome illusion of the end of the historic process. Zoroastrianism made a contribution to eschatology in the basic tenet that the present conflict between good and evil would be resolved in the end of days by the eternal victory of the good.

It is against the above background of the sixth-century scene that all the religions of the East are to be evaluated down to the Greek period. Judaism happens to be not only historically the most important, but also the best recorded, of those religions.

A return to Judah would at best be most difficult. Not only would the Jews have to experience the miracle of getting back from afar, but the land had been occupied by encroaching neighbors who partially filled the vacuum left by the exiles. (The extent of the vacuum is attested not only by the biblical account but also by the numerous mounds never resettled since 586.) And yet, despite all the discouraging odds, the Jews could not regard their exilic status as permanent. Just as the prophets had foretold their defeat and exile, they had also predicted the return of the remnant. The fulfilment of the one, guaranteed that of the other. Besides, if God would not restore this remnant as He had promised, that would mean the triumph of the heathen over Yahwe—which was unthinkable.

The historic cultic religion of Yahwe had ceased because sacrifice was legitimate only in the Jerusalem Temple. Accordingly, prayer, the sabbath and circumcision received

added prominence. The institution of the decentralized syna-
gogue, in which prayer took the place of sacrifice, dates to
this period. Yearning for Zion while exiled by the waters of
Babylon evoked some of the finest psalms in the Psalter.

The first political sign that encouraged the exiles was in
561 B.C. when Evil-Merodach elevated Jehoiachin and treated
him with respect.

The great prophet of the Exile is Ezekiel, the architect of
the Restoration. The first verse of his book contains a date in
terms of Jehoiachin's exile. The fortieth chapter opens with
a double date in terms of the first exile (597) and the destruction of Jerusalem (586). Ezekiel, mindful of his nation's
plight was not merely looking back at past woes. Chapters 40
to 48 are the blueprint for the New Jerusalem of the Restoration. With Ezekiel, Jewish Apocalyptic comes into its own.
The exposition of extravagant visions as keys to the future
had modest origins in the remote past. Ezekiel made Apocalyptic a major form of religious expression in Judaism. It was
to become the essence of books in both Testaments—such as
Daniel and Revelation—let alone a host of books (still in the
course of discovery) among what is known as Apocrypha and
Pseudepigrapha.[1]

Like the former prophets, Ezekiel was concerned with
spiritual values and divine justice. He could not conceive of
the just God punishing his contemporaries for the sins of their
ancestors. For Ezekiel, both the living and their ancestors
were alike guilty for the plight of the Judeans. Salvation was
coming but not for the sake of the guilty living or the guilty
dead. Salvation for Judah was inescapable for the sake of
God's own name. The heathen had to be shown that God was
supreme and looked after those who believed in Him. The

---

[1] See R. H. Charles, *The Apocrypha and Pseudepigrapha of the Old
Testament*, Oxford, 1913. Additional pseudepigrapha have been found
recently in the cave of Ain Feshkha near the Dead Sea.

return to Zion was thus a necessary consequence of God's nature.

Ezekiel mapped out the construction of the Second Temple and the regulations of its priesthood, which was limited to the descendants of Zadok. Other priestly families, such as those that had been associated with the high-places, were to be lowered in rank to Levites. While the Zadokite priests were to serve God, the Levites were (so to speak) to serve the priests. (This subordinate role of the Levite, made it hard to round up levitical volunteers, when the restoration came.) Ezekiel laid great stress on the Temple rituals and laws of purity, particularly the purity of the priests, who had to be pure for their sacred duties. Unlike the other prophets, Ezekiel emphasizes the cult as well as ethics and morals. Postexilic Judaism, whose architect he was, was destined long to remain a religious community rather than a political entity.

The Age was one of restorations. Nabonidus was restoring ancient cults all through his Mesopotamian Empire. The Twenty-sixth (or Saite) Dynasty in Egypt was devoted to reviving the glories of the great Eighteenth Dynasty. Into this pattern fit the Judeans who aimed at restoring the Davidic Dynasty on Zion.

The restoration came sooner and more suddenly than any one expected. There would have been no Zionist restoration under the Neo-Babylonian Empire. But in 539 Cyrus the Great conquered Babylon without shooting a single arrow. The Babylonian Empire disappeared and the Achaemenian Empire ruled the East down to the Egyptian frontier. Cyrus's policy of restoring exiled men and gods fulfilled the Jews' desire to return home. In 538 Cyrus issued an edict that Jewish exiles could return with the sacred vessels (taken from the First Temple by Nebuchadnezzar) and with royal permission to construct a Second Temple on Zion (Ezra 1). Dreams had come true. 42,360 Judeans plus 7337 slaves and 200 singers,[2] and livestock[3] returned to Judah (Ezra 2:64-67). Shesh-bazzar, the Prince of Judah (Ezra 1:8), was made the Persian governor of Judah and the predicted restoration was at hand.

The prophet of the return is the author of chapters 40-55 in Isaiah.[4] He offers consolation with such buoyancy of spirit that he is the most blithe author in the Bible and perhaps in all religious literature. Earlier prophets had scolded the people for their backsliding. But Deutero-Isaiah (as the prophet is called in scholarly literature) offers only a joyous message. Israel's mission is to convert all the gentiles. The whole world including Cyrus (whom he calls the anointed of the Lord in 45:1) will know that Yahwe is supreme and has alone shaped history. For Deutero-Isaiah there is no issue of Yahwe versus other gods, but only of Yahwe versus lifeless idols made by men's hands. Yahwe, the God of Israel must become, through missionizing, the God of all mankind. Jewish missionizing had presumably already won converts some of whom went to Zion with the returning exiles.

The change of the nation into a church inevitably brought with it disappointment to those who had looked for a glorious restoration of a Judean Kingdom which would be the center of world affairs, and to which all the nations of the earth would submit, and whose people would be the one people that all the others would join.

[2] The low status of the singers is reflected in their being listed after the slaves. The gatekeepers and *nethinim* were also petty Temple personnel of low status (note their position in Ezra 2:70).

[3] Domestic animals are often included in ancient censuses; e.g., Ugaritic texts 305:4; 329:18-19.

[4] Different compositions by different authors were often combined by the Hebrews. The different collections that make up the Book of Proverbs are fortunately supplied with titles. Frequently, however, titles are omitted (e.g., Genesis 1:1). It may be that Isaiah 40—55 was attached to 1—39 because of the Messianic theme they have in common.

The returning exiles found Judah badly run down in the half century of desolation that followed the catastrophe of 586. Remnants of clans in the south gladly attached themselves to the returnees, not just for the help they could give but more especially for the protection they would thereby receive. There had encroached upon Judean soil squatters from the surrounding peoples such as the Edomites, Moabites, Ammonites, Philistines and particularly the Samaritans. The latter were specially hostile, partly in reaction to Judean exclusiveness which prevented the returnees from embracing the Samaritans into the orthodox fold. The prophesied remnant that was to usher in and preside over the Messianic Age did not have to be large but it did have to be pure and consist of the select few of the Chosen People who had remained true to Yahwe. While this ideal was not adhered to strictly, it did contribute to the Judean rejection of the Samaritans. (There were, indeed, some *gerim,* that is people who, though not of pure Judean extraction, identified themselves with the Judeans, by whom they were accepted.)

The towns had each a group of elders with authority in local affairs. These elders could on occasion convoke popular assemblies. One tenth of the men were drafted by lot for service in Jerusalem, to shoulder the onerous duties of soldiering as well as building. Their numbers were augmented by gallant volunteers [5] so that in all about three thousand men devoted themselves to the important task of restoring unhappy Jerusalem to a fitting capital.

The Highpriest in Jerusalem was Jeshua, the grandson of Seraiah who had served as the last Highpriest in the First Temple prior to the destruction in 586. Building operations went ahead in spite of the havoc wrought by drought and

---

[5] Unless the word "volunteers" (Nehemiah 11:2) is a euphemism for "draftees," much as we call soldiers "enlisted men" even though they be drafted. (The reconstruction above is composite for about 530-430.)

famine (Haggai 1:6, 10 ff.; 2:16 ff.). The painful difficulties that confronted the returned remnant made it obvious that salvation was not yet at hand. Patience may have been inspired by the view that seventy years (Zechariah 1:12) would intervene between the disaster of 586 and the real Restoration, which would therefore first come around 516.

Shortly after Cyrus conquered Babylon, he installed his son Cambyses as governor in Babylonia. Thus Cambyses, as crown prince, gained valuable experience in administration. When Cyrus lost his life in 528 during a military campaign, Cambyses became king and in keeping with the customs of his land and people, he married his own sisters Atossa and Roxana.

Cambyses set himself to execute the great unfinished project of his father: the conquest of Egypt. Amasis had been succeeded by Psammetichus III, who had many Greek allies. However, Greek loyalties were divided and some Greeks gave aid to Cambyses. The Phoenician cities were brought effectively into the Persian sphere and the Nabatean Arabs supplied water for Cambyses' troops in the hazardous desert that separated Judah and Egypt.

The Judeans probably cooperated with Cambyses and in no case placed obstacles in his way. Indeed Cyrus may have facilitated the Restoration to Zion with a view to setting up a friendly state on the Egyptian border that would some day aid his armies in conquering the Nile. Relations between the Achaemenian government and the Jews were always good; certainly at this time as we shall soon see. Yet no reference to Cambyses exists in the Bible or in Jewish tradition. The reason is probably that he did not affect Judean welfare.

The decisive battle was fought at Pelusium in the northeast part of the Delta. The end of Egyptian autonomy came in 525 when Cambyses captured Memphis. The conqueror wanted to push on to Carthage but his Phoenician allies refused to turn against their daughter colony.[6] Instead, Cambyses marched to Ethiopia. En route he found the colony of Jews at Elephantine, an island in the Upper Nile, where a temple to Yahu (= Yahwe) was already in existence.[7] Upon Cambyses' conquest the colony became a military outpost of the Achaemenian Empire. Those Jews remained faithful to their Iranian masters in spite of dire difficulties with the resentful native population. They were also faithful to their ancestral God. The Elephantine Jews have left an important group of fifth century B.C. Aramaic papyri which we shall have occasion to discuss presently.

Cambyses became a Pharaoh and is so depicted on Egyptian monuments. He has also left hieroglyphic texts in the Egyptian manner. Though he favored some Egyptian temples, he reduced the income of many others, thus incurring the hatred of their priests and devotees.

In 522 B.C., Cambyses' kinsman Darius, then only twenty-eight years old, served Cambyses as a spearbearer in Egypt. In that eventful year Cambyses left Egypt for home. Cambyses' brother Smerdis (or a Magian named Gaumata who impersonated Smerdis whom Cambyses had slain—according

[6] Friction between a mother country and its offshoots does not mean that one would be willing to attack the other. Frequently the awareness of kinship is stronger than all other considerations. It was probably for such a cause that Jeroboam II (like several other strong kings of Israel) never harmed Judah, although he vanquished his neighbors on virtually every side and could easily have conquered Judah, as far as military considerations went. Friction between Britain and her English-speaking dominions does not mean that the dominions will not stand by the mother country in a crisis. Nor does the accumulation of differences between Britain and the U.S.A. mean that they will not support each other with blood in any serious war for the foreseeable future. Only ignorance of this basic historical fact could have misled the Axis into trying to secure U.S.A. neutrality early in World War II by offering the U.S.A. a free-hand in (i.e., the conquest of) Canada, Australia and New Zealand. One does not stab his mother in the back even for material advantage.

[7] Perhaps the colony had been founded by Judeans who fled from Nebuchadnezzar's invasion and conquest. Egypt and Judah were at that time allies.

to Darius's account) revolted and seized the throne. By canceling three years of taxes and levies, that Smerdis won some popular support. On the other hand, his centralizing of the cult occasioned the hostility of those devoted to local shrines. Cambyses died in 521 leaving the rebellious Smerdis as king, but Darius boldly returned to Persia where he gathered an army and proceeded to Media, where he slew Smerdis. Down to 519, Darius had to quell a whole series of revolts throughout the Empire; for in time of central weakness, empires tend to disintegrate into their component parts under local nationalistic leadership. Darius's account of the rebellions and his victories over them is told in his large autobiographical inscription on the rock walls of Behistun. The text is the most extensive and important of the royal Achaemenian inscriptions. It is, like so many of those inscriptions, trilingual, with versions in Old Persian, Elamite and Babylonian. The decipherment of the Old Persian, which is closely related to Sanskrit and the sacred texts of the Zoroastrian Parsees in India, was the key to the Babylonian version, which in turn opened up all of Accadian and eventually Sumerian literature. Elamite, being unrelated to any well known language, is still only partially deciphered. For interprovincial purposes, Aramaic was used, especially west of Iran. Thus part of Darius's autobiography has been found in Aramaic among the Elephantine papyri. Darius recognizes Ahuramazda as his god. However, there is no reference in any of the Achaemenian inscriptions to Zoroaster. The nature of the Empire made it appropriate for the emperor to have the title "King of Kings" (still used by the Shahin-Shah "Of-Kings the-King" in Iran). It is to this period that Yahwe's title "King of the Kings of Kings," still used in the Jewish prayer book, dates.

While the Judeans took no part in the revolts, many of the Judeans must have regarded those revolts as the disintegration of the World Empire that would be replaced by their own Messianic Kingdom. It may have been such a line of thought that induced the prophet Haggai to instruct Zerubbabel, grandson of Jehoiachin, to begin constructing the Second Temple on the first of the month of Elul 520, while the rebellions were in progress. But whatever illusions of glory any Jews may have cherished, they were rudely dispelled when Iran won and every spark of revolt was extinguished. The gentile World Empire was more firmly established than ever and common sense showed that Judah, far from being the center of the world, would have to remain a little province in a great gentile order. Darius, to be sure, upheld his predecessors' policy of permitting the Jews to reëstablish their commonwealth with a Temple. Indeed the only tangible result of the restoration was the completion of the Temple (and a modest one it was!) on the third of Addar 515.

External conditions were good. The Empire provided the basis for trade and public security. But such blessings were small consolation for a frustrated people, whose dreams of their own Messianic World Order had vanished into thin air.

# Chapter XVII
# THE PASSING OF NEAR EAST
# ANTIQUITY

THE Judean community did not possess the power to extricate itself from its poverty and impotence. Its piety went unrewarded (Isaiah 58:3) and even wicked pagans fared better than God's people (note Malachi 3:14-15). Help was to come from the richer Jewish community of Babylonia. There in the East many Jews prospered and some entered government service in which they achieved high positions close to the king. Since the eastern Jews lived among gentiles, they clung all the more tenaciously to their religion. Some doubtless made pilgrimages to Jerusalem (cf. Zechariah 6:10). However their devotion to the Jewish religion did not blind them to the reality of a great, stable World Empire in which there could be no real restoration of the Jewish nation or state. Thus they were loyal citizens of the Achaemenian Empire and as Jews were interested in Jewish religion rather than Jewish statehood. They used their influence effectively with the Persian government so that Artaxerxes I in 458 authorized Ezra to proceed to Judah to establish the Law of the God of the Heavens (Ezra 7:12, 21, 25).[1]

Ezra was accompanied on the long road to Jerusalem by some 1760 Babylonian Jews including not-too-enthusiastic Levites (8:15 ff.) and other Temple servitors like the Nethinim (verse 20). The community they found in Judah was pious but badly off. The few well-to-do were concerned

[1] That Achaemenian kings took such steps affecting minority religions is also known from Darius II's permit in 419 for celebrating the Passover in Elephantine.

with worldly affairs and were entirely too intimate with those outside the fold, including the Samaritans. Ezra decided on a reform that included the putting aside of foreign wives and their children. This brought on the hostility of the non-Judeans, notably of the Samaritans. Thus it became imperative to rebuild the walls of Jerusalem (cf. Ezra 4:13, 21) against the possibility of attack. But Rehum, the governor of Samaria, together with his associates and subjects, convinced Artaxerxes that the walls were preparative to rebellion and to the cessation of paying taxes to the King. The upshot was that the walls of Jerusalem were wrecked anew and Ezra lost his prestige and efficacy as a leader. (See Nehemiah 1:3.)

Late in 446 (?) B.C., Nehemiah,[2] a Jew highly placed in the Persian court, heard of the sorry state of affairs in Jerusalem. He appealed to the King, who dispatched him there as Governor of Judah. Ezra was a rather impractical cleric lacking the personality for effective leadership. Nehemiah, on the other hand, was a practical, clear-headed and model layman with the desire and power to help the church. He reached Jerusalem in 445 and, after looking the dilapidated walls over, summoned the leaders of the people and inspired them to begin enthusiastically the arduous task of reconstruction. Rich and poor responded. Even men like the Highpriest Eliashib, who had opposed Ezra's reform, responded to Nehemiah's call. Nehemiah gained considerable popular support among the poor by proclaiming a remission of debts. Again the

---

[2] I follow the traditional view that Ezra's mission preceded Nehemiah's. However the sequence and chronology of the two leaders have been hotly contested by inconclusive arguments on both sides. The subject is covered with objectivity and full documentation by H. H. Rowley, "The Chronological Order of Ezra and Nehemiah," *Ignace Goldziher Memorial Volume,* I, Budapest, 1948, pp. 117-149. My adherence to the older view is not prompted by tradition alone. More cogent are considerations arising from the fact that the practical administrator Nehemiah would be needed to straighten out the failure of the impractical scribe Ezra, rather than vice versa.

Samaritans tried to block the rebuilding program. Thus San-ballat and Tobias (both of whom had connections through marriage with influential Judean families) and Geshem the Arab tried to incite an attack on the builders and capture Nehemiah but all such machinations were foiled and the task of reconstruction was energetically completed in fifty-two days.

Nehemiah resisted the attempt of Judean fanatics to revive Messianic pretensions for which there could be no place in the Persian Empire. Neither Nehemiah himself, nor any scion of the Davidic House (such as Zerubbabel of whom we hear no more) emerged as the anointed of the Lord. Tactfully Nehemiah (12:38) remained in the background at the popular convocation that he assembled, for as Governor he did not want his presence to create an atmosphere of government pressure. His aim was fulfilled by the decision of the people to prohibit business on the sabbath and holidays, to enforce the sabbatical year with its remission of debts (a boon for the poor debtor class), to contribute each a third shekel head tax to the Temple, to render first fruits and other emoluments to the priests, and tithes to the Levites. These decisions on the 24th of Tishri 445 (?) were in a sense the foundation of Judaism that lasted down to the creation of the modern state of Israel. National aspirations, which had proved unrealistic, were deferred to the far-off Golden Age of the Messiah. For the time being, Judah would content itself with its church, as a church state, which Josephus (*Contra Apionem* 2:165) later termed a theocracy. No more pretenders to the Davidic throne appeared on the scene. Tribute was paid to the Empire which attended to external politics, military affairs and the security of life and property. But autonomy in religion (and in other internal affairs such as justice) had been secured for Judah by the Religious Party, whose most influential leaders were Babylonian Jews.

In the ecclesiastical state of Judah, where the Temple was the *raison d'être,* the priests soon became the wealthy elite who assumed the leadership over the council of elders for administration and justice. The Highpriest, who alone was acknowledged to have direct contact with Yahwe, mediated between God and the people. The function of the laity was to support the Temple so that its service should be kept up. Laymen had to be content with the role of spectators and worshipers blindly obedient to the divine Law.

Nehemiah's work of 445 (?) proved to lack sufficient momentum. After the distinguished layman departed, public laxity set in. Accordingly he returned to Judah in 433 (?). This time he ordered the gates of Jerusalem closed on the sabbath to prevent merchants from entering to profane the holy day. Intermarriage, some of which was unpreventable, foreshadowed the doom of Hebrew as the spoken language. Priests were illegally taking the tithes that were the Levites' due. The Highpriest was much too closely allied with Samaritan chiefs including Tobias whom he invested with the collection of priestly income and to whom he assigned a room in the Temple. A grandson [3] of Eliashib married the Samaritan Sanballat's daughter and preferred to leave Judah than to give up his wife and Samaritan contacts. In any case, Nehemiah (13:28) expelled him but tactfully refrains from giving his name. It has been plausibly suggested that he was none other than Manasseh, the first Highpriest in Shechem in accordance with a tradition (Josephus, *Antiquities* 11:302 ff.) containing a kernel of historic truth. In any case it was in that period that the rupture between Samaritans and Jews became irreparable and that the Samaritan heresy became firmly established. The fact that Samaritans and Jews were close neighbors with the same faith, Law and ritual made them deadly enemies. The only difference between

---

[3] A son of Jehoiada son of Eliashib.

them was the identification of God's Holy Mountain. Though the Samaritans were numerically significant for centuries (as is for example witnessed by the New Testament) they could have no future, because their religion and hope were those of the Jews, and withal they were not Jews. History was to show that the continuity of the Jewish people depended on the Diaspora and not on the Palestinian community. The Samaritans, without any share in the Diaspora, were thus doomed to the extinction now confronting their tiny remnant in the twentieth century A.D.[4]

The Judean highpriesthood did not have a model record. Eliashib's grandson Johanan murdered his own brother Jesus (= the anglicized Greek form of Jeshua or Joshua) in the Temple to hold on to the highpriesthood which Jesus wanted to take away from him with Persian help. As a punishment the Persian governor Bagoaz laid a tax of fifty drachmas on the daily sacrifice of a lamb.

The incorporation of new blood from the outside, although against the professed policy of the Commonwealth, was instrumental in strengthening the Jews to the extent that they could surmount the early obstacles that beset them. Gradually the Jews expanded into Philistia (1 Chronicles 2:55 ff., 4 and 8; Nehemiah 11:25 ff.) and later, in Greek times, into Transjordan and Galilee. The official view prohibited the admission of Moabites and Ammonites into the congregation of God (Nehemiah 13:1) but there was a more liberal view against such discrimination (Isaiah 56:3). The expansion of the Jews meant that the Highpriest, presiding in Jerusalem over the assembly of ecclesiastical and civil leaders, was growing in importance with the spread of his followers.

As the end of the Book of Nehemiah shows, Judah was set up strictly as an ecclesiastical entity. The community

[4] A tiny Samaritan remnant around Shechem (= Nablus) still clings to its claims and to its service under the leadership of a Highpriest.

there was not the main stream of Jewry. On the other hand, the Diaspora was ever widening. From Babylonia, Jews spread to Susa, Media, westward and to all the provinces of the World Empire (Esther 3:8; 8:17; 9:2-3, 16). Those Jews, no matter how separated they were, retained their Jewish identity so that they were different from the rest of the population (Esther 3:8). As is sometimes the case with minorities,[5] the Jews were enterprising and successful, including in government service. Since the Jews were not bound by close ties to their gentile neighbors, they were free to serve the king without conflicting loyalties. Thus men like Nehemiah or Mordecai[6] were in a position to serve their king well, to attain positions of influence and to secure royal protection for their coreligionists when necessary. This, of course, stirred up jealousy and hatred so that with the Diaspora appears antisemitism. As long as the Hebrews were a nation on their own soil, they had normal feuds and friendships with their neighbors, like all other nations. But antisemitism is a product of the Diaspora, as exemplified by Haman, the villain in the Book of Esther.

While it lies beyond the scope of our investigation to give a detailed account of the Achaemenian Empire,[7] it is fitting to outline its origins, culture and history.

Indo-Europeans appear on the Near East scene shortly after 2000 B.C. While their chief representatives are the Hittites, the Mitannian kings and gods often bear Indo-European names. The Hyksos hordes included Indo-Euro-

[5] The Friends and Mormons in America, and the Parsees of India, are modern examples of such minorities.

[6] Regardless of the historicity of the story of Esther, the book is reliable as a mirror of Achaemenian times. We have every reason to believe that Jews like Mordecai, who attained high positions at court (like Nehemiah), were not rare.

[7] The most recent book on the subject is the posthumous (and in many ways unfinished) work of A. T. Olmstead, *History of the Persian Empire*, Chicago, 1948.

pean warriors. With the Indo-Europeans the horse, effectively used for pulling the war chariot, entered the Near East and revolutionized the art of warfare. The Iranian plateau was to become a great stamping ground of the Aryans (as we may call the segment of the Indo-Europeans to which the Iranians belong).

As is the case with so many countries, the earliest written records on Iran are cuneiform. In 836 B.C. Shalmaneser invaded the mountains of western Iran and subdued, among others, a few Median tribes.[8] The height of Assyrian power in western Iran came under Sargon who in 715 exiled the Median chief Dayuku and forced over twenty Median city states to pay tribute in Nineveh. By 713 those tributaries increased to forty-odd. The Sargonid kings continued the Assyrian grip on Media until the decline that set in toward the close of Assurbanipal's long reign (668-626?), when Media first emerges as a great power. Under Cyaxares, Median sovereignty extended from Iran to Asia Minor and had a rival on the world scene only in Babylonia. Cyrus of Persia upset the equilibrium when he rebelled against his Median master Astyages the son of Cyaxares, and within three years defeated him at Pasargade (in Persis) and later captured the Median capital of Ecbatana. Since Cyrus disregarded the treaties made by Media, he was opposed by a coalition that included Nabonidus of Babylon, Amasis of Egypt, Croesus of Lydia and the Spartans. By vanquishing Croesus in 546 B.C., Cyrus's borders were extended to the Mediterranean. His victory over Nabonidus in 539 made him master of Western Asia down to the Egyptian border. Cambyses in 525 added Egypt to the Empire and pushed up the Nile into the Dark Continent until his expedition against the Ethiopian Kingdom of Napata and Meroe came to grief

[8] The Medes (like the Persians) are a division of the Iranians.

but not before he established the span of the Achaemenian realm "from India to Ethiopia" (Esther 1:1).

The phenomenal success of the Iranians was due in part to strong leadership and to the effective use of archers, whose shower of arrows kept the enemy at a distance. Iranian infantrymen carried lances and daggers for engaging the foe at close range, while the cavalry, skilled by the long attachment of the Aryans to the war horse, supplied maneuverability when it was needed. Iranian military successes were first checked by the Greeks at Marathon. The Greek phalanx proved to be fatal to the Iranians whose hail of arrows was at last answered; for with the phalanx Alexander the Great ended the Achaemenian Empire.

While Darius I and to a lesser extent Xerxes I made minor extensions in the imperial borders, the limits of the Empire were basically established by Cyrus and Cambyses.

The Achaemenians had the majestic plan to rule rightly over a united world. The mild treatment they accorded their conquered subjects is admirable. The Persians of the homeland enjoyed a privileged position. They offered "first fruits" and other gifts to the king, but not outright taxes. In exchange for those offerings, given on holidays, the king would present his fellow Persians with gifts. To be sure, the privilege of being Persian went hand in hand with the duty to render military service.

The number of Achaemenian capitals seems at first confusing. In the district of Pasargade, Cyrus built a town, palace and tomb; the tomb is still standing almost intact near the modern village of Murghab. Upon the conquest of Babylonia, however, Babylon became the real capital of the Achaemenian Empire and it was from there that the kings generally ruled the Empire during the winter months. Darius I and Artaxerxes II erected great palaces at Susa (in Elam) which was also used as a capital during the winter months.

The story of the Book of Esther is set in Susa. Darius I, however, replaced Cyrus's Persian [9] capital at Pasargade with a new capital of unprecedented splendor at Persepolis.[10] There the king celebrated and received homage on the New Year, which down to the present is the greatest occasion on the Iranian calendar (and is now celebrated for no less than thirteen days). Other kings, notably Xerxes I, embellished and augmented the buildings of Persepolis. Ecbatana was also a capital, probably in the hot summer when Babylon and Susa are unbearable [11] but Ecbatana, at an elevation of over 6000 feet, is comfortable. It was by Mount Elvend, south of the city, that Darius and Xerxes built residences. Both monarchs lavished so much effort on constructing the royal residences at Persian Persepolis and Median Ecbatana, perhaps with a view to cementing the union of the Medes and Persians on which Achaemenian prowess was based.

The king had seven counselors (Ezra 7:14; Esther 1:14). Under Darius I the realm was divided into twenty satrapies each of which was subdivided into administrative provinces; note the 127 provinces ascribed to Xerxes in Esther 1:1. We have seen in the case of Judah how such districts enjoyed a great measure of autonomy, often under native sons. Yet, at the same time there was an atmosphere of despotism because there were occasions (however rare they might be)

[9] By Persian I here mean pertaining to Persis (= the modern province of Fars), the homeland of the Achaemenians.

[10] Persepolis was the "home" residence of the king in his native province. It was too remote to serve as a capital of the Empire, for which a more central location (such as Babylon's) was called for.

[11] Well-to-do natives keep cool by seeking refuge in deep cellars. American veterans of the Persian Gulf Command do not have to be convinced of the summer heat in the area. Around Dizful (near Susa), there are flies in winter but none in mid-summer when the heat is too much for them. More than one Army doctor, on his first day of duty there, took a patient's temperature, set the thermometer down for a minute (not realizing the room temperature was between 110° to 120° Fahrenheit) and when looking at it, fearfully marveled at how the patient was alive with a temperature in excess of what the thermometer is made to indicate.

when the central government or the satraps would strip the helpless subjects of their rights and privileges.

Court officials and the troops were paid in kind and were fed at government expense ("they ate at the king's table" as the idiom goes). They also received land grants and other royal gifts as a reward for meritorious service. Greek mercenaries, however, were paid in coinage. Thus for them and certain other enterprises the king had to have money. The governors took contributions for their table at which officials ate (Nehemiah 5:14). Gold was minted only by the king, but less precious metal could be cast into currency by local rulers such as satraps.

The Book of Esther is a valuable mirror of the Achaemenian court and times. The scene is laid in Susa the capital during the reign of Xerxes (Esther 1:1-2). The author knows of the seven nobles who enjoy the intimacy and confidence of the king (Esther 1:14). He also knows that in Iran, the Law was immutable (8:8).[12] He is familiar with the channels of empire administration (8:9). The Book is full of Persian words. But it has escaped the attention of scholars that Esther gives the earliest evidence of a distinctively Iranian institution that has survived down to modern Islamic times in Iranian Shiism, as the doctrine of *kitmân* or *taqiyya* which we may translate as "dissimulation." This doctrine permits one to deny his religion and pose as a member of another religion to avoid personal danger. Thus, Iranian Shiites are allowed to pose as Sunnites, when they make the pilgrimage to Mecca which is in the hands of Arab Sunnites who on occasion show violent antipathy toward Shiites. In Iran itself religious minorities often pose as Shiites for self-preservation. Thus sometimes Jews and Christians, and fre-

[12] As we have noted above, the Judeans began their unbroken tradition of regarding the Law as final only in 621 B.C. Among the gentiles, the Achaemenian Kings of the Medes and Persians are the first on record to regard the Law so strictly.

quently Bahais, parade as Shiites. Westerners who have been
raised to admire martyrdom and to frown upon denying
one's faith, consider "dissimulation" a vice; but in Iran it
fits into the regulated *mores*. Esther (2:10) hides her Jewish
affiliations without any qualms very much in the spirit of
Iranian dissimulation; and when the tables are turned and
the Iranian majority have reason to fear the Jews, the Iranian
gentiles pretend to be Jews (8:17).[13] The doctrine of dissimulation, instead of being an Islamic innovation, may well be
an Iranian survival in Shiism.

Darius commissioned a Carian captain named Scylax to
explore the Indus River. After doing so, Scylax circumnavi-
gated Arabia and sailed to Suez. He wrote the narrative of
his itinerary in Greek. Darius completed the canal from the
Nile to Suez and celebrated the feat in texts pointing out
that it had become possible "for ships to sail direct from the
Nile to Persia via Saba (= South Arabia)." Thus the
Indian and Egyptian extremities of the World Empire were
connected by water.

We have noted how tolerant the Achaemenians were in
matters of religion. This secured local support throughout
the empire for the government through the various priest-
hoods. With slight lapses, Iranian favor toward the Jews
can be traced from reign to reign. Cyrus authorized the
Restoration; Darius I confirmed it; Artaxerxes I in sponsor-
ing Ezra and Nehemiah enabled them to bolster it.

Zoroastrianism was geared to tolerance for it made a
place for foreign gods as helpers of Ahuramazda. This, to
be sure, resulted in other religions influencing Ahuramazda-
ism. Although Zoroastrianism from the start was a missionizing religion, it was checked at the Iranian borders by the

[13] Rather than "became Jews" as the English translations would have
it. The verbal conjugation (known as "hithpael") can convey the meaning of pretending.

fact that its sacred writings were not available in translation. Judaism, on the other hand, developed a facility for translating the Hebrew Scriptures, into Aramaic Targumim (as the Aramaic versions are called) and, under the Ptolemies, into Greek. While Judaism eventually gave up its missionary work, it provided Christianity with a ready-made apparatus for reaching the gentiles through translation, first in Greek, then in Latin and finally in innumerable modern languages (many thus provided with a written language for the first time). Zoroastrianism, in spite of its failure to become a world religion, has many features that anticipate Christianity. The effective dualism, whereby the good god Ahuramazda is now battling, but in the end of days will conquer, the evil deity Ahriman is if anything clearer cut than New Testament dualism, where God's influence is prominently opposed to Satan's. Furthermore, Zoroastrianism had the motif of the Savior, who in the end of days will help Ahuramazda triumph over the forces of evil. Yet it can be shown that Christianity inherited such features from Judaism, not from Zoroastrianism.

As so often happens in religion, minor gods become more popular than the head(s) of the pantheon. Just as the young Baal eclipsed the old El and the maiden Anath eclipsed the mother goddess Asherah; in Iran Anahita, the goddess of the springs,[14] and Mithra, the sun-god,[15] grow in importance so that Artaxerxes II and III (unlike the earlier kings) mention them in addition to Ahuramazda.

A World Empire must be international. This is reflected in

[14] On the Iranian plateau the scarcity of water naturally favored her rise to prominence.

[15] Love of the sun is common enough in many parts of the world but nowhere more than in Iran down to the present. Iranian students abroad have been known to become so depressed by rain and fog, and miss their native Iranian sunshine so much, that in extreme cases they have committed suicide.

Iranian art. Cyrus's constructions at Pasargade are relatively national Persian, whereas those of Darius and Xerxes at Susa and Persepolis have incorporated more Babylonian, Greek and Egyptian elements; plus elements from Asia Minor in the rock sculptures around Persepolis. The fusing of these elements into an organic unity make Persepolis one of the greatest accomplishments in world architecture. The Achaemenians followed Babylonian precedent not only in architecture and design but in the policy of employing foreign craftsmen. Since the art and artisans were those of a World Empire, when the Empire collapsed, its art perished with it.

Although the Persians controlled the Empire, their success depended in great measure on Greek armies and Greek generals. Not only Greek mercenaries but also Greek traders and artisans spread Greek civilization. An index of what was taking place in the Empire is supplied by the coins of Phoenicia and Asia Minor, where the art and inscriptions on the coins witness the impact of Hellenism. Greek leaders became increasingly aware of the shame whereby Greek talent was being exploited for maintaining an Empire for Iran. The Greeks, talented though they were, were cursed with disunity. By playing off one Greek faction against the other, Iran neutralized Greek potentialities.

Darius I (521-485) and Xerxes I (485-465) came to grips with Greece and failed so that the Aegean Sea became the focal spot of the world scene. Corruption and intrigue grew apace in Iran to the detriment of the Empire. Thus Xerxes I was murdered by his Vizier Artabanus. Artaxerxes I (465-425) has been alluded to as probably the king of that name in whose reign Ezra's and Nehemiah's activity took place. The ephemeral reigns of Xerxes II and Sogdianus fell in 425-424. Darius II (Nothus), who ruled from 424 to 404, is of special interest since Elephantine papyri date from his reign. It was he who authorized the Jews of Elephantine to celebrate the Passover in 419. In his fourteenth year (410) some Egyptians and Persians inflicted a disaster on the Jews of Elephantine. They destroyed the temple there and carried off the sacred cult objects. Jedoniah, the head of the community, and his associates wrote a long letter in 407 stating that the destroyed temple dated from before Cambyses' Conquest (525) and that they had written to the Jerusalem Highpriest Johanan (cf. Nehemiah 12:22, 23) but had gotten no reply. It is probable that the Jerusalem Highpriest did not favor the existence of rival temples, but did not dare say so because a government tolerant in religious affairs could scarcely be expected to allow a church to suppress its adherents in other parts of the Empire. Besides, the Samaritans whose leaders were also influential in Persian circles in Palestine, had a temple. What was most important, however, was the undeniable fact that Jerusalem depended on the exiles of Babylonia for support, so that the Highpriest could scarcely afford to deny the right of Jews outside Palestine to have a place of worship. Disapproving of the Elephantine temple, but not daring to maintain the principle of Jerusalem exclusivism, perhaps the best way out was to leave Jedoniah's letter unanswered. Jedoniah also wrote to Deliah and Shelemiah, the sons of Sanballat, which shows that as seen from Egypt, the Samaritans no less than the Judeans were reckoned as coreligionists of the Elephantine Jews, who had left Palestine before the irreparable break in Judeo-Samaritan relations had developed. From 410 to 407, when the letter was written, the Elephantine Jews were in mourning for their demolished temple. Finally the permit came from Deliah and Bagoaz, the Persian governor in Palestine, to rebuild the Elephantine temple.

In the reign of Artaxerxes II Memnon (404-359) the

Empire faced dissolution [16] but Artaxerxes III Ochus (359-338) reunited the Empire to its full limits. His barbarism led him to exterminate nearly all of his own family before he himself was poisoned by the eunuch Bagoaz. After the short reign of Arses (338-336), who resented Bagoaz's power and was therefore poisoned by him, Darius III (336-330) came to the throne. It was in the same year (336) that Philip of Macedon, who had united some of Greece, set out to liberate the Greek cities from Iranian domination but was assassinated before he could fulfill his plan. Philip was succeeded by his brilliant son Alexander in the same year that Darius III became king. In 334 Darius reconquered Egypt which had revolted. An eye witness might little have realized that the great Achaemenian Empire that had dominated the world for over two centuries was about to vanish. In that same year of 334 Alexander set out with his army, and a staff of scientists and authors, to conquer the Persian Empire. His father had begun his plan to strengthen Macedonia by incorporating his immediate neighbors. Then he launched on the Crusade so dear to the hearts of all Greek nationalists: to free the Greek cities. Alexander not only fulfilled his father's plan but proceeded on the grander project of conquering the Achaemenian World Order. After subjugating Asia Minor, he pushed on through Syria and captured Tyre in 332. Tyre, on a fortified isle just off the coast, had resisted every earlier attack and siege; but Alexander joined it to the mainland by a causeway so that it is now a little cape instead of an island. Thence he moved south to Gaza and to Egypt, which he annexed to his rapidly growing empire. At Gaugamela, near Erbil in Assyria, he defeated Darius's army in 331. As a finishing touch he burned Persepolis in 330 thus

[16] For example Egypt regained its independence under Nekhtenebef (378-360) and his son Jedhor (360-359) and the latter's nephew Nekhtharhebi (359-340).

avenging the Persian burning of Greek Athens. It lies beyond our subject to go into the details of Alexander's short-lived empire, that upon his death split into several divisions. Judah see-sawed between the Ptolemaic and Seleucid kingdoms in what had been Alexander's empire. Greek Europe and the Near East fused more intimately than ever before and the union was destined to produce glorious results ranging from the science of Alexandria to the Christianity modestly born in Jewish Palestine but sensationally spread among gentiles on all three continents of the Old World.

The Hellenistic Age, ushered in by Alexander, wrought profound cultural changes throughout the East.[17] Thus alphabetic scripts replaced the old native systems of writing with the result that Babylonian cuneiform died out in the first century A.D. and left the burden of literacy to Aramaic. Egyptian eventually began to be written in Greek letters and entered the Coptic stage of the Egyptian language. Knowledge of the hieroglyphs persisted into Roman times but then lapsed into oblivion. Both cuneiform and hieroglyphic texts remained closed books until they were deciphered in the nineteenth century.

Greek influence on the art and science of the Near East is unmistakable (although Near East influence on Greek art and science had far earlier beginnings and continued in Hellenistic times). However, when Islam swept the East, linguistically it did not destroy Hellenism but rather the survivals of the pre-Hellenic East. Outside of a Hellenistic uppercrust and a number of Greek cities (notably Alexandria) the Semites of Asia were still speaking not Greek but Aramaic; the Egyptians were speaking not Greek but their native Coptic; the North Africans were speaking not Latin but their

---

[17] The Hellenistic Age may well be regarded as the pivotal era of western civilization. Into it funneled the mainstreams of the past: Babylonian, Jewish, Iranian, Egyptian, Greek, Roman, etc. Out of it came Islamic, Medieval and eventually our Modern civilization.

native Berber. Accordingly today, the diminishing speech islands of Semitic Asia are Aramaic about to be engulfed in a sea of Arabic. Moreover the surviving Christians have Syriac more often than Greek liturgies. Coptic is no longer spoken but the fact that the still sizable Christian church surviving in Islamic Egypt is Coptic, not Greek, shows that Islam conquered a predominantly Egyptian, not Greek, Nile Valley. Northwest Africa is becoming solidly Arabicized under Islam but Berber (akin to the ancient language of the Libyans with whom the Egyptians fought) is the language that, though slowly dying, lingers on in the mouths of millions. But while the languages of the ancient Near East are vanishing under the impact of Arabic, the spirit of the ancient Near East lives on in the Islamic East of today. Without knowing it the Arab in Canaan still calls rain-fed land *baal,* little realizing that in that word the fertility god of his Canaanite ancestors lives on. Much more important is the fact that old Mesopotamian law, incorporated by the Jews of the Babylonian Exile, has been transmitted on Babylonian soil to Islam, whose *Fiqh* (Legal System) is largely the heir of the ancient East.[18] Many other manifestations of the persistence of antiquity could be pointed out; perhaps the most important (and most elusive) survival lies in the realm of social psychology.

By the Hellenistic Age, the period of the Old Testament is virtually over.[19] The Jews, in admitting books to the Canon, regarded the Achaemenian Age as the last in which books could be divinely inspired. Daniel, by claiming to have

[18] The influence of Greek and Roman law on Jewish and Islamic jurisprudence should not be exaggerated through ignorance of ancient Near East law.

[19] The Hellenization of Judaism is abundantly evident not only when it is in Greek dress, such as in the writings of Philo or Josephus. Even in normative rabbinic Judaism, the wisdom of the sages, in form and to a lesser extent in content, is more akin to the teachings of Epictetus than to the wisdom literature of the Old Testament.

been written by a man whose career spanned Nebuchadnezzar's and Darius's reigns, managed to enter the Canon
even though it is of the Greek age. The book contains such
grotesque errors concerning the Neo-Babylonian and Achaemenian Empires, that as a historic source for those periods,
Daniel is of quite limited value. One of the *faux pas* is that
Belshazzar (erroneously called the son of Nebuchadnezzar)
was the king of Babylon when Cyrus conquered it. Actually
the Babylonian king was Nabonidus but since Daniel is
widely read as a biblical book, there are probably more people
who think Prince Belshazzar was the king than there are
people who have ever heard of Nabonidus.

While it has been in vogue to date various parts of the
Old Testament to Hellenistic times, there is really very little
that can be convincingly attributed to any time after the
passing of the Achaemenians. The notable exception is Daniel
which has Greek words (3:5, 7, 15) and references to Greek
history. The book, which is a unity as it stands, follows the
ABA pattern; starting in Hebrew, continuing in Aramaic,
and ending in Hebrew. The Aramaic is idiomatic and smooth;
the Hebrew is artificial and inelegant; because the author
knew Aramaic as a living language but Hebrew as a stilted
dead language. But to detach the poor Hebrew from the
good Aramaic (or to insist that the Hebrew portions [20] are
translated from Aramaic) is to shut our eyes to the stylistic
plan of the book in ABA form. The King of Greece (Daniel
8:21) refers to Alexander the Great and the Four Kingdoms
(8:22) refer to the major parts into which his empire was
fragmentized after his death. The purpose of the book is
eschatological: to discover what will happen in the end of
days (2:28) when God's incorruptible Kingdom, which He

---

[20] Aramaisms are due to the fact that the author's language was
Aramaic and he thought in Aramaic when his knowledge of Hebrew was
inadequate.

will never forsake to the gentiles, shall smash the tyrants of the earth and abide forever (2:44). In Daniel, the latest book of the Old Testament, appear phenomena not to be found in early Hebrew literature. The anonymity of angels (as we have noted in the periods of the Patriarchs and Judges) has given way to the beginning of a complicated angelology destined to take hold in Judaism, Christianity and Islam. Thus Michael is the guardian angel of Israel (12:1). The early idea that all men went alike to spend eternity in a dreary Sheol has now given way to the idea that the worthy will be resurrected for life eternal while the wicked are destined for everlasting damnation (12:2). The frustrations of the Jewish people had evoked these new developments. Apocalyptic extravagances were fostered to perpetuate the hope that earthly tyranny would be replaced by the Kingdom of God on earth. Men had so little satisfaction in a world full of dislocations, that a personal afterlife was created to help them bear the agony of this world.

The merging of the Near East with classical Europe brings us to the close of Near East antiquity, including the end of Old Testament history. The last of the native empires (namely, the Achaemenian) was the largest of the ancient Near East. But it was the small Jewish minority in that Empire that was to exert profound and ever-renewed influence on the world of the future.

# APPENDIX ON LITERATURE AND
# HISTORIOGRAPHY

TRIBAL and illiterate people are often prompt to celebrate current events in song. When I first visited Palestine in 1931, I heard Arab villagers already singing ballads about the Muslim-Jewish riots of 1929. In antiquity, epic celebration of history often preceded prose accounts. The Greeks had their Homer long before their Herodotus and Thucydides. The King of Battle epic proclaimed the conquests of Sargon of Accad before there were any prose annals of the Assyrian kings. Even after a nation gets scribes to transform speech into more permanent records, there is often a long lag until the urge arises to supplant epic history with the more factual prose history. The epic precursors leave their mark on prose historiography; the origin of poetic literature therefore impinges on the origin of historic writing.

The ancient epics of which we have actual transcripts embrace notably those in cuneiform and those ascribed to Homer. As we have noted in Chapter VII, the impact of cuneiform tradition was brought to bear on the Ionians via the Hittites and other Asianic people. This influence is in keeping with the general trend of cultural progress from east to west in antiquity. But there is an important exception to this trend: the highly civilized Caphtorians invaded the Asiatic mainland and so constitute a cultural movement from west to east in both halves of the second millennium. The Caphtorian impact in craftsmanship is universally recognized; but it is equally true that the Caphtorians made literary contributions to Canaan. Moreover, the close connections between the literature of Ugarit and Homer are due in large measure to the Caphtorian element that spans them. Also the fact that Ugaritic, of all known literatures, lies closest to the Old Testament is due not only to the circumstance that both lie in Canaan but also in part because Caphtorian influence bridges Ugarit and Judah.

That not only the poetry but even the prose of the Old Testament betrays epic antecedents has been evident from formal considerations. An excellently documented statement of the situation has been given by the late Professor U. Cassuto in *The Goddess Anath,* Jerusalem, 1951. He points out that the advanced literary stage of even the earliest Hebrew literature is due to the fact that the Hebrews on entering Canaan adopted the already highly developed literary tradition of the land. It may be added that the literary development in the inland and marginal Canaanite territory conquered by Judah was not so highly polished as in the cosmopolitan port of Ugarit. This explains why Hebrew poetry is less stylized and more spontaneous than Ugaritic poetry.

To illustrate the vestiges of epic form in the transformed prose Hebrew version, we need cite only a single example. In Mesopotamian, Ugaritic and Homeric epics there are verbatim repetitions of speeches (first as given to, and then as delivered by, the messengers) or actions (first as instructions, then as fulfilment). Joab, sending a messenger to inform David of Uriah's death, predicts in epic fashion David's response (2 Samuel 11:20-21). However, in our abbreviated prose version, the predicted response is not delivered by David.

That the epic forerunners of the Hebrew prose narratives are attested formally is too well known to require further demonstration here; but that they are attested also in content is sufficiently new to warrant as adequate a documen-

tation as it is possible at present to give of an important
subject still in its infancy.

The interrelations of the surviving expressions of ancient
epic are evident not only from the details (cf. Chapters VI-
XI) but also from basic motifs. Gilgamesh, Achilles and
Keret are, though of at least partly divine extraction, destined
to die. Moreover, their anticipated death is the subject of
epic regret. Gilgamesh and Achilles (whose actual deaths
are suppressed with artistic restraint) are compensated with
immortal fame. Keret's mortality, however, is compensated
with the continuance of his line through progeny. The latter
solution of the classic tragedy of man's futile quest for personal immortality is already hinted in the Gilgamesh Epic,
where Gilgamesh (X: iii: 1-14) is told to give up his wild
goose chase for divinity and content himself with the comforts and realities of wife and child. Furthermore, the twelfth
and last tablet of the Gilgamesh Epic stresses Enkidu's
message from the underworld to the effect that a man's welfare post mortem is in direct proportion to the sons he has
left on earth.

The Ugaritic treatment of the topic of progeny can be
outlined in some detail: There may be difficulty in securing
the right bride (thus in Keret). The progeny is promised by
divine annunciations and blessing (Keret and Aqhat). The
biological process is supplemented with religious rites: incubation, direct divine revelation to the prospective father as
to the necessary sacrifices. After sons are born, there is a
preference for the youngest at the expense of the firstborn
(in Keret). We are thus confronted with the fact that the
Ugaritic legends of Aqhat and Keret reflect a pervading
element of the patriarchal narratives; to wit, the divine
promise of progeny. Difficulty in securing the right bride
is overcome by Isaac and Jacob. Annunciations start with
Hagar before Ishmael's birth. Divine blessings with promise

of progeny typify the narratives of all three Patriarchs. Abraham (quite like Keret and Daniel) receives direct instructions from God as to the proper rituals, which are combined with incubation (Genesis 15:1-12). And after the birth of sons, the junior may be preferred to the senior; thus Jacob is preferred to Esau (as subsequently Perez to Zerah, Ephraim to Manasseh and David to all his brothers). However, all claim to divine ancestry or to personal immortality is lacking in the patriarchal narratives. The quest for immortality is realistically and completely solved through progeny. Preoccupation with the birth of a son remains a theme in the history of notable men down to the end of the Period of the Judges. In the case of Samson, the annunciation is still via a divine entity; in the instance of Samuel, the prediction is through the priest Eli, reflecting the development whereby direct communion between laity and God became supplanted by mediation of divine messages through priests and prophets.

The direct mingling of men and gods is of a piece in Ugarit and the patriarchal narratives. Thus Abraham and Sarah, quite like the Ugaritic Daniel and his wife Dnty, entertain god(s) for dinner in natural fashion. When we come to Moses, the contact is shrouded in a supernatural aura. Samson's parents, to be sure, serve a sacrificial meal to a deity but it is consumed supernaturally and not like the dinners served to the divine guests of Daniel or Abraham. In the Bible, crass personal contact between men and God is gradually eliminated so that even His words must be mediated by His special human representatives, the prophets. The earlier direct relationship between men and gods is common to all the epics: Mesopotamian, Ugaritic, Greek and "Proto-Patriarchal". The later barriers grew hand in hand with factual historiography and ecclesiastical vested interests.

If the Patriarchal Cycle is the epic of The Birth of a
Family, the Exodus is that of The Birth of a Nation. The
essential historicity of the Exodus should not be questioned.
It fits into the general framework of Egypto-Asiatic relations,
whereby famine in Canaan impelled Semites repeatedly to
seek bread in the Nile Valley regardless of the price. The end
of any famine in Canaan might be the signal for many an
exodus. That *the* Exodus is handled in an epic manner no
more disproves its historicity than does Homer's manner
disprove the historicity of the Trojan War. Often the epic
manner calls for elaborating specific details whose historicity
is banal rather than marvelous. What could be more common-
place than a supply of bread before a planned mass movement?
Yet this is singled out for epic celebration in Keret: 79-84,
171-5. Accordingly the prominence given to the baking of
*maṣṣā*[1] "unleavened bread" in the Exodus was evoked by
the repertoire of the epic tradition in which the Exodus was
celebrated.

Of course there are epic features that do not fit into the
matrix of reality. Thus when we read that the clothes of the
Israelites did not wear out for the forty years they wandered
in the wilderness, we are dealing with the same motif we
meet in the Gilgamesh Epic (XI:244-5, 246), whereby
Gilgamesh is equipped with a garment that will remain new
and show no sign of wear throughout his long and arduous
journey from the abode of Utnapishtim to his native city
Erech. Once we get a feeling for these epic features, it is
easy to single them out of the biblical narrative. For example,
the Ten Plagues have an unmistakable epic ring. However,

[1] That *maṣṣā* has no satisfactory etymology suggests it is a loanword.
That it is the same word as Greek *maza* is well-known, but the prevalent
view that it is borrowed from Semitic because it has no Indo-European
etymology, is weak on account of the lack of a Semitic etymology as well.
Indeed its presence in Hebrew and Greek suggests a Caphtorian origin
because Caphtorian influence spans Israel and Greece sufficiently early.

it is not my purpose to set up criteria (no matter how sound) and base thereon a hypothetical system for analyzing the Hebrew text so as to detach the epic features. It is rather my aim to confine my observations to specific elements controllable from extrabiblical sources; and in this spirit we continue our investigation.

The Conquest, though basically factual, has epic features. We shall note only one, that happens to contain nothing supernatural: the ruse whereby the Gibeonites use stale bread (Joshua 9:12) to convey the impression of a long lapse of time in their supposed wanderings. This reechoes an old motif. Gilgamesh (XI: 200-28) is convinced that he has slept a week, by a loaf baked for him on each successive day; the seven loaves displaying the signs of age ranging from mold to freshness.

The crowning epic cycle in Old Testament history is the Hebrew "Shahnameh", the Epic of Kings celebrating the rise of the monarchy that under Saul stood up against Philistine tyranny, and under David shook off the yoke of tyranny and achieved the glory of empire. David's greater accomplishment and his founding the first and only enduring dynasty explain why he and he alone merited epic treatment par excellence. Like Keret ( :9), David was one of eight brothers (1 Samuel 16:10-11). Moreover, the fact that David is the youngest who eclipses all his elder brothers is an epic motif we have already discussed but which we may briefly amplify by pointing out that it is particularly applicable in Ugaritic epic royal succession (128:I-II). Furthermore, the dual tradition that he was the seventh (1 Chronicles 2:15) or the eighth (1 Samuel 16) son points to a poetic origin with the device of climaxing "7" with "8" parallelistically. No one will question David's historicity, but neither will any open-minded orientalist fail to see that the *manner* of recounting his anointment in 1 Samuel 16 reflects dramatic epic form.

Like Keret who must win the hand of a princess by war, David must slay many a Philistine to win the princess Michal as his bride. Furthermore, the fact that David loses her and has to regain her (2 Samuel 3:14) suggests that when the Ugaritic bard tells that Keret's (:12-14) rightful bride departed, it does not mean she died but that his destined wife has somehow or other left him and must be rewon. (In other words, Keret's marital history, as far as the story goes, is monogamous.) The epic of King Keret also relates his suffering in consequence of sin. We may compare David's suffering for his sin with Bathsheba. That the child's fatal illness lasts for the epic number of seven days (2 Samuel 12) reflects a poetic original. Keret's disaster involves the welfare of his realm which faces famine (126:III); cf. David's errors, which confront his realm with a choice of disasters including famine (2 Samuel 24:13).

With David the nation comes of age. Genuine triumph makes epic exaggeration less necessary. The institution of government scribes makes possible annalistic records with heavy inroads on less accurate popular epics. Moreover, the consciousness of historic significance evoked among the Hebrews a historiography not to be equalled anywhere in the world until half a millennium later under the Fifth Century Greek historians Herodotus and Thucydides.

David's narrative combines earlier epic with later historiography. With Solomon the epic elements diminish and annalistic elements increase. After the division of the kingdom, many of the traditional epic features disappear. Schematic numbers for the reigns vanish after the forty years each of David [2] and Solomon. Preoccupation with the birth of a son and heir, though it must have remained common

---

[2] Epic round numbers may be broken down in the course of prosification. Thus David's epic "40" is broken down into his 7 years at Hebron plus 33 at Jerusalem. Similarly, the epic "70" members of Jacob's household are broken down into 66 + 2 + 2 in Genesis 46:26-27.

enough in real life, is no longer considered worthy of inclusion in the history. Romantic marriage [3] (which certainly could not have died with David in Israel) is no longer mentioned. Annunciations are eliminated from secular life and confined to the sphere of religion.[4] Post-Davidic history is virtually devoid of the old Canaanite epic content, however much the language continues to reecho the epic tradition in expression and style.

The catastrophe of 586 did not strip the Jews of their conviction that their history had eternal significance and hope. From after that date there are two comprehensive histories in the Bible, compiled from earlier sources: (1) from Genesis through Kings, and (2) Chronicles. Both start human history with Adam. The Genesis-Kings account cannot be a haphazard, unedited collection. Each successive book takes up where the preceding one leaves off. The last event in Kings was the hope-inspiring event of Jehoiachin's elevation. Accordingly, restored nationhood under Davidic kingship was still cherished as a workable ideal. The last event in Chronicles is the Edict of Cyrus authorizing the return to Zion. By this time the international situation had ruled out all practical prospects for real national independence. The restoration could be ecclesiastical but not in terms of Davidic sovereignty. Hence the ecclesiastical orientation in the Chronicler's history. The fact that Ezra and Nehemiah are supposed to follow Chronicles must have been obvious to the men responsible for the present Hebrew order in which Chronicles follows Ezra and Nehemiah. For Ezra opens with a repetition of the last statement in Chronicles thus picking up the narrative before going on. May it not be that the

---

[3] Since romantic marriage is absent from pre-Ugaritic epics (e. g., Gilgamesh), its presence in Ugarit, the Bible and Homer point to a Caphtorian origin. Cf. *Journal of Near Eastern Studies* 11, 1952, p. 213.
[4] The first purely religious annunciation in Canaan occurs in Ugaritic text 77 :7.

present arrangement resulted from a desire to close the Hebrew Bible on a hopeful note: the Edict of Cyrus?[5] Ezra ends with affairs on Zion in a sorry state. Nehemiah ends his book on the middling note that while all was not rosy, he had done his best. Nehemiah would be an uninspiring "finis"; Ezra, a quite hopeless one. The choice of Chronicles with which to close the Old Testament made for a happy ending even though chronological considerations call for the order Chronicles-Ezra-Nehemiah.

To evaluate the historical books of the Old Testament the student would do well to bear in mind the whole as well as the parts. Both the Genesis-Kings and the Chronicles-Ezra-Nehemiah "Histories of the Hebrew People" have embraced many a transformed epic, such as the Epic of Creation, the Deluge, the Birth of a Family, the Birth of a Nation, the Epic of Kings, etc. Why and how the transformations were effected should be among the questions foremost in the minds of biblical students today.

[5] It was Joan K. Gordon who called this to my attention.

# INDICES

## Biblical References

298

## Ugaritic References

# INDICES

## Homeric References

**ILIAD**

| | |
|---|---|
| 1:297 | 93 |
| 1:320 ff. | 99 |
| 1:348-363 | 93 |
| 1:544 | 90 |
| 2 | 98 |
| 2:1-15 | 94 |
| 2:23-24 | 94 |
| 2:60-70 | 94 |
| 2:157-165 | 95 |
| 2:173-181 | 95 |
| 2:303 | 99 |
| 5:382-404 | 98 |
| 5:860-861 | 93 |
| 6:290 | 89 |
| 8:563 | 97 |
| 10:540 | 92 |
| 11:182 | 90 |
| 11:592 | 97 |
| 11:720 | 97 |
| 11:745 | 97 |
| 12:66 | 97 |
| 13:716 | 97 |

**ILIAD**

| | |
|---|---|
| 18:372-379 | 96 |
| 18:478-613 | 96 |
| 19:404-417 | 98 |
| 22:69 | 95 |
| 22:75-76 | 93 |
| 22:167 | 90 |
| 24:144-158 | 95 |
| 24:171-187 | 95 |

**ODYSSEY**

| | |
|---|---|
| 4:590-591 | 97 |
| 5:87-91 | 90 |
| 5:95 | 91 |
| 7:179 | 91 |
| 7:183 | 91 |
| 9:40-42 | 97 |
| 9:548-549 | 97 |
| 13:53 | 91 |
| 13:294-299 | 94 |
| 14:78 | 91 |
| 15:14 | 92 |

**ODYSSEY**

| | |
|---|---|
| 15:67 | 92 |
| 15:148-149 | 91 |
| 16:11 | 92 |
| 16:158 | 99 |
| 16:159-163 | 98 |
| 16:299 | 93 |
| 17:291-319 | 95 |
| 17:483-487 | 91 |
| 17:548 | 93 |
| 19:592-593 | 99 |
| 20:14-16 | 93 |
| 20:49 | 97 |
| 20:299 | 98 |
| 20:309-310 | 97 |
| 20:318-319 | 97 |
| 21:352-353 | 96 |
| 21:362-365 | 98 |
| 22:30 | 93, 94 |
| 22:37 | 97 |
| 22:57-59 | 92 |
| 22:287-291 | 98 |
| 23:335-337 | 96 |
| 24:128 | 99 |

## Vocabulary

**HEBREW**

| | |
|---|---|
| abrek | 125 |
| admoni | 112 |
| barabbim | 200 n. 16 |
| beqaʻ | 112 |
| bosheth | 158 n. 6 |
| ʻemeq | 179 n. 1 |
| ephah | 213 |
| gerim | 264 |
| hodesh | 174 n. 15 |
| hodesh ha-abib | 173 n. 15 |
| ʻibr(îm) | 76 n. 2 |
| kaf | 140 |
| kobaʻ | 108 n. 14 |
| maṣṣā | 293 |
| maṣṣebôth | 181 |
| meliṣim | 199 n. 7 |
| nethinim | 263 n. 2 |
| qanim | 38 n. 31 |
| qedesha | 240 n. 12 |
| qinnim | 38 n. 31 |
| qnym | 38 n. 31 |
| qobaʻ | 108 n. 14 |
| seren | 108 |
| shibboleth | 141 |
| sibboleth | 141 |
| teraphim | 117, 142, 148 |
| urim | 150 |
| yad | 140 |
| Yehudi | 209 n. 5 |
| yerah | 174 n. 15 |

**PHOENICIAN**

| | |
|---|---|
| brbm | 200 n. 16 |

**UGARITIC**

| | |
|---|---|
| Ḥkpt | 108 n. 14 |
| Ḥqkpt | 108 n. 14 |
| l- | 92 |
| lsmm | 97 n. 10 |
| tdmm | 96 |

**BABYLONIAN**

| | |
|---|---|
| awilum | 72 n. 13 |
| mushkenum | 72 n. 13 |
| qadishtu | 240 n. 12 |
| wardum | 72 n. 13 |

**SUMERIAN**

| | |
|---|---|
| ensi | 62, 66, 156 |
| lugal | 62 |

**ARABIC**

| | |
|---|---|
| Fiqh | 285 |
| kitmân | 278 |
| leben | 52 |
| suyl | 193 |
| shaṭāra | 114 n. 27 |
| taqiyya | 278 |

**GREEK**

| | |
|---|---|
| maza | 293 n. 1 |

**PERSIAN**

| | |
|---|---|
| Shahin-Shah | 267 |

**"ARYAN"**

| | |
|---|---|
| mariannu | 74 |

**DANUNITE?**

| | |
|---|---|
| Kryntrysh | 200 |

# GENERAL INDEX

Abel, 24
Abigail, 149
Abijah (son of Jeroboam), 180
Abijah (King of Judah), 182
Abijam, 182
Abimelech (of Gerar), 108, 109, 113
Abimelech (of Shechem), 140-141
Abishag, 167, 168
Abishai, 161, 162, 164
Abner, 146, 154-155, 164
Abraham, 75, 91, Chap. VIII: passim, 189, 292, etc.
Abram, 29
Absalom, 159-164, 167
Accad, 28, 35 n. 27, 64-66, 79, 289
Accadian, 3, 4, 32, 61, 89, 93, 248, 267
Achaemenian(s), 2, 4, 6, 9, 248, 262 ff.: passim
Achilles, 33, 96, 98, 291
Achish, 148, 150, 151, 168
Adadnirari III, 208
Adah, 24
Adam, 23, 24, 25, 40, 296
Adana, 198-200
Adapa, 40
Addar, 268
Adonijah, 167-168
Adoniram, 165, 170
Adoram, 165, 178
Adullam(ite), 121, 148
Aegean, 74, 281
Agamemnon, 94, 191
Ahab, 94, 184-195, 211; House of —: 206
Ahaz, 221-222, 234
Ahaziah (King of Israel), 191-192
Ahaziah (King of Judah), 194-195
Ahijah, 180
Ahimelech, 148
Ahinoam, 150
Ahitophel, 160-162
Ahmosis I, 56
Ahriman, 280
Ahuramazda(ism), 279-280
Ai, 132, 134 n. 9
Ain Feshkha, 261 n. 1

Akhetaton, 77
Alexander, 12, 276, 283-284, 286
Alexandria, 284
Ali Baba, 59
alphabet, 4, 5, 42-43, 80, 81, 284
Amarna, 118; — Letter 289 18-20: 109 n. 15
Amarna Age, 60, 74, Chap. V: passim, 81, 100, 103, 108
Amasa, 162, 164
Amasis, 257, 258, 265, 275
Amaziah (Bethel priest), 212-213
Amaziah (King of Judah), 208
Amenemhet I, 50, 51, 52
Amenemope, 129
Amenophis III, 60, 75
Amenophis IV, 60, 75-77
Amittai, 210
Amman, 158
Ammon(ites), 108, 141, 175, 186, 207, 241, 256, 264, 273
Amnon, 158-159
Amon (King of Judah), 236, 241
Amon (Egyptian god), 50, 77-78, 129, 246
Amon-Re, 50
Amorite, 6 n. 7, 70, 133, 174, 218 n. 15
Amos, 127, 207, 211, 212-216, 219, 232, 233, 251; Book of —: 182, 210
Anahita, 280
Anath (goddess), 82, 85, 86, 93, 140, 145 n. 16, 280
Anath (parent of Shamgar), 137
Anathoth, 234 n. 8
Anatolia, 74, 76 n. 2, 79, 201, 217
annunciations, 84, 105, 291, 292, 296
antonymic pairs, 21 n. 3, 22-23, 97-98
Anu, 35
Apiru, 76
Apocalyptic, 261, 287
Apocrypha, 261
Apsu, 30
Aqaba (Gulf of), 172, 174, 208

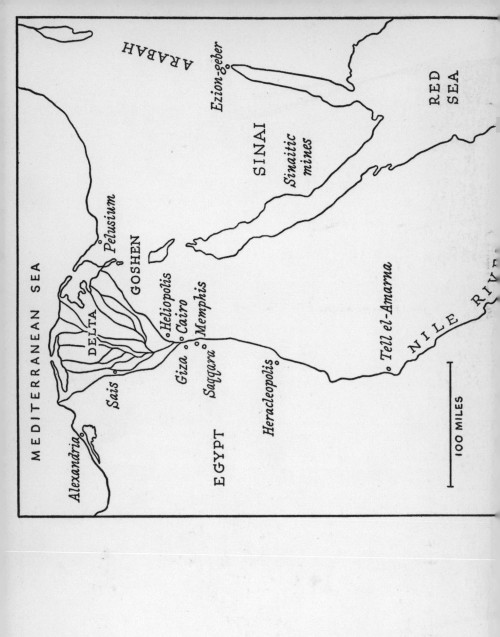